THE RAPE OF THE NILE

Tomb Robbers, Tourists, and Archaeologists in Egypt

BRIAN M. FAGAN

Charles Scribner's Sons, New York

NOTE

There is no one uniform system of Egyptian nomenclature in use among Egyptologists. We decided to use that adopted by William C. Hayes in *The Scepter of Egypt,* The Metropolitan Museum of Art, New York, 1953, as his spellings appear to be in widespread use.

Copyright © 1975 Brian Fagan

Library of Congress Cataloging in Publication Data

Fagan, Brian M.
  The rape of the Nile.

  Includes index.
  1. Egyptology—History. 2. Egypt—Antiquities.
I. Title.
DT60.F27   932   75-11857
ISBN 0-684-14235-X

1 3 5 7 9 11 13 15 17 19 C/MD 20 18 16 14 12 10 8 6 4 2

Printed in the United States of America

But every woman shall borrow of her neighbour, and of her that sojourneth in her house, jewels of silver, and jewels of gold, and raiment: and ye shall put them upon your sons, and upon your daughters; and ye shall spoil the Egyptians.

Exodus 3:22

For the Fox and the Vicar,

with love and affection, and because of many
good times

CONTENTS

PART ONE: TOMBS, TOURISTS, AND TREASURE

PART TWO: THE GREATEST PLUNDERER OF THEM ALL

PART THREE: ASSAULT ON ANTIQUITY

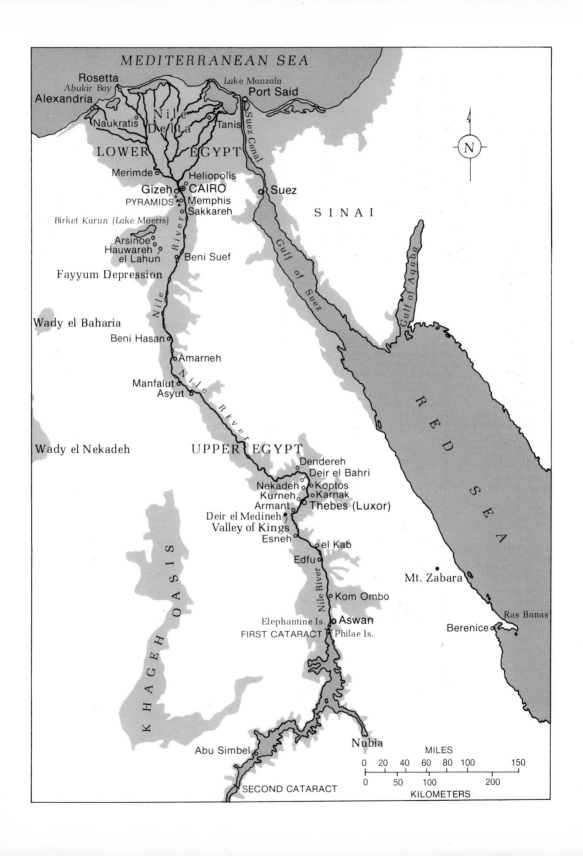

THE CHRONOLOGY, DYNASTIES, PHARAOHS, AND MAJOR EVENTS AND CULTURAL DEVELOPMENTS OF ANCIENT EGYPT

DATES	DYNASTIES	PRINCIPAL PHARAOHS*	MAJOR EVENTS AND CULTURAL DEVELOPMENTS
3100 B.C.	Unification of Upper and Lower Egypt, Early Dynastic Period I and II	Narmer (Menes)	Emergence of Dynastic civilization and of the major institutions of Egyptian government and religion. Capital of Egypt eventually established at Memphis. Royal tombs at Abydos and Sakkareh
2686 B.C.	Old Kingdom III to VI	Zoser, Snofru, Khuf-wy, Kha'ef-Re, and Men-ku-Re	Pyramid burial for pharaohs. Construction of the pyramids of Gizeh. Eternal life a royal prerogative
2181 B.C.	First Intermediate Period VII to XI		Disintegration of the state and internal dissention. Eventually Thebes prevails. Expansion of the cults of Osiris and Amun-Re
2050 B.C.	Middle Kingdom XI and XII	Various Montu-hotpes and Amun-em-het I. Sesostris I and II	Extension of Egyptian sphere of influence into Asia and Nubia. Amun becomes a major god

Date	Period / Dynasties		
1785 B.C.	Second Intermediate Period XIII to XVII		Hyksos rulers in Lower Egypt are eventually toppled by the Thebans. Horse and chariot are introduced to the Nile Valley
1580 B.C.	New Kingdom XVIII to XX	Many important rulers, including Ah-mose, Thut-mose I–III, Amun-hotpe II–IV, Queen Hat-shepsut, Sethy I, and Ramesses II–III. Tut-ankh-Amun, in fact a minor ruler, reigned briefly during the New Kingdom	The height of Egyptian power and prosperity. Empire extends into the Euphrates region and deep into Nubia. Valley of Kings comes into use as a royal burial place. Karnak and Luxor the scene of much temple building
1085 B.C.	Late Period XXI to XXX	Numerous rulers, among them 12 kings whose reigns exceeded 20 years	Country sundered by political disputes. Eventual conquest of Egypt by Persians and others
525 B.C.		Conquest of Egypt by Persian King Cambyses	
332 B.C.		Alexander the Great visits the Nile Valley	
305 B.C.		The Ptolemies	Dendereh, Edfu, Kom Ombo, and Philae. Period of great influence for Greek rulers of Egypt. Library at Alexandria achieves great importance
30 B.C.		Roman occupation of Egypt	Egypt becomes part of the Roman Empire after the death of Antony and Cleopatra

*For reasons of clarity, only the most important rulers are mentioned by name. Dates of their reigns are occasionally given in the text, or they can be obtained from any book on Ancient Egypt. The chronologies used in this table are a digest of various time scales proposed by different scholars and should be regarded as approximations, expecially for the earlier dynasties.

A Note on the Illustrations

The photographic research for *The Rape of the Nile* took me into many fascinating byways of Egyptology and nineteenth-century history. I have tried to balance contemporary portraits, lithographs, and photographs against modern shots of major sites. Anyone developing a pictorial survey of Egyptology is bound to rely heavily on *La Description de l'Egypte,* for the exquisite illustrations are a fascinating kaleidoscope of early nineteenth-century Egypt. Scenes of Egyptian life are to be found in David Roberts' *Egypt and Nubia* (1846), illustrations with a keen eye for detail and often with a pleasingly romantic touch. Stanley Lane Poole's *Social Life in Egypt* (London, 1884) includes some pleasing views of Cairo. Tourist drawings of the Nile are plentiful but often of

xiii

dubious quality. I found the illustrations in Amelia Edwards' *Thousand Miles up the Nile* a little disappointing, and some of the best material is found in travel books published by Bible and Tract societies. One excellent example is the Reverend Samuel Manning's *Land of the Pharaohs: Egypt and Sinai Illustrated by Pen and Pencil* (London, 1876), which comes complete with Biblical texts, moralizings, and numerous lithographs of the tourist in Egypt, many of which appear in this book.

PART ONE: TOMBS, TOURISTS, AND TREASURE

The Valley of Kings

1 The Destruction of the Pharaohs

"One can imagine the plotting beforehand, the secret rendezvous on the cliff by night, the bribing or drugging of the cemetery guards, and then the desperate burrowing in the dark, the scramble through a small hole into the burial chamber, the hectic search by a glimmering light for treasure that was portable, and the return home at dawn laden with booty." So wrote the great British Egyptologist Howard Carter soon after he had discovered the magnificent tomb of Tut-ankh-Amun in 1922. "We can imagine these things," he added, "and at the same time we can realise how inevitable it all was."

Howard Carter was writing about the Valley of Kings, the desolate and rocky valley to the west of Thebes chosen as a royal burial place for the

3

Tomb of Nakhte at Thebes
XVIII Dynasty
A festival scene (*opposite*)
Female musicians

Egyptian pharaohs for at least four hundred years
after the sixteenth century B.C. The pharaohs were
buried in rock-cut tombs with carefully concealed
entrances, while their elaborate mortuary temples
were built near the Nile close to Thebes. The dry
climate of Thebes has preserved for us—and generations of tomb robbers—the rich furniture of the
royal tombs of the New Kingdom, including inlaid
furniture, ceremonial thrones, thousands of funerary statuettes or *ushabtis*, magnificent sarcophagi,
and fine alabaster vessels. Children's toys, jewelry,
regalia of state, even linen shrouds throw a fascinating light on the daily life of the long-dead
kings. The pharaohs of the XVIII to XX dynasties,
princes, and high officials were laid to rest in the
Valley of Kings, while other royal personages were

5

buried in nearby side valleys and in the adjacent hills. The tombs of the nobles were in the cliffs and hills facing the Theban plain. Their bodies, and those of hundreds of other more privileged Egyptians wealthy or important enough to be buried with the prospect of an afterlife, were buried in rock-cut tombs, caves, or clefts in the rocky hills in brightly painted mummy cases.

An almost hereditary group of necropolis workers was permanently employed to work on royal tombs, living in a special village at Deir el-Medineh. There are records of strikes and pay disputes, of absenteeism and family quarrels. The tombs of nobles were prepared by other craftsmen, whose villages are almost unknown to archaeologists. Even so, for the royal families, the nobility, and those able to afford it, there was a feeling of continuity with some form of life in the afterworld, a feeling that was reflected in considerable expenditure on tombs, temples, and their contents.

Yet the Egyptians themselves, through motives of greed rather than piety, were the first to desecrate their dead and destroy the mummies of many pharaohs. Tomb robbing was a well-organized pastime in the Thebes necropolis. The tombs of the pharaohs were ransacked for their treasures by cunning and well-armed grave robbers who often worked in close collaboration with corrupt priests and well-bribed officials. Most of the royal tombs of the Valley of Kings had probably been opened illegally by professional thieves by the end of the XX Dynasty. The depredations of these robbers were so severe that most of the royal treasures vanished forever long before the archaeologist or antiquarian came to Thebes and completed the work of destruction.

The royal burials of the Valley of Kings were probably left in comparative peace during the reigns of the great pharaohs of the XVIII and XIX dynasties (1570–1180 B.C.), kings such as Sethy I and Ramesses II, who ruled Egypt and a large for-

6

eign empire as well. A closely supervised officialdom maintained the royal tombs and prevented
much large-scale looting. But toward the end of
the XX Dynasty the pharaohs were much weaker,
petty officialdom less thoroughly watched. The
custodians of royal tombs and cemeteries were
lax in their duties and a wave of tomb robbing
began. During the reign of Ramesses IX (1142–1123
B.C.), a major law case involving tomb robbing
was heard in the courts at Thebes, the records of
which have been preserved on surviving papyri.

The case involved the mayors of the two
Thebes. Pa-ser, the mayor of eastern Thebes, was
an honest but rather officious local bureaucrat
who became concerned at the constant rumors of
royal tomb robberies which floated across the
river from Thebes of the Dead on the other bank
of the Nile. Perhaps he was anxious to ingratiate
himself with higher authority, or to discredit his
hated rival Pa-wero, mayor of the sister community where the royal graves lay. Whatever his motives, Pa-ser started an official investigation into
tomb robbing, a subject that officially lay outside
his responsibilities. Soon he was uncovering all
manner of disturbing testimony, including eyewitness accounts of royal grave robberies. Graphic
details of surreptitious robbery were extracted
from various witnesses who described how they
pried open the entrances of royal tombs.

> Then we found the august mummy of the king. There
> were numerous amulets and golden ornaments at his
> throat, his head had a mask of gold upon it, and the
> mummy itself was overlaid with gold throughout. . . .
> We stripped off the gold which we found on the august
> mummy of the king and the amulets and ornaments,
> and the coverings in which it rested.

Pa-ser took his damaging testimony to Kha-em-
wese, the local vizier, and demanded an offical
inquiry into the state of the royal tombs. Vizier
Kha-em-wese sent an official commission on a
tour of inspection. They found that one royal

**A royal mummy. The inner
coffin of Tut-ankh-Amun.**

7

grave, that of King Sekhem-Re Shed-towy, son of Re Sobk-em-saf, had been violated as well as some priestesses' tombs lying to the west of the city. Pa-ser's witnesses were questioned anew. They now protested their innocence and denied their earlier testimony. The result of the inquiry was a disaster for Pa-ser, who had underestimated the extent to which Pa-wero controlled the thriving robbery business. The vizier dropped all charges against the tomb robbers, probably with relief, as it seems certain that he was up to his neck in the racket as well.

Pa-wero rejoiced at his easy victory over his rival and gloated quietly at home for a while. Then a few months later he collected together "the inspectors, the necropolis administrators, the workmen, the police, and all the laborers of the necropolis" and sent them to the east bank for a noisy celebration. The crowd marched up and down in raucous triumph, paying special attention to Pa-ser's house, a proceeding that the unfortunate mayor tried to ignore with a dignity that well became him. But eventually his impatience got the better of him, and he rushed off to complain to the pharaoh's butler, who resided at the temple of Ptah nearby. Pa-ser poured out his troubles, reiterated his charges and claimed he could prove them. Then he lost his temper and threatened to take his story directly to the pharaoh. This was a grave mistake, for his threat involved a gross breach of bureaucratic etiquette that implied that the vizier himself was involved in the robberies. The butler carried the story to Kha-em-wese, who promptly convicted Pa-ser of perjury and told him to stop making a nuisance of himself.

But Pa-ser was not so easily silenced. He continued to bombard the vizier with evidence relating to tomb robberies. A year later, even high officialdom could not disguise the violations that had taken place, and a fresh inquiry was convened, this time by a new vizier, Nebmare-nakht. Forty-five tomb robbers were brought before the court.

Fortunately the high points of the testimony have survived on a series of famous papyri that were—ironically enough—sold on the illegal antiquities market in Thebes in the late nineteenth century. The witnesses were placed on oath, and then beaten to extract true confessions. The evidence was damning. The incense roaster of the temple of Amun recounted how he was approached by a group of robbers at night while asleep. "'Come out,' they said, 'We are going to take plunder for bread to eat.' They took me with them. We opened the tomb and brought away a shroud of gold and silver. We broke it up, put it in a basket, brought it down and divided it into six parts." The various accused were beaten on the soles of their feet or tortured with a screw until they either confessed or corroborated each other's testimony.

The scribe of the Necropolis was examined with the stick [until] he said: "Stop! I will tell. This silver is [all] that we brought out. I saw nothing else." He was examined with the birch and the screw . . . Nesy-amenope, the scribe of the Necropolis, said to him: "Then the tomb from which you said the vases of silver were taken is [yet] another tomb. That makes two [tombs] besides the main treasure." He said: "That is false. The vases belong to the main treasure I have already told you about. We opened one tomb and only one." He was examined again with the stick and the birch and the screw [but] he would not confess anything beyond what he had [already] said.

Although the penalties handed out to these particular tomb robbers were extremely harsh, any reduction in the tempo of grave robbery can at best have been temporary, for there are scattered records of later trials. Nothing could stop the voracious tomb robbers.

Even the tombs of the great XVIII Dynasty pharaohs were emptied of their riches, despite the opposition of dedicated priests and officials who were determined to protect the dead pharaohs from destruction. The bodies of kings were moved

9

from tomb to tomb, from sarcophagus to sarcophagus, after repeated defilement of royal mummies. Ramesses II and Sethy I themselves were moved several times. Eventually the robbers became so daring that the priests obtained a strong, confidential guard and moved every known royal mummy to safe hiding in one of two caches, either in a secret tomb in the Valley of Kings or in a cleft in the hills overlooking Thebes. This time they managed to evade the tomb robbers for three thousand years, until the late 1870s, when the cache was discovered by accident but saved for science.

The wealth and stability of Ancient Egypt was proverbial in the Mediterranean world of four thousand years ago. A rich literature tells of the deeds of the pharaohs. We know their names, have some knowledge of their personalities, and can gaze on their well-preserved treasures. Most people have heard of Ramesses II and Tut-ankh-Amun. Artistic traditions and works of art have survived in bewildering glory and amazing quantity despite the depredations of ancient and modern treasure hunters. Vivid writings and character sketches give us insights into the daily life of the Egyptians, into the court scandals and *causes célèbres* of a long vanished age. But three thousand years after the apogee of Egyptian civilization a mere pittance of the riches and glory that made up the world's longest lasting civilization remain for archaeologist and tourist to admire.

The tombs and great monuments of Ancient Egypt have been under siege ever since they were built. The Egyptians themselves used them for building stone. Theban tomb robbers were followed by religious zealots and quarrymen who eradicated inscriptions and removed great temples stone by stone. Arab treasure hunters tunneled around the pyramids in search of gold. The Sphinx was used for target practice. Then came the travelers and antiquarians in search of curiosities or commercial gain. Some measured the pyramids; others bought mummies and tunneled in the

Ramesses II

10

tombs of Sakkareh. Napoleon Bonaparte came to the Nile in search of an empire and left with the first record of Ancient Egypt, a record that caused a sensation in Europe. By 1833 the monk Father Géramb was able to remark to Pasha Mohammed 'Ali that "it would be hardly respectable, on one's return from Egypt, to present oneself in Europe without a mummy in one hand and a crocodile in the other." Indeed, by Géramb's time a craze for things Egyptian had taken Europe by storm. Diplomats and tourists, merchants and dukes, all vied with one another to assemble spectacular collections of mummies and other antiquities. Architecture and fashion were strongly affected by the new fad. Egyptology became a fashionable subject for the wealthy and the curious. At the same time as the French genius Jean François Champollion was deciphering hieroglyphs, hundreds of travelers were despoiling the very civilization he sought to understand.

During the past two thousand years Ancient Egypt has effectively been destroyed, both by the Egyptians themselves and by a host of foreigners, many of them arriving in the Nile Valley in the name of science and nationalism. The loss to archaeology is incalculable, that to Egyptian history even more staggering. As a result of the looting and pillage of generations of irresponsible visitors,

The pyramids of Gizeh and the Sphinx at sunset. From *La Description de l'Egypte.*

11

Howard Carter presiding at the opening of the burial chamber of Tut-ankh-Amun

the artifacts and artistic achievements of the Ancient Egyptians are scattered all over the globe, some of the most beautiful and spectacular of them stored or displayed thousands of miles from the Nile. Fortunately something has been saved from the wreckage by the dedicated work of modern archaeologists and by the efforts of the Egyptian government during the last hundred years. We cannot in all conscience blame those who

12

looted Ancient Egypt. In retrospect they were
merely mirroring the moral and intellectual climate of their times. The Egyptians were motivated
by profit, by the need to make a good living. The
foreigners were driven by dreams of treasure and
wealth, by incentives of profit and the driving lust
to own the exotic that has been such a pervasive
feature of Western civilization. But at least the
efforts of the foreigners have made the world
aware of the glories of Ancient Egypt in a super-
ficial way. The brightly painted mummies of Egyptian pharaohs and their subjects are commonplace
in European and American museums. Everyone
has seen at least a picture of a hieroglyphic inscription or the pyramids. In these days of swift
jet travel and well-organized package tours, many
of us have been lucky enough to gaze on the bat-
tered remnants of Ancient Egypt on the banks of
the Nile. We are probably stimulated to visit
Egypt by a chance visit to a museum or the reading of a book on the Ancient Egyptians. Yet the
artifacts we see in London, New York, or Paris
were, many of them, obtained by people whose
interest in antiquity was accompanied by a fatal
curiosity, reinforced with gunpowder, picks, and
other destructive instruments. It is one of the tragedies of history that our knowledge of Ancient
Egypt is derived in large part from artifacts recovered during centuries of pillage and tomb robbing among the rock-cut tombs and pyramids of
the Nile.

2 The Father of History and the First Tourists

"This country is a palimpsest," wrote that remarkable Victorian lady Lucie Duff-Gordon from Luxor more than a century ago, "in which the Bible is written over Herodotus, and the Koran over that." And a palimpsest it is, of conquests and tourists, of dedicated travelers and hard-working archaeologists. The story of the discovery of Ancient Egypt owes as much to travelers' tales as it does to the fine words of professional scholars and leisured antiquarians. Even the Ancient Egyptians believed that their civilization was the oldest of all civilized institutions. Indeed, the stability and power of the pharaoh's government was proverbial. The Greeks and Romans were fascinated by the great temples and mighty pyramids that still dominated the banks of the Nile and had ob-

14

viously been there for centuries. The basic institutions of religion and government were thought by the Greeks to have stemmed from the Ancient Egyptians, the inhabitants of a country full of strange wonders.

"There is no country that possesses so many wonders, nor any that has such a number of works that defy description," remarked the Greek historian Herodotus, who visited the Nile in about 460–455 B.C. Herodotus wrote one of the first lengthy accounts of the curiosities and antiquities of the Nile, only a few centuries after the decline of the greatest Egyptian pharaohs. His *Histories* have fascinated scholars and Egyptologists for centuries.

Herodotus' writings show clear evidence of a profound, if at times inaccurate, knowledge of the Ancient World. His reputation as a historian stood high even in his own times, for he was invited to read his works in public before the Athenians. Fortunately, the *Histories* have come down to us in their entirety. They are a collation of observed facts, folk tales, myths, genuine history, and delightful curiosities. Herodotus himself emerges from them as a thoroughly gullible and likable man, with a penchant for accurate observation and an infinite capacity for admiration and wonder. The nine books of the *Histories* do not, of course, measure up to modern historical standards, for their author was much given to exaggeration and was uncritical about his sources. But the essential accuracy of his anthropological observations has been proven by archaeologists on many occasions. He took the trouble to describe Egypt at great length, for he seems to have been more enthusiastic about the Egyptians than almost any other people that he met.

In traveling up the Nile, Herodotus merely followed a well-trodden route. The Nile floodplain is crisscrossed by canals and irrigation works; before the days of roads, railways, and airlines, it was laborious to traverse. All governmental business

"The cliffs of the Nile"

and commercial activity passed up and down the river in barges and sailing vessels, while simple canoes of papyrus reeds served the villagers' needs. Few foreigners ventured into the arid wastes of the deserts which pressed onto the Nile Valley. There was little to see, and the caravan journeys could be arduous in the extreme. So the itineraries of most visitors to the Nile remained basically unchanged for centuries, a journey up the river from Alexandria to Aswan, with stops at the pyramids, Karnak, and Thebes. Thus far the journey was straightforward enough, even in Herodotus' time.

A mass of information and misinformation resulted from Herodotus' leisurely journey. He turned his data into one of the most famous passages of the *Histories*, probably the earliest sys-

16

tematic account of the Nile Valley and its wonders. It is difficult to separate the author's personal observations from the hearsay and myth which he collected, but Herodotus seems to be at his best when describing the geography of the Nile. He speculated as to the cause of the annual flood. "Of the sources of the Nile no one can give any account," he remarked; ". . . it enters Egypt from beyond." Yet he went on to say that people said that the floods were caused by melting snow, a theory that was proved correct more than two thousand years later, although Herodotus disbelieved the tale.

Like so many other Classical visitors, Herodotus professed a reverence and enthusiasm for Egyptian institutions. The Egyptians, he observed, were religious to excess, worshiping a large assembly of

Wall relief in the temple of Sethy I at Abydos: Ramesses II and a prince capturing a bull

gods, from whom, he surmised, the Greeks derived at least some of their own divinities. The cat was held in great reverence and buried in special cemeteries, as were other domestic animals. And, like so many visitors after him, Herodotus was fascinated by the burial customs of the Ancient Egyptians. He described how the embalmers drew out the brain through the nostrils with an iron hook and then cleaned out and preserved the corpse over a period of seventy days. Then, he observed, "the relatives, when they receive the mummified body, make for it a wooden case, shaped like a man; and having put the body inside and sealed it up, they stand it in a sepulcher, upright against a wall." Later investigators have confirmed the essential accuracy of Herodotus' account, which, perhaps, he observed firsthand.

From burial customs he passes to agriculture and fishing, to the hunting of crocodiles and Egyptian boats. No detail large or small escaped the eye of this remarkable traveler. His historical researches, however, left a lot to be desired. Herodotus recounts the legends of origin of the Egyptian state, the story of Menes, the first ruler of a unified Egypt, and tells how the priests showed him king lists recording the names of 350 kings, lists perpetuated in Manetho's *History of Egypt*. The fragmentary historical narrative in the *Histories* is based on hearsay and legend, and the author himself admits as much. But unfortunately his successors simply accepted Herodotus as gospel truth, and, as so often happens, historical myths became dogmatic fact, slavishly copied by centuries of historians.

Yet Herodotus was in an unusual position. Of all the many travelers and historians who have visited Egypt in the past three thousand years whose works have come down to us, Herodotus is the nearest to the great pharaohs themselves. He talked to priests and worshipers who were actively carrying on the traditions of millennia of religious devotion. The monuments of the Nile

were in a far better state of preservation than
they are today, before the disastrous inroads of
archaeological plunderers, despoiling Christians,
and quarrying Muslims. So his account is a vivid
one, perhaps too vivid, of a remarkable and exotic
river valley which he and other educated men
reasonably accepted as the cradle of their own
civilization. The Egyptians themselves came alive:
we read of their drinking bouts, of the story of
the theft of the thief's body, and of complex religious ceremonies, with Herodotus at our side occasionally admonishing us: "Such as think the
tales told by the Egyptians credible are free to accept them for history. . . ." His admonitions were
timely, but were largely ignored by Herodotus'
successors and generations of scholars and historians.

Herodotus' credibility has been castigated by
modern scholars, not least among them the great
French Egyptologist Auguste Mariette. "I detest
this traveler," he wrote, complaining that Herodotus visited Egypt when the ancient language was
still spoken and thus could have asked all sorts of

**The pyramids of Gizeh and
the Sphinx in modern times**

19

key historical questions and received accurate answers. Instead he "tells us gravely that a daughter of Cheops built a pyramid with the fruit of prostitution. . . . Considering the great number of mistakes in Herodotus . . . would it not have been better for Egyptology had he never existed?"

In a sense Mariette is right, for Herodotus' account of Egypt is the first factual description to survive, and the many inaccuracies, stemming in large part from Herodotus' liking for the fanciful and marvelous and his gullible acceptance of tall stories told by temple caretakers, were perpetuated for centuries. Yet British Egyptologist Sir Alan Gardiner's assessment of Herodotus as the "Father of History" and a "great genius" is probably fairer, for he was experimenting with what at the time was a totally new literary art form.

When the Romans occupied Egypt in 30 B.C., the Nile Valley became a prosperous and stable province of the greatest empire the world had known. The awesome security of the Roman Empire blanketed Egypt, although old religious ways were tolerated and even revered. Roman interest in Egypt was predominantly political and exploitative. The power of the empire depended to a great extent on first-rate communication systems and security for the traveler. For three and a half centuries the Roman world was at peace. A rich and leisured class enjoyed an easy life of travel and luxury, passing in safety to even the remotest corners of the empire. Thousands of tourists flocked to Egypt and other parts of the Near East in search of education, entertainment, or religious edification.

The Roman tourist took ship at Ponzzolez for Alexandria, or crossed to Carthage and then traveled to the Nile by coast road. Either route was safe and speedy, for the imperial business used the same communication networks. Constant and uninterrupted traffic crisscrossed the Mediterranean. Marble, linen, papyrus, glass, and perfumes, as well as passengers, were carried in ships which sometimes reached a length of 53 meters and dis-

20

placed more than 2,000 tons. Upon arrival at Alexandria one could travel by river to the Ethiopian frontier or use the post road which ran alongside the Nile. At Koptos, well-maintained mail roads followed the Ancient Egyptian route across the desert to the Red Sea ports of Berenice and Myoshormos, important coastal ports and trading stations in the Arabian and Indian Ocean trade.

The extraordinary stability of Roman Egypt was based on a political system that was superimposed on the native cultures. In France and Britain, for example, the local people sought to become Romanized as quickly as possible, adopting the customs and institutions of their conquerors. But the Egyptians remained aloof, worshiping their age-old gods, cultivating their fields as they always had, perpetuating the mysterious hieroglyphs of earlier times. A distinctive way of life of tremendous antiquity continued to survive comparatively unscathed, surrounded by the lasting monuments of religious and political institutions that extended back into the distant past. The security of Roman rule enabled the tourist to move around freely in this strange country.

The centralized administration of the Roman Empire made constant travel between Rome and Alexandria, and between the governor's headquarters and provincial towns, essential. Government delegations, ambassadors, military conscripts, individual citizens seeking redress, all shuttled to and fro from Egypt to Rome. But many people traveled to the Nile simply to enlarge their intellectual horizons or out of curiosity. Direct inquiry was the best way of learning about history, geography, and the arts of philosophy, religion, and magic which everyone knew were developed to a high pitch in Egypt. Alexandria had an international reputation for scholarship and medicine. Famous teachers were available for the traveler. The sick could be cured. Then there were the notorious pleasure resorts at Alexandria. Ptolemy Soter's celebrated temple of Serapis at Kanopos was famous

The Ramesseum at Thebes

throughout the Ancient World for its extravagant and orgiastic rituals. The cult of Serapis was an amalgam of the worship of two Egyptian gods, Osiris and Apis, a sacred bull.

Tiring of Dionysian pleasures, the tourist could then venture southward up the Nile to another world, where the monuments of antiquity overlooked fertile fields and centuries-old irrigation systems. Although the more serious traveler might examine hundreds of temples, most tourists followed an itinerary which took them from Alexandria to Memphis, the pyramids, the Valley of Kings, and the lovely island of Philae. These places were easily visited by boat or road. Numerous small inns catered to the needs of the weary traveler. Private contractors hired out their boats

22

or pack animals to organized parties of visitors, many of them armed with their Herodotus or Egyptian geographies written by other authors. They recorded their journeys in numerous graffiti scratched on ancient monuments. Their authors sought to inform and to entertain, to titillate with fantasy and myth, and to embrace all manner of information. Antiquities like the pyramids were only part of a general corpus of information presented to the uncritical reader. Most writers added little to Herodotus, for they plagiarized the great historian's work unmercifully.

The Greek author Diodorus Siculus lived in the Nile Valley from 60 to 57 B.C. and was one of the first people to write about the huge seated figures of Amenophis III on the floodplain at Thebes. The Greeks named these spectacular statues the Colossi of Memnon, after a Homeric hero. Ramesses II's nearby temple, the Ramesseum, became known as the Memnonium. Diodorus admired the Ramesseum and its courts with its statues of the king. He found an inscription on one of the figures, which he quoted, attributing the temple correctly to Ozymandias, the Greek equivalent of User-ma'et-Re, the actual name of Ramesses II: "My name is Ozymandias, king of kings; if any would know how great I am and where I lie, let him surpass me in any of my works." Many centuries later Percy Bysshe Shelley (1792–1822) was inspired by a "traveler from an antique land" who described two "vast and trunkless legs of stone" in the desert. "My name is Ozymandias, king of kings: Look on my works, ye Mighty, and despair!" he wrote, a short poem that is among the immortals of the English language.

The Greek geographer Strabo (64 B.C.–C. A.D. 22) was a contemporary of Diodorus Siculus. He accompanied Aelius Gallus, a Roman prefect of Egypt, on his expedition to Upper Egypt in 25 B.C. Strabo's *Geography* is an enormous compilation of factual information about the Roman world. Egypt fills much of his seventeenth book. The account is mainly geographical, a catalog of towns and resources. Archaeological sites are treated like other features of the landscape. At Memphis, he visited the site of the Serapeum. "One finds also [at Memphis] at the temple of Serapis, in a spot so sandy that the wind causes the sand to accumulate in heaps, under which we could see many sphinxes, some of them almost entirely buried, others only partially covered." Nearly two thousand years later, French archaeologist Auguste Mariette used Strabo's account to rediscover the Serapeum. Strabo's party paused to admire the great Colossi at the Ramesseum at Thebes. Next they examined some inscriptions on obelisks in Luxor and Karnak, one of which was later given to King Louis XVIII by Mohammed 'Ali in the nineteenth century and now stands in the Place de la Concorde in Paris. "Above the Memnonium," remarked Strabo, "are tombs of kings, which are stone-hewn, are about forty in number, are marvelously constructed, and are a spectacle worth seeing." This is one of the first references to the Valley of Kings, for so long the scene of archaeological rape and pillage. Strabo ends by castigating Herodotus and others for "talking much nonsense, adding to their account marvelous tales, to give it, as it were, a kind of tune or rhythm or relish." Strabo was not the first Egyptian traveler to find reality different from history.

The first stop for the Roman tourist venturing upstream was the pyramids at Gizeh, still adorned with their magnificent casing stones, later removed by the Arabs to construct the public buildings of Cairo. Many travelers were moved to inscribe their names on the casing stones, a thoroughly human failing which has vandalized ancient monuments throughout history. The Egyptian examples provide, in themselves, a fascinating historical kaleidoscope of pithy observations and reactions to the marvels of antiquity. The earliest recorded inscription dates to about A.D. 1475, for the older inscriptions were removed with the

24

casing stones, although we know from the travels of Rudolph von Suchem, a monk who visited the pyramids in 1336, that earlier inscriptions did exist.

Near the pyramids of Gizeh lay the Sphinx, which was buried in drifting sand. Pliny the Elder was one of the first Roman authors to describe this most famous of Egyptian monuments. There were other tourist attractions, too: the temple of Apis at the ancient and flourishing town of Memphis, the famous "Labyrinth" at the Fayyum, a vast palace of Amun-em-het III (1850–1800 B.C.). The Labyrinth was so named on account of its many courtyards and rooms which caused imaginative Greeks to compare it to the mythical Cretan Laby-

Crocodiles on the Nile. "It is a timid, shy creature, and is said to have been driven away by the noise of the steamboats."

rinth. "It has twelve courts, all of them roofed," wrote Herodotus; ". . . the passages through the houses, and the varied windings of the paths across the courts, excited in me infinite admiration, as I passed from the courts into chambers, and from the chambers into colonnades, and from the colonnades into fresh houses, and again from these into courts unseen before." Herodotus felt that the Labyrinth was even more wonderful than the pyramids for there were far more distinguished buildings at Luxor. Nearby were the sacred crocodiles of the Fayyum, fed from priestly hands, strictly as a tourist attraction. No traces of the Labyrinth survive today. When the great Egyptologist Sir Flinders Petrie excavated at the site in 1889, he found only a few columns and architraves and numerous chips. For centuries lime burners had camped among the ruins and slowly reduced them to shredded rubble.

From the Labyrinth the traveler pressed on upstream to Luxor and Karnak, where he walked through the vast hall of pillars at Karnak and ven-

Karnak: Hypostele Hall of Sethy I and Ramesses II

The Colossi of Memnon near
Thebes. From *La Description
de l'Egypte.*

tured into the desolate Valley of Kings, burial
place of the pharaohs. There, the deep burial
chambers of the pharaohs quarried into the hills
of the valley were an exciting adventure. By the
time the Romans came, many of the tombs had already been opened and plundered. The tourist
could venture into the mysterious chambers and
inscribe his name by torchlight on the walls of
the desecrated tomb. But Diodorus complained:
"We found nothing there except the results of pillage and destruction."

But it was the two vast seated statues of Memnon on the floodplain near the Valley of Kings
which were one of the highlights of any visit to
the Nile. The Greeks had identified these seated
Colossi with the mythical King Memnon of Ethiopia, son of the Dawn, who had assisted the Tro-
jans against Achilles. Like the Labyrinth, the Colossi had received their name from a well-known

27

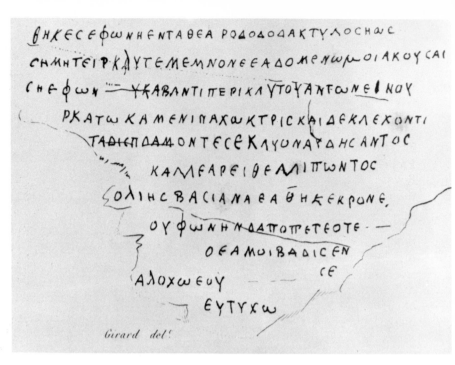

ΒΗΚΕΣΕΦωΝΗΕΝΤΑΘΕΑ ΡΟΔΟΔΟΔΑΚΤΥΛΟCΗωC
CΗΜΗΤΕΙΡΚΑΥΤΕΜΕΜΝΟΝΕΕΑΔΟΜΕΝωμ ΟΙΑΚΟΥCΑΙ
CΗΕΦωΝ ΥΚΑΒΛΝΤΙΠΕΡΙΚΛΥΤΟΥΑΝΤωΝΕΙΝΟΥ
ΡΚΑΤω ΚΑΜΕΝΙΠΑΧωΚΤΡΙCΚΑΙΔΕΚΛΕΧΟΝΤΙ
ΤΑΔΙΕΠΟΔΑΜΟΝΤΕCΕΚΛΥΟΝΑΥΔΗCΑΝΤΟC
ΚΑΛΓΑΡΕΙΘΕΛΛΙΠωΝΤΟC
ΖΟΛΙΗCΒΑCΙΑΝΑΒΑΘΗΚΕΚΡΟΝΕ,
ΟΥΦωΝΗΜΔΑΠΟΠΕΤΕΟΤΕ
ΟΕΑΜΟΙΒΑΔΙCΕΝ
ΑΛΟΧωΕΟΥ   CΕ
ΕΥΤΥΧω

Girard del.

A Greek inscription on the foot of one of the huge statues, recorded by the authors of *La Description*

character of common legend, a familiar historical landmark identified among a landscape of unfamiliar gods and pharaohs. In fact the two seated statues are effigies of Pharaoh Amenophis III and stood in front of his vast mortuary temple, which had already been quarried away by Roman times. Both statues had been badly damaged in antiquity, most recently by an earthquake in 27 B.C., but this did not prevent the northern statue of the pair from emitting mysterious sounds in the early morning. Tourists flocked to hear and speculate about the strange noises. Some compared them to human voices, others to a harp string. Strabo was more cynical. He suspected that the local priests had installed a mechanism to cause the sound. Without question, however, the moaning was caused by expansion of the stones in the early morning heat of the sun or some related natural phenomenon. The humble and the mighty gathered at dawn to hear the statue speak.

The Memnon was not so obliging to the Emperor Hadrian, who visited the statue in A.D. 130. He remained silent the first day, but spoke to the emperor and empress on the second, an event that caused an accompanying poetess to inscribe some commemorative verses on the statue in praise of Memnon and, of course, the Emperor Hadrian. The Memnon's later refusal to speak for the Emperor Septimius Severus in A.D. 202 was fatal. Severus sought to conciliate the god by restoring the head and torso, an act that silenced the statue forever.

We do not know what damage Roman tourists did to the Egyptian past. There are no official records of a widespread trade in antiquities. Nor, seemingly, had the apparent medicinal properties of Egyptian mummies been recognized. But the obelisk, a slender pinnacle of granite carved with hieroglyphs, proved of overriding interest to the Romans. Strabo's obelisks were but two of several removed by Roman emperors. Constantine the Great (A.D. 306–337) was a great looter of obelisks. He caused a granite obelisk erected at Thebes by Thut-mose III in the fifteenth century B.C. to be removed to Alexandria. Bureaucratic inertia delayed the monument at the Egyptian coast until after Constantine's death. It found its way to Istanbul, where it was erected in the Hippodrome near the Hagia Sophia Mosque on the orders of Emperor Theodosius I in A.D. 390. There it still stands. The other was eventually brought to Rome and erected in the great Circus Maximus. In due course it fell down, but was reerected by Pope Sixtus V in 1587. The slender proportions and exotic hieroglyphic inscriptions on these obelisks seem to have excited the Romans, for they copied the architectural form with their own cruder obelisks. No one was able to comprehend the significance of Egyptian obelisks, although the soldier and naturalist Pliny the Elder (A.D. 23–79) suggested they were symbolic representations of the sun's rays. A leisurely inspection of the obelisks in Rome con-

The Emperor Hadrian

29

vinced him that the hieroglyphic inscriptions comprised "an account of natural science according to the theories of the Egyptian sages." The same author contemptuously dismissed the pyramids "as a superfluous and foolish display of wealth on the part of the kings."

The obelisk in the Campus Martius was put to use by Augustus as a form of calendar to mark the sun's shadow and the lengths of days and nights: "A pavement was laid down for a distance appropriate to the height of the obelisk, so that the shadow cast at noon on the shortest day of the year might exactly coincide with it. Bronze rods let into the pavement were meant to measure the shadow day by day as it gradually became shorter and then lengthened again." "But," added Pliny, "the readings thus given here for about thirty years have failed to correspond to the calendar."

The Roman interest in Ancient Egypt seems to have stemmed from plain intellectual curiosity about a civilization assumed to be the oldest in the world. While, no doubt, some prominent Romans, like the Emperor Hadrian, bought some antiquities for their gardens, already adorned with Greek statuary, and the tomb robbers of Thebes continued their nefarious business unmolested, many Roman tourists must have aspired to the hopes of an Alexandrian visitor inscribed on one of the temples at Philae: "Whoever prays to Isis at Philae becomes happy, rich, and long-lived."

Obelisks of Thut-mose I and Queen Hat-shepsut at Karnak

Diorite head of Amun-hotpe III. XVIII Dynasty.

3 "Mummy Is Become Merchandise"

Some fifty years after Constantine the Great had removed the obelisks from Thebes, a French nun named Lady Etheria ventured to Egypt as part of a lengthy progress through the holy places of the Near East. Somewhat bolder than her contemporaries, she visited Alexandria, passed by the pyramids, inspected the dwelling places of hermits, and gazed on the Colossi of Memnon at Thebes. "Nothing else is there now save one great Theban stone in which two great statues are cut out, which they say are the statues of holy men, even Moses and Aaron, erected by the Children of Israel in their honor," she wrote. Lady Etheria passed on into history, but was satisfied with her observation. By Etheria's time, the Bible was the primary literary source in the civilized world, a safe and secure archive of philosophy and information which was capable of explaining the strange ways of the world.

Lady Etheria was traveling in unsettled and changing times, when the great academic centers of the Classical world were in decline or turning inward on themselves. Egypt had not escaped the winds of change, for the decline of Roman power and the rise of Christianity had brought many

"The Island of Philae, a view showing several monuments." From *La Description de l'Egypte.*

"A general view of Edfu."
From *La Description*.

changes in traditional economic and religious
ways. Christianity itself came to Alexandria in the
first century A.D., in the hands, so it is said, of
St. Mark. A small group of converts soon mush-
roomed into a large congregation of Christians
who refused to worship the emperor as a god in
his own right, a campaign of revolt that led to
appalling persecutions and many martyrdoms. But
in A.D. 313 Constantine the Great recognized Christianity as one of the official religions of the empire, and the influence of the Alexandrian Christians grew all-powerful on the Nile. The new
religion was at first a religion of townsfolk, of educated Alexandrian Greeks and minor tradesmen.
But in the fourth century the scriptures were
translated from Greek into Coptic, the language
most commonly spoken by Egyptians. A cult of
monasticism, a quest for spiritual perfection
through retreat from the secular world, emerged
among small communities of monks and hermits
who spread the new doctrines to the common
people. Christianity among the poverty-stricken
Coptic peasants began, perhaps, as a form of anti-
colonial protest against a sinful world dominated
by elitist town dwellers.

34

The Coptic Christians were far from unified in
their beliefs or traditional customs, but were all
committed to a new order of religious institutions
which did not tolerate the old. While the Roman
tourist had been curious about Egyptian religious
beliefs, the native Copts were determined to ex-
punge all traces of ancient, heretical ways. Their
zeal was encouraged by none other than Emperor
Justinian himself, who ordered the beautiful temples of Isis on the island of Philae closed in the
sixth century A.D. The temple statues were removed to Constantinople, presumably to commemorate his piety in converting the heathen. The
ceremonial panoply of Ancient Egyptian religion
was now illegal, and the symbols of the ancient
religion regarded as evil and sinful. So the inscriptions and faces, heads, hands, and feet from
fine friezes on temple porticos were ruthlessly
obliterated with hammer and chisel in the name
of God. In 397 the fanatical Patriarch Cyril and
his armies probably destroyed the Serapeum at
Memphis, one of the great Roman tourist attractions. The ruins were covered with drifting desert
sand and uncovered only in the nineteenth century.

The neglected temples of the pharaohs stood empty on the floodplain, occupying valuable agricultural land, or higher ground which was never flooded by the annual inundation. Some were destroyed for building stone, for hewn stone blocks are admirable building materials in a country desperately short of wood. There was no need to quarry fresh granite when large numbers of beautifully cut and squared blocks were available for the taking from the ruins of a disused temple. Even the Ancient Egyptians themselves had recycled their building stone. Much of modern Cairo was built from carefully hewn stones from nearby temples and pyramids which were dismantled piecemeal by quarrymen. Where man did not quarry away the stone or deface temple inscriptions, nature took over. Desert sands drifted over the Sphinx. Agricultural land was in short supply on the Nile floodplain, so the people built their villages on patches of higher ground, including the roof of the great temples of Horus at Edfu, deeply buried under drifting sand. The roof of the temple was occupied for centuries by peasant farmers who were completely ignorant of the significance of the building they had commandeered. Lady Etheria and her contemporaries glimpsed Ancient Egypt just as it was entering a long slumber, an oblivion which lasted for centuries.

The far-from-gentle Christians were followed by conquering Arabs, who defeated the Byzantine rulers of Egypt. The small Muslim army was led by the soldier-poet 'Amr, who wrote of Alexandria that he had captured a city "that contains 4,000 palaces, 4,000 baths, 400 theaters, 1,200 greengrocers, and 40,000 Jews." But the city was a shadow of its former learned self. Most of the great library had been destroyed in a civil war two and a half centuries before. At first Egypt was little more than a military province of the expanding empire of Islam, but the new religion spread slowly along the banks of the Nile as more agricultural settlers, bureaucrats, and Islamic scholars settled in Egypt.

The mosque of ibn Tulun, Cairo, founded in the ninth century A.D.

36

Seated statue of Amun-hotpe III in black granite from Luxor. XVIII Dynasty.

The cultured scholars of the new order marveled at the temples and pyramids, but they came from an even more alien culture which had no appreciation of the history or cultural achievements of its new colony. Without this historical sense they were at a loss, nor could the Copts, ignorant of hieroglyphs or older religious ways, enlighten their new masters. So the scholars shrugged and ascribed the works of Ancient Egypt to giants or magicians long departed from the banks of the eternal river. Some thought of the pyramids as Joseph's granaries used for storing corn in years of plenty, a theory already propounded by the Roman author Julius Honorius before the fifth century. Others thought they were treasure houses of long-dead kings. The great Arab geographer 'al-Masudi wrote that the Great Pyramid contained "the image of a sheik, made of green stone, sitting on a sofa, and wrapped up in a garment." Unfortunately, the statue could not be moved. Some rather adventurous souls, bolder than 'al-Masudi, entered the pyramids in search of treasure during the Middle Ages. Temples and pyramids became quarries for building stone or were dismembered in a frantic quest for legendary treasure.

For centuries the Arabs pursued treasure hunting with a curious intensity, rivaled only by that displayed by nineteenth-century antiquities collectors. It was so widely practiced in the fifteenth century that treasure hunting was classified as a taxed industry. People dug everywhere using secret magical incantations and techniques which, if effective, would be just the thing for a modern archaeologist to use in amplification of his electronic detection methods. Guidebooks to treasure hunting included complicated directions to tomb areas, such as one cemetery complex near Heliopolis which was visible to a treasure hunter if he performed "fumigations" at a certain point. *The Book of Hidden Pearls and Precious Mysteries* and other such jewels of treasure-hunting lore were regarded as vital parts of the treasure hunt-

38

er's safari kit. The instructions given in these handbooks would delight any amateur chemist:

> You will uncover some masonry. Break it, perform continuous fumigation, and you will find a sloping way that will lead you to a chamber containing a corpse covered by a cloth of woven gold and wearing golden armour. . . . The incense should be compounded of agalloche, stigmatas of saffron, dung, carob kernels, sycamore figs. Take a *mithqal* of each of these ingredients, grind them fine, moisten them with human blood, roll them into pellets and burn them as incense . . . the talismans and the hiding places will thus be discovered.

Not everyone was taken in by the nonsense, least of all that wise and sober Arab writer Ibn Khaldoun, who mocked the treasure hunters and their magic in the fifteenth century. "Suppose that a man did want to bury all his treasures and to keep them safe by means of some magical process," he wrote. "He would take all possible precautions to keep his secret hidden. How could one believe, then, that he would place unmistakable signs to guide those who sought the treasure, and that he would commit those signs to writing?" Despite Ibn Khaldoun's scorn, treasure hunters blasted and probed their way through Ancient Egypt well into the nineteenth century, undeterred by murders and thefts, or by repeated failures. As late as 1907 Gaston Maspero, then director of antiquities in Egypt, arranged for the publication of *The Book of Hidden Pearls* at a very low price so that it was freely available as a worthless publication for the most gullible.

The outside world knew little of the Egyptians and even less of their ancient civilization, for the governors of Egypt did little to encourage foreigners to visit the Nile. Christians were far from welcome once Islam took root in the country, as the Catholic monk Bernard the Wise found to his cost in 870. He and two companions had to bribe their ship's captain to put them ashore at Alexandria at all. Then the governor in Cairo cast them into jail

Pompey's Pillar at Alexandria

The Sphinx (*opposite*)

until "after six days it occurred to us by the help of God to give him 300 Denarii each." After gazing at Joseph's granaries (the pyramids), the pilgrims withdrew hastily to Jerusalem without any further archaeological inquiries. None of the various pilgrims who strayed from the regular stamping grounds of such travelers in the Holy Land could be described as dispassionate observers, for they almost invariably interpreted the pyramids and other monuments in terms of the Hebrews and the biblical story. A few educated and cultured Muslims were able to contribute far more intelligent and perceptive observations. One such was an Arab doctor from Baghdad, Abdel Latif, who taught medicine in Cairo in about 1200. At that time there were few Europeans in Egypt, and the superintendent of buildings in the city was busily quarrying away the smaller pyramids within easy reach of Cairo to construct a defense wall around the citadel. Latif ventured about two-thirds of the way into the upper part of the Great Pyramid, which he found crowded with treasure hunters armed with their pet handbooks and incantations. The much-trampled passageways were choked with bat droppings and infested with a noxious stench. Latif fainted away in horror and emerged in a highly fearful state. But he was not too shocked to admire the fine hieroglyphs on the casing stones and the Sphinx. "This figure is very beautiful," he wrote, "and its mouth bears the seal of grace and beauty. It could be remarked that it smiles in a gracious manner." He ventured also to Memphis, where he described the ruins of the huge Roman city. "It requires a half-day's march in any direction to cross the visible ruins," he wrote. Six hundred years later, all that remained were a few mounds of earth and some fragmentary statues.

The educated European of five hundred years ago had access to almost no reliable information on Egypt at all, except for travelers' tales and hearsay brought home by returning Crusaders

40

A sakieh or waterwheel, painted by the celebrated Victorian artist David Roberts

during the preceding centuries. He could, however, turn to *The Voiage and Travaile of Sir John Mandeville, Knight,* purportedly an accurate guidebook for pilgrims to the Holy Land, illuminated by the personal experiences of its devout author. This entertaining volume, a mine of information compiled from Classical sources, fables, folklore, and highly unreliable travelers' tales, was soon regarded as the ultimate authority against which other accounts were checked. In fact, Sir John Mandeville never existed and the author, one Jean d'Outremeuse, never visited the Nile at all. The whole work was a complete fabrication. This deliberate—and highly successful—literary fraud was widely quoted, especially on account of its description of the pyramids. "And some men say that they be sepulchres of great lords, that were

42

sometime, but that is not true, for all the common rumour and speech is all of the people there, both far and near, that they be the garners of Joseph," was Mandeville's verdict on the pyramids—perhaps, indeed, a majority view, but not one shared by Brother Felix Fabri of Ulm, Germany, who actually gazed on the pyramids and sensed that they were "marvelous sepulchral monuments of the ancient kings of Egypt."

Firsthand accounts of the Nile were still few and far between. Most people turned to the writings of the great Leo Africanus, a Catholic and a scholar whose wanderings over northern Africa in the early sixteenth century are of the greatest interest to African historians. Leo traveled all the way up the Nile to Aswan and the First Cataract, observing the life on its banks and the antiquities, which were not, however, his primary concern. His *History and Description of Africa,* as indispensable to the prospective traveler as Mandeville, makes only cursory mention of the pyramids and describes Memphis as a "citie that seemeth in times past to have beene very large." At Manfalut:

Near unto Nilus stand the ruins of a stately building which seemeth to have beene a temple in times past, among which ruins the citizens finde sometimes coine of silver, sometimes of gold, and sometimes of lead, having on the one side hielygraphick notes, and on the other side the pictures of ancient kings.

It was only the most determined of travelers who succeeded in reaching Egypt. The sea voyage across the Mediterranean, perhaps in a Venetian or Turkish galley, might take weeks. Brother Felix Fabri complained of drunken passengers who interrupted his Sunday sermons, and the loathsome occupation of all seamen: "the hunting and catching of lice and vermin."

He had returned from Egypt on a Venetian spice galley, a vessel engaged in regular trading with the Alexandrines. The spices as well as other

Painted wooden models of offering bearers—girls bearing baskets of wine, meat, and live ducks. Tomb of Meketra, Thebes. XI Dynasty.

43

Mummy of Meryet-Amun

commodities came overland from the east and were funneled into Europe through Alexandria. Then in 1517, a few years after the Portuguese had opened up the Cape of Good Hope route to the east and monopolized the spice commerce, Egypt was invaded by the Turks and became a province of the Turkish Empire. The new ruler, Selim I, confirmed earlier diplomatic treaties with France and Spain and granted a measure of religious protection to non-Muslims. It was now reasonably safe to travel in Egypt, if one managed to escape the attentions of pirates on the way to the Nile. A steady stream of pilgrims, diplomats, and merchants made their way to Alexandria and farther inland in search of holy places, political advantage, or commercial opportunity. Many of these travelers were preoccupied with their commercial or religious objectives and were little concerned with scientific observation. But there were some more objective observers. In 1533 Dr. Pierre Belon of France, a botanist, ventured inside the pyramid of Cheops and inspected the Sphinx, which by this time had been mutilated—by Sheik Mohammed in 1300.

But it was the mummy that excited the most attention from the speculators. Anyone who visited Egypt was confronted with Ancient Egyptian mummies. References to the processes of embalming were commonplace in Classical literature accessible to literate explorers. The Egyptians themselves broke up mummy cases for firewood and sold the corpses for medicinal purposes, for by the sixteenth century "mummy" had become a highly prized drug. The word "mummy" is derived from the Persian word *mummia* (Arabic: *mumija*), a term for pitch or bitumen. Pissasphalt from the Near East had long been regarded as useful for a cure for cuts and bruises, and for the treatment of fractures, nausea, and a host of other ailments. The appearance of pissasphalt closely resembled that of the bituminous materials used by the Ancient Egyptians in the mummification process.

44

When supplies of pissasphalt were hard to come by, it became common practice to substitute the materials found inside the bodies of Egyptian mummies for the real thing. From there it was an even shorter step to substitute the dried flesh of the mummy for the hardened bituminous materials found in the body cavities.

Mummy had a long and respectable antiquity as a medicinal substance. As early as the tenth century A.D., Arab doctors were describing the properties of a medical specific that had obviously been in use for centuries. The Arab historian and doctor Abdel Latif, whom we have already met describing the Sphinx's smile, was evidently familiar with mummy: "The mummy found in the hollows of corpses in Egypt, differs but immaterially from the nature of mineral mummy; and where any difficulty arises in procuring the latter, may be substituted in its stead." A flourishing trade in mummified human flesh had arisen. The medicinal substance was exported as entire mummies or in fragments packaged in Cairo and Alexandria, whence merchants sent the dried substance all over western Europe. Peasant villagers dug up the tombs and transported mummy to Cairo, "where," recorded Abdel Latif in 1203, "it is sold for a trifle. For half a dirhem I purchased three heads filled with the substance. . . . This mummy is as black as pitch. I observed, when exposed to the strong heat of the sun, that it melts." Another Arab writer recorded in 1424 how

people who had made a large pile of human corpses were discovered in Cairo. They were brought before the provost, who had them tortured until they confessed that they were removing the corpses from tombs and were boiling the dead bodies in water over a very hot fire until the flesh fell off; that they then collected the oil which rose to the surface of the liquid to sell it to the Franks, who paid twenty-five pieces of gold a hundredweight for it.

Numerous foreign merchants traded in mummy, for the potential profits were enormous. The Ger-

Mummy of XI Dynasty, with mask

45

A jeweled collar with pectoral from the tomb of Tut-ankh-Amun

man traveler Johann Helferich of Leipzig, who visited Egypt in 1565, was so anxious to buy some mummies that he dug the sand out of several tombs in a fruitless search for ancient corpses. But few were as ambitious as John Sanderson, an energetic agent for the Turkey Company, who spent a year in Egypt in 1585–1586. Sanderson lived in Alexandria, visited the pyramids and the Sphinx, and studied commercial opportunities in Cairo. But he spent much time at the famous Memphis mummy pits. The enterprising Sanderson was quick to cash in on the Ancient Egyptians. He bought more than 600 pounds of mummified flesh and a whole body for export to England. Such an enormous shipment of mummy was unusual, but Sanderson simply bribed his way out of Egypt accompanied by his consignment and "divers heads, hands, arms and feet for a sheive." The market value of mummy in Scotland in 1612 was eight shillings a pound, so Sanderson made quite a profit. A French physician, Guy de la Fonteine of Navarre, investigated the mummy trade of Alexandria in 1564 and found clear evidence of fraud and use of modern corpses to satisfy an apparently insatiable demand for mummy. Many of the merchants who exported the substance cared little about the sources of mummy. Indeed they marveled that Christians, so particular about their diet, could actually eat the bodies of the dead. Mummy was practically a patent medicine. Even King Francis I of France carried a small package of mummy with him as an emergency precaution. But not everyone was happy about mummy. "This wicked kinde of Drugge, doth nothing helpe the diseased . . . it also inferres many troublesome symptomes, as the paire of the heart or stomacke, vomiting, and strike of the mouth," fumed one writer.

The Egyptian government sought to restrict the wilder excesses of the mummy trade by levying harsh taxes on traders and forbidding the shipping of corpses out of Egypt. Apparently the ships

46

that carried mummies met violent storms so fre-
quently that the superstitious crews regarded a
cargo of mummy as unacceptably dangerous. But
the threat of shipwreck and government regulations did not prevent fraud and the export of
mummy; indeed it persisted in medical use until
the early nineteenth century.

The great philosopher Sir Thomas Browne was
very explicit: "Mummy is become merchandise,
Mizraim cures wounds, and Pharaoh is sold for
balsam." Even in Mark Twain's day, mummy was
remembered, if only in a humorous context. On
the Egyptian railroad, he recalled in *Innocents
Abroad,* "the fuel they use for the locomotive is
composed of mummies three thousand years old,
purchased by the ton or by the graveyard for that
purpose, and . . . sometimes one hears the profane
engineer call out pettishly, 'D——n these plebe-
ians, they don't burn worth a cent—pass out a
king.'" Even in the 1970s there is a regular, although very insignificant, demand for mummy
among those who deal in magic and the occult. It
is rumored that genuine powdered Egyptian
mummy can be bought at some New York drug-
stores for forty dollars an ounce.

4 "He Will Make a Collection"

Since the most beautiful monuments of antiquity appear to have survived the perils of so many centuries solely to be judged worthy of a place in your Eminence's libraries and cabinets, may I assure your Eminence that in order to procure for them so glorious a shelter, that I have already written throughout the Levant to impose the necessary orders in all places where there are Consuls of France that they seek with great care all such things as may be worthy of this honour.

Ambassador du Houssay had good reason to take care to write in this vein to Cardinal Richelieu from Cairo in 1638, for he was merely pandering to the taste of the French nobility and the king himself for the exotic and curious. This taste for collecting antiquities was relatively new, a phe-

Hunting scenes from a tomb painting

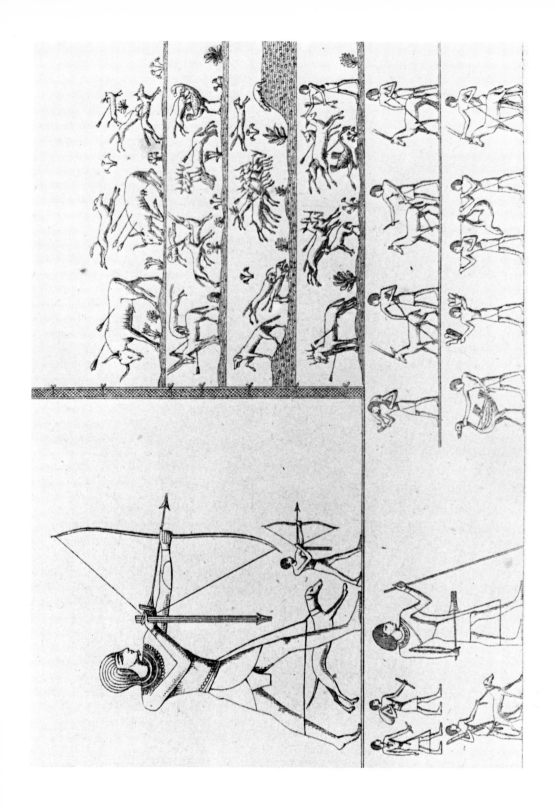

nomenon which arose in part from the emancipation of people's minds during the Renaissance. Ancient manuscripts were dusted off and collected as the new learning sparked an excitement about the diversity of mankind and the history of human achievement. It was not long before new and learned dissertations on the state of the world were gratifying the literary tastes of cultivated gentlemen. But, with the exception of the obelisks in Rome and Constantinople, few Egyptian antiquities were to be seen in Europe. Mummy was in common use, so presumably the general public was aware of the Ancient Egyptians' unusual burial customs. In 1615 the celebrated Italian traveler Pietro della Valle brought back the first Mesopotamian cuneiform tablets to reach Europe. He also purchased fine mummies at Sakkareh. Casual purchases such as these became increasingly commonplace in cabinets of curiosities and royal collections.

The serious business of collecting antiquities had really begun in the sixteenth century, when some Italian cardinals and the Medici Prince Cosimo I (1519–1574) had acquired large collections of antiquities, including a few Egyptian pieces. Travelers on the Grand Tour of Mediterranean lands, a cultural phenomenon of the seventeenth and eighteenth centuries, purchased sculpture and statuary from Greek and Roman temples for their gardens and cabinets. Early collectors were polymathic in their interests, with little sense of quality or geographic specialization. Coins, mummies, Indian scalps, baskets, Polynesian axes, and papyri were all part of a cabinet of curiosities. Considerable sums were lavished on collections of exotic statuary and artifacts, which were often viewed by large crowds. Collecting antiquities, in short, had become a highly acceptable and potentially lucrative activity, both for the collector and for the dealer who supplied him.

"I never saw a place I liked worse," wrote the Scottish explorer James Bruce of Cairo in 1768. He

added that "it afforded less pleasure and instruction than most places" and possessed antiquities which "less answered their description." Bruce's views of Cairo were not shared by the many curious and wealthy travelers who visited the city after the sixteenth century. A new breed of visitor now ventured to the Nile in the wake of the merchant and pilgrim—the antiquarian in search of intellectual enlightenment and the antiquities themselves. A flurry of leisured diplomatic activity had accompanied the Turkish annexation of Egypt, and many diplomatic visitors came to Cairo, some of them to settle for long periods of time. Both new diplomats and more transient visitors were taken on a well-trodden tourist circuit to the pyramids and the mummy pits of Sakkareh. They visited the bazaars in Cairo, where they were able to examine completely bandaged corpses and marvel at the blackened limbs and shriveled faces of age-old Egyptians. The curio dealers were only too glad to supply the visitor to Cairo or Alexandria with amulets, scarabs, papyri, or even complete mummies—for a consideration. Even if prices seemed high, one could sell one's purchases in Europe at an enormous profit.

The French kings and their noblemen were probably the most avid collectors of antiquities during the seventeenth and eighteenth centuries.

Dancing girls in Cairo painted by David Roberts in the mid-nineteenth century. "They are often extremely handsome," he wrote, "and among them are certainly to be found the finest women in Egypt. But they are never admitted to a respectable hareem, for they are the most abandoned of courtesans."

"A Fellah's hut with land divided into squares for irrigation"

Special parties of scholars were sent to Mediterranean lands in search of coins, manuscripts, and all manner of antiquities. Their undigested collections provided a catalyst for more detailed inquiry. A more serious objective was part of the specific instructions to Father J. B. Vansleb, a German in the service of Louis XIV who received orders to seek "the greatest possible number of good manuscripts and ancient coins for His Majesty's library." Vansleb was to make a description of the peoples of Egypt and "of the different manner of burial of divers peoples."

Father Vansleb had an eventful journey, consoled by a "kilderkin of wine" which he guarded jealously from his fellow travelers. He tried to measure the pyramids with long pieces of string, but was unable to complete the task because of drifting sand. At Sakkareh he had himself lowered into the mummy pits, where he acquired some mummified birds in earthenware pots. These he sent back to Paris with some Arab manuscripts, including one which described "the hiding places of all the treasures in Egypt." Disguising himself in Turkish dress, he traveled upstream from Cairo, only to be forced back because of threats on his life. Vansleb was known to be an emissary of the king of France, and the Turks feared that Louis XIV might have designs on Egypt. He abandoned his intention of going to Ethiopia, a mission that had been entrusted to him, and wrote to France complaining of the barbarity of the people and the tyranny of the Turkish authorities. In June 1672 he resumed his travels and nearly lost his life while attempting to visit the Coptic monasteries of St. Macarious in Lower Egypt. His wine cask was the problem. A zealous Turkish magistrate incited some young people to ask Vansleb for a drink, a demand with which he refused to comply, pointing out that Muslims were forbidden wine. The following day he was ambushed by three young ruffians who tried to throw his precious barrel into the Nile. Vansleb snatched for his kilderkin;

A coffeehouse on the outskirts of Cairo. "Loungers are satisfied to sit hour after hour, sipping a cup of coffee, or of sherbet, or listening to the dismal tones of a *tarabookah.*"

53

his Nubian servant, a man "of stout heart," cast one of the thugs into the Nile, and the incident ended with a fine of ten piasters for drinking alcoholic beverages. He appealed to the local kachif for protection and an escort. Instead the kachif said he would accompany him to the monastery himself, and moved Vansleb to his house. Vansleb was now seriously worried, for the kachif had a reputation for timely assassinations. Fortunately one of the kachif's servants, whom Vansleb had tipped well some time before, came secretly and warned him to leave at once. Vansleb "had no further desire for sleep" at this news, stole quickly out of the village, and bribed a boat captain to take him aboard. Moments after they had cast off, the kachif and thirty horsemen came galloping along the bank in frustrated fury. The perils of the king's service were almost too much for Vansleb, who retired to Constantinople to finish a book on the history of the Church in Alexandria before returning to France in 1676. There he was censured for not persevering with his journey to Ethiopia.

But it was the local diplomats who became the most ardent collectors. Diplomatic duties in Cairo or Alexandria were hardly arduous. The collection of antiquities offered a lucrative sideline, especially through local contacts forged in government service. Benoit de Maillet, one of the first of a new breed of diplomatic antiquarians and collectors, was French consul in Egypt from 1692 to 1708. He visited the interior of the Great Pyramid more than forty times, corresponded with scholars in France, and developed an outline scheme for the exploration of Ancient Egypt which acted as a blueprint for Napoleon's expedition a century later. "We are told," he reported, "that there are still in Upper Egypt temples of which the blue or gilded vaultings are still as beautiful as if they had just been finished; there are idols of a prodigious size; columns without number. " His diplomatic reports recommended that an accurate map

Benoit de Maillet (1656–1738). This portrait appeared in his *Description de l'Egypte* **(1735).**

54

of Egypt be compiled and that "persons wise, curious, and adroit" should be encouraged to make a scientific exploration of the Nile Valley at a slow and deliberate pace. Just over a century later, Napoleon Bonaparte's savants carried out de Maillet's recommendations. De Maillet's successor, Le Maire, was another keen antiquarian, as was Paul Lucas, a goldsmith's son who came to Egypt on his own account to buy gems, coins and curios. He later became an agent for Louis XIV, ordered in 1716 to "endeavour to open some pyramid in order to find out in a detailed manner all that this kind of edifice contains." But Lucas never opened a pyramid. Instead he collected mummified birds at Sakkareh and took a leisurely voyage upstream past Thebes, where he admired the "vast palaces, magnificent temples, these obelisks, and the prodigious number of thick columns that are still standing," as he drifted slowly past.

Schooled in Classical literature and widely read in travelers' tales, some of the more ambitious of European tourists now traveled to Cairo, inspected the pyramids at Gizeh, and allowed themselves to be pushed and shoved into the burial chambers. Nearly every traveler complained about the heat and stench inside the pyramids. Some fainted away from heat exhaustion; others, too plump for the narrow defiles, stuck in the passages, to the discomfort of their companions. Local Arabs would help them climb up the outside, assisting them from step to step of huge boulders. To travel farther upstream along the Nile, the tourist struck a bargain with the skipper of a dahabeah, a type of sailing vessel that had plied the waters of the Nile as far upstream as the First Cataract and beyond for centuries. The tourist of two hundred years ago merely plugged into the local transportation system and visited the monuments at Thebes, Aswan, and other localities near the Nile. Until the advent of the railroad, motorcar, and airplane, no other logical means of transport existed for either tourist or local traveler.

55

A booth in the Cairo bazaar sketched by the Victorian tourist and writer Amelia Edwards and entitled "In the Name of the Prophet—Cakes"

Every traveler paused in the bazaars of Cairo, too. Merchandise from all parts of the Arab world was for sale in the city, to say nothing of European trade goods and the products of Black Africa. Great caravans arrived and departed from Cairo every day, and the bazaars were alive with the bustle and never-ceasing ebb and flow of the world's commerce. Antiquities had been for sale in the bazaars of Cairo for centuries, as curiosities, as jewelry, and in the form of gold and other raw materials stolen from ancient tombs and offered on the open market. The occasional traveler purchased a shipment of mummy, or even a complete body. Most tourists departed with at least a scarab, statue, or amulet. But the serious collector of antiquities was still a rarity, except

56

for the odd royal emissary or a leisured gentleman making antiquarian inquiries on his own account. A lucrative market in antiquities was already in being, but it was not on the scale that was to develop in later centuries, when the great museums of Europe began to vie with one another in building collections of Egyptian antiquities. But even the demand for mummies kept the villagers of Sakkareh more than busy with grave robbing, for the market for the dead was seemingly insatiable and more profitable than agriculture. Elsewhere, the destruction of temples and pyramids for building stone proceeded apace. Richard Pococke, a British traveler who visited Egypt in 1737, was moved to lament: "They are every day destroying these fine morsels of Egyptian Antiquity; and I saw some of the pillars being hewn into mill-stones."

In a sense Ancient Egypt was familiar territory to Christians. Its pharaohs had been the hated oppressors of the Israelites, whose escape from bondage under Moses was familiar to every Bible reader. The "itineraries" of antiquarians and other travelers were eagerly devoured by a gullible public. Egyptian antiquities became prized possessions, exceptionally unusual possessions of con-

Richard Pococke's drawing of the Sphinx, 1743

**Statue of Amun-em-het III. XII
Dynasty.**

siderable social prestige and market value in an
alien society. Even the most miscellaneous collections excited considerable interest. In 1723, for example, one Thomas Serjeant brought a "parcel of
Egyptian Gods lately come from Grand Cairo" to
a meeting of the Society of Antiquaries in London. The members were fascinated by "a brass
Osiris, a brass Harpocrates, a Terminus, a naked
brass figure distorted of better taste, Isis and bam-
bino, a little Egyptian priest, a cat, a stone beetle,
a curious beetle with wings and hieroglyphics in a
curious paste of blew colour." The demand for
Egyptian antiquities inevitably outstripped the
supply, so prices rose, more people bought antiquities in Cairo and in auction rooms, and a new
and lucrative trade came into being. Now there
were full-time collectors, and the craze to collect
was becoming a public concern. European countries were gradually forming their own national
museums, repositories for their own cultural heritages as well as those of other nations. One of the
first was the British Museum, established by an
act of Parliament in 1756. An important nucleus of
its collections was a vast agglomeration of artifacts and curiosities collected by Dr. Hans Sloane,
an eminent physician and one of the founders of
the museum. Some Egyptian lamps, papyri, and
other small artifacts were included in Sloane's collection, acquired, like all early collections, through
extensive travel and purchase from dealers.

By this time, it had occurred to some visitors
that it would be worth digging for antiquities on
their own account. Permits were obtained from
the Turkish authorities to empty tombs and excavate around temples in search of inscriptions and
statuary. Such excavations were sometimes richly
rewarded with mummies and fine grave ornaments, but they were fraught with peril. The Arabs
were convinced that Europeans had special magical spells under their command which would enable them to locate the richest caches of gold and
jewels. In at least one instance, reported by the

famous English traveler William George Browne, a Moroccan and a Greek were murdered in a temple at Thebes, simply because the Arabs suspected that they had brought spells for treasure hunting with them. When any "treasure" was found, there was fierce rivalry for possession and profit. Collectors, dealers, local authorities, and the government all claimed their stake in any important discovery. When the French vice-consul at Alexandria shipped three statues to Paris in 1751, local envy was so intense that even the indifferent authorities claimed the finds by fiat. "Only by the use of tact, maneuver and money" was he able to remove the statues. These types of transactions were to become common as the local people cashed in on temple and tomb with a brazen neglect for historical tradition and a thirst for profit, fueled by a persistent and growing foreign demand.

But many people were simply curious about Ancient Egypt and its marvels. Some travelers spent extended periods of time in the Nile Valley wandering from temple to temple recording the inscriptions and beautiful frescoes that highlighted the dramatic architecture of Egyptian temples. King Christian VI of Denmark was so interested in Egypt that he sent a special expedition out to the Nile. Frederick Lewis Norden, an artist and marine architect, was chosen as leader and traveled deep into Upper Egypt. He tried to reach the Second Cataract, but was forced to turn back at Derr in Nubia. Norden was a thoroughly sober and hard-working observer of the Egyptian scene who recorded a mass of information on Egyptian monuments. His *Voyage* was published in 1755 and was widely read by both scholars and the general public. For the first time, the public at large had access to a corpus of plans and drawings of Egyptian monuments that were both vivid and accurate.

Norden was interested in the details of ancient life, a departure from earlier preoccupations with

Frederick Norden (1708–1742). "The reader seems to accompany the author in his voyage, and to share all his pleasures without undergoing the fatigue and dangers."—Norden's English editor.

59

Norden's drawing of the Sphinx, 1755

legend and fantasy. He admired the magnificent frescoes of the Battle of Kadesh executed in the temple at Luxor by order of Ramesses II and examined fine tomb paintings that were as fresh as the day they were painted, preserved by the dry atmosphere of the Egyptian climate. Norden found the Arabs preoccupied with treasure and magic. "Travellers must think themselves happy in being allowed to contemplate the ancient edifices, without daring to stir any thing. I shall never forget what a crowd of people was assembled, while we were mooring at Aswan, in order to see, as they said among themselves, expert sorcerers in the black magic art." His advice to prospective travelers was to the point: "Begin by dressing yourself in the Turkish manner. A pair of mustachios, with a grave and solemn air, will be very proper companions by which you will have a resemblance to the natives." The "sober and continent" antiquarian is advised to steer clear of prostitutes, for they will give him a memento "indelible by time, place, or mercury."

60

Norden's magnificent descriptions and fine drawings were all very well, but they threw almost no new light on the history of the Egyptians themselves. They remained a shadowy people, known only from their spectacular monuments and the writings of Herodotus and other Classical writers, sources that had been worked to death by author after author. No one knew how old the Egyptians were, nor had anyone been able to decipher hieroglyphs. Clearly, the decipherment of Ancient Egyptian writing would unleash a cascade of information about what was still considered to be the world's oldest civilization. Many people had tried to translate hieroglyphs, but their efforts had been in vain, largely because they assumed that Greek writers were correct in assuming that heiroglyphs were picture writing and that the symbols expressed mystical concepts.

The speculations that surrounded hieroglyphs were quite extraordinary. One worthy scholar believed that the Egyptians had founded a colony in China and that hieroglyphs were developed from Chinese script. Bishop William Warburton of

Norden sails past the pyramids

The entrance into the Greate Pyramis

Gloucester argued more soberly that the Egyptians used their script for day-to-day purposes and not for mystical objectives. He showed how the script had evolved from a form of picture writing into a simpler hand used on a daily basis. But to study Ancient Egypt was to become intensely frustrated. The hieroglyphs were apparently unintelligible; most of the principal monuments that were still above ground had been visited and reported upon by more than a few scholars. Large-scale excavation was beyond the resources of any one traveler, and no foreign government had thought to organize such investigations. The serious scholar was baffled, and the treasure hunter still unaware of

62

the tremendous riches that awaited discovery at Thebes, in the Valley of Kings, and elsewhere.

Only the philosophers flourished, not least among them the Comte de Constantin François Chasseboeuf Volney, who spent four years in Egypt and Syria studying the history and political and social institutions of both countries. He paused to admire the pyramids and deplored the extravagance of the despots who built these and other massive structures at the expense of the slavery of their fellow countrymen. "While the lover of the arts may wax indignant when he sees the columns of the palace being sawn up to make millstones," he wrote, "the philosopher cannot help smiling at the secret malice of fate that gives back to the people what cost them so much misery, and that assigns to the most humble of their needs the pride of useless luxury." Volney was more than a moralist, or even an intellectual revolutionary, for his book was an excellent campaign handbook for generals and a prized possession of one of history's greatest adventurers, Napoleon Bonaparte, who organized the first massive assault on the ramparts of Ancient Egypt.

5 "A Dead Language You Cannot Understand"

By the late eighteenth century, Europe and the United States were beginning to feel the effects of accelerating technological innovation. The discovery of steam power and the use of coal had begun to transform industrial production. On the political scene, the American and French revolutions had excited the imagination of intelligent observers on both sides of the Atlantic. But Egypt remained an obscure and half-forgotten country on the fringes of the Mediterranean. Ruled in name by the Turkish sultan, it was controlled in practice by the Mameluks, aristocratic mercenaries interested in little but the proceeds of harsh taxation. Their country remained an area of negligible political importance—hot, dusty, and entirely alien to European eyes. Yet even in the eighteenth century Egypt was respected for its original contributions to civilization and for the high antiquity of its institutions. And its geographical position was of key importance, for to control Egypt was to threaten the busy land routes to rich British possessions in India.

General Napoleon Bonaparte was the man who pushed Egypt into the center of the world stage. French interest in the Nile had been on the in-

French soldiers on parade in the desert. From *La Description de l'Egypte.*

Napoleon Bonaparte by J. Guerin

crease since the 1770s, partly because of political lobbying by much harassed French merchants in Egypt, foreign exiles in a hostile country. Many government officials believed that Egypt had tremendous commercial potential and feared a British takeover of the strategically important Nile Valley. They had good reason for apprehension, for the Ottoman Empire, based on Constantinople, was weak and corrupt, to the extent that European politicians had dubbed it "the sick man of Europe." Other countries were starting to detach outlying portions of the Turkish sultan's territories. Egypt, under only nominal rule by the sultan, was a natural candidate for annexation. The French were slow to contemplate any political initiatives, partly because of domestic upheavals and also for financial reasons. But when Napoleon Bonaparte had concluded his bloody conquest of Italy with the Peace of Campo Formio in 1797, his restless and ambitious mind turned to new projects whose boldness and success would further his political ambitions. Napoleon became obsessed with the East, a strange fascination that was to grip many politicians of the next century, among them Benjamin Disraeli and Napoleon III. His ruthless mind turned toward ideas of worldwide conquest, toward the creation of a great French empire centered on the Orient and ultimately on India, where the British had expelled the French in the mid-eighteenth century.

By April 1798 Napoleon had been authorized to mount an expedition to seize Malta and Egypt and to build a canal at the Isthmus of Suez. On May 19, 1798, he sailed from Toulon with a fleet of 328 ships and an expeditionary force of 38,000 men to conquer Egypt, landing at Abukir Bay near Alexandria on July 1. The expedition was accompanied by the members of a special Scientific and Artistic Commission carefully selected by Napoleon to provide a cultural and technological background to his ambitious plans for the colonization of the Nile Valley. The Commission consisted of 167 sci-

66

entists and technicians, soon nicknamed "The Donkeys" by the military. Napoleon's Scientific and Artistic Commission had been set up on the general's own initiative. In the spring of 1798 Napoleon had attended a meeting of the Institute of France attended by the leading scientists of the Republic. He harangued them on the importance of Egypt to contemporary scholarship and intellectual life, and pressed for a strong intellectual backing for his new campaign.

The chief recruiter of the savants was Claude-Louis Berthollet, a physician and chemist, who succeeded in assembling a remarkable group of talented men around him. Jean-Michel de Venture was a distinguished Orientalist, Etienne Geoffrey Saint-Hilaire a zoologist and lifelong friend of the celebrated paleontologist Jacques Cuvier. Saint-Hilaire's ideas foreshadowed some of Darwin's evolutionary theories. Gaspard Monge, mathematician and chemist, was a fervent republican and a steel and gunpowder expert; his most recent appointment had been to a different body, a "Government Commission for the Research of Artistic and Scientific Objects in Conquered Countries." This Commission had followed in the wake of Bonaparte's armies in Italy and examined art collections, museums, and libraries, deciding which objects were to be ceded to the French Republic under the terms of peace treaties. One has only to tour the Louvre to see how efficient the Commission was—the expropriated works include the *Mona Lisa*. Monge was obviously a highly qualified recruit for the Commission.

Then there was Dominique Vivant Denon, artist extraordinary. Denon had been the supervisor of a collection of antique gems under King Louis XV and had also, it was rumored, been a favorite of Madame Pompadour. For a while he filled a post at the French Embassy in St. Petersburg, Russia, and was much admired by Catherine the Great. His career as a diplomat gave him a wide experience of the world and a broad knowledge of the

Monge

Vivant Denon

67

arts of eighteenth-century Europe. He was fond of women, a sparkling conversationalist, and a member of the French Academy. At the time of the French Revolution he was living in Florence, pursuing a leisured life among art treasures and friends whom he enjoyed. Immediately upon hearing the news of political upset, he returned to France only to find that he was on a list of proscribed names and that his real estate and financial holdings had been confiscated by the revolutionary authorities. Denon was reduced to poverty and vegetated in the Paris slums eking out a bare existence by selling drawings and the eighteenth-century equivalent of picture postcards. Fortunately, however, he came to the notice of a well-known painter of the French Revolution, Jacques Louis David, who employed him as a minor functionary in his studio. Through this connection, he won the good will of a number of revolutionary leaders. Denon's diplomatic skills soon came again into public view and, indeed, were remembered from an earlier time. The revolutionary authorities eventually restored Denon's properties to him at the direct order of the notorious Robespierre. The artist cum diplomat soon met Napoleon and the Empress Josephine and was high in the favor of senior French scientists. Denon's reputation was not only firmly based in scientific circles, however. His *Oeuvre Priapique,* a collection of vivid pornographic etchings, highly explicit even by French standards of the time, was popular reading among the intelligentsia. It was to this talented and skillful artist that a major portion of the illustrative responsibility of the Commission's work was assigned. Fortunately for Egyptology, Denon's skills were guided by a rapturous enthusiasm for the antiquities of the Nile and everything Egyptian.

The Commission's work was the most lasting result of one of Napoleon's most unsuccessful campaigns, for it accomplished an immense amount of scientific research in three years of work. Fortunately, the members were well prepared for their

huge task, bringing with them from France a large
library that contained a copy of practically every
book ever published about the Nile and many
crates of scientific apparatus and measuring instruments. The work of the Commission started
soon after Napoleon reached Cairo on July 21,
1798. He took immediate steps to set up an Egyptian Institute in the capital, housed in an elegant
Cairo palace. Napoleon himself took an active interest in its activities and attended many of the
Institute's regular meetings.

Napoleon in Cairo

The headquarters of the Egyptian Institute in Cairo. From *La Description.*

Drawing water from the Nile. A series of explanatory sketches from *La Description.*

Three years of astonishingly prolific and fruitful scientific activity ensued. Scientists from totally different academic disciplines worked harmoniously together, united by a common fascination about a new and virtually unknown country. They exchanged local knowledge and stimulated one another's creativity by chance conversations and regular seminars. The scientists were deeply involved in the administration of Egypt, too, serving on committees and medical commissions, or answering the myriad of practical questions thrown at them by Napoleon and his generals. Yet pure research held pride of place, with important papers read at regular seminars—on the technical processes used by Egyptian craftsmen, on experimental agriculture, and, a topical subject, contributed by minerologist Deodate Gratet de Dolomicu,

70

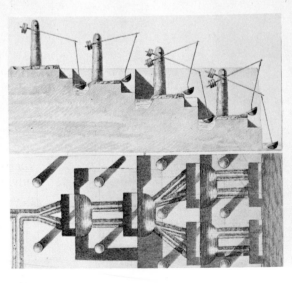

on the "selection, conservation, and transportation of ancient monuments" to be shipped to France.

A great sensation was caused at a meeting on July 19, 1799, when a letter from the mathematician Lancret announced the discovery at Rosetta of "some inscriptions which may offer much interest." The inscriptions were preserved on a basalt tablet found by an unknown French soldier working on the fortifications of Fort Rachid near the town of Rosetta. Fortunately the officer in charge of the work detail, one Captain Bouchard, recognized the importance of the find and sent it to the Institute. The Rosetta Stone is made of a tablet of fine-grained basalt, inscribed with three columns of script, the first consisting of hieroglyphs, the second written in demotic, a late cursive Egyptian script, and the third in Greek. The Greek inscription was promptly translated and found to record a decree of the Egyptian priesthood in 196 B.C. Here, the savants immediately realized, was the potential clue to hieroglyphs, the key to a detailed understanding of Ancient Egypt.

The greatest contributions made by the Institute were in the fields of geography and Egyptology. The first detailed map of Egypt produced by its cartographers was not published until after Napoleon's reign, but it formed the basis of the other scientific work carried out by the Commission. When General Desaix was dispatched up the Nile in pursuit of Murat Bey in August 1798, he was joined by Vivant Denon, by now a hardened and indefatigable traveler, who was able to discover and record with uncanny accuracy the glories of Ancient Egyptian architecture and sculpture by the banks of the Nile. Denon had spent his early months in Egypt sketching and observing the local scene, attending meetings of the Institute, and busily recording his impressions. He was rapturous about the pyramids: "The great distance from which they can be perceived makes them appear diaphanous, tinted with the bluish tone of the sky,

General Desaix

The Rosetta Stone on display in the British Museum

73

and restores to them the perfection and purity of the angles which the centuries have marred." His expectations for the perilous journey with Desaix were boundless, for, as he wrote later: "I was about to tread the soil of a land covered since immemorial times with a veil of mystery . . . from Herodotus to our own times, all the travellers were content to sail up the Nile rapidly, not daring to lose sight of their boats, and leaving them only in order to inspect, hastily and uneasily, the objects closest to shore." The right man had arrived in the Nile Valley at the right moment.

Denon's precise, and perhaps rather stiff, record of the major monuments of the Nile was a remarkable tour de force carried out under incredibly difficult conditions. Desaix's army was making forced marches of 25 to 30 miles a day, constantly in danger of raids from marauding warriors. At Hermopolis Denon was given but a few minutes to make a sketch of a temple. But at Dendereh he was more fortunate. The army lingered in admiration at the magnificent temple for a day. Denon was enraptured: "Pencil in hand, I passed from object to object, drawn away from one thing by the interest of another . . . I felt ashamed of the inadequacy of the drawings I made of such sublime things." The sun set, and Denon remained oblivious, wrapped in artistic rapture, until his commanding officer, General Belliard, himself escorted him home to the distant army at a gallop.

Then, on January 27, 1799, they rounded a bend of the Nile and came in sight of the temples of Luxor and Karnak. The division came to a spontaneous halt and burst into applause. "Without an order being given, the men formed their ranks and presented arms, to the accompaniment of the drums and the bands," wrote a lieutenant on the expedition. Denon was already sketching, conscious of a great and emotional moment when an entire army paid a spontaneous tribute to antiquity. Wherever the army went, Denon went too, riding furiously in search of monuments and

"Artist's impression of the interior of the Temple at Dendereh." From *La Description.*

74

sketching under fire or even when in danger of capture. Desaix eventually reached Aswan, where he visited the islands of Elephantine and Philae.

Denon's work aroused tremendous enthusiasm for archaeology, especially among the hydraulic engineers charged with improving Egyptian agriculture. The engineers were soon neglecting their own dull work and making a beeline for temples and tombs recording architectural features, hieroglyphic inscriptions, and all the magnificent panoply of Ancient Egypt. Pencils ran out, lead bullets were frantically melted down as substitutes, and a vast body of irreplaceable information was recorded for posterity. At the same time, small antiquities by the hundred were removed from temple and tomb.

Napoleon's expedition to Egypt was perhaps doomed to military failure from the beginning, largely because of the vulnerability of its seaborne communications. Admiral Nelson's naval victory in Abukir Bay on August 1, 1798, destroyed much of Napoleon's fleet, but the expedition dragged on for another year. General Desaix overran Upper Egypt and Napoleon won a land victory against the Egyptians but, despite these successes, misery, hunger, Egyptian eye disease, and many other misfortunes dogged the French. Finally, on August 19, 1799, the emperor abandoned his army and fled from Egypt in a fast ship. The army soon surrendered to British forces and the abortive expedition was over. Historically, however, the greatest consequences of the expedition were in awakening Egypt's political leaders to the importance of their remote country in European politics, and in creating a dramatic explosion of knowledge about Ancient Egypt that emanated from the discoveries of Napoleon's Scientific Commission.

The extraordinary results of the Commission's researches took many years to prepare for publication. Denon himself returned to Paris to an enthusiastic reception. He was made the first director of the Louvre and founded the Egyptian collections of that great institution, continuing to collect works of art for the French national collections throughout the remainder of Napoleon's political career. His *Voyages dans la basse et la haute Egypte* was published in 1801 and soon became a best seller translated into several languages.

Then, eight years later, the first volume of the monumental *Description de l'Egypte* appeared, eventually to be published in twenty-four volumes between 1809 and 1813. The sumptuous and magnificently illustrated folios caused a sensation in European cultural and scholarly circles. They depicted the riches of Egyptian antiquity with a vivid accuracy that had never been witnessed before. The delicate lines and colors of paintings and inscriptions were brilliantly executed on a large-scale format which made every minor detail spring to the entranced eye. It is difficult for us living in a world of instant communication and of easy familiarity with the pyramids and other antiquities of the Nile to understand the tremendous impact of the *Description.* Here for the first time was revealed a marvelous, flourishing early civilization whose monuments had stood the test of thousands of years of wars and neglect. Temple after temple, pyramid after pyramid, artifact after artifact— Denon and his colleagues laid out before a delighted public a romantic and exciting world of exotic and fascinating antiquity. Unfortunately, however, the authors of the *Description* were unable to ascertain the significance of their discoveries, largely because no one had been able to translate hieroglyphs into a modern language. Yet, the most important discovery of the entire expedition, the Rosetta Stone, eventually provided the key to the unraveling of the puzzle of Ancient Egypt.

From the museum point of view, the finds of the French expedition were of extraordinary value and rarity. The British Museum, for example, contained but a handful of Egyptian antiquities, most of them mummies, scarabs, and small ornaments.

But the savants of the Commission had acquired an enormous new collection of Egyptian antiquities, many of them of great beauty. The knowledge obtained from the Commission's work was more significant than its collections. Although they did not discover any new sites or spectacular temples, the work of the French was so accurate and was published so beautifully that the general public was able to appreciate the extraordinary range and quality of the antiquities of the Nile. The French expedition and its publications provided a catalyst not only for further study of Ancient Egypt and the decipherment of hieroglyphs, but also for a ruthless scramble for Egyptian antiquities. This scramble was flamed by popular enthusiasm for the exotic and by an increasing familiarity with Egypt among soldiers and diplomats.

The scramble for antiquities began with the French expedition itself, for the savants and their precious collections were corralled in Alexandria when the paranoid General Menon surrendered the city to General Hutchinson and the British

"Karnak: a view of the entrance and the temples from the south." From *La Description*.

army. Menon was one of those persons who cannot conclude an agreement of any sort without recrimination and debate. No sooner had the military agreement been signed than Menon and Hutchinson began to dicker over the savants and their collections. The British claimed all the antiquities under a clause of the capitulation agreement. Menon stated that the Rosetta Stone, the prize of the whole collection, was his personal property. But the scientists, led by the zoologist Geoffrey Saint-Hilaire, declared that they would rather follow their collections to England than give them up. Menon was obliged to grant their request with ill grace: "I have just been informed that several among our collectors wish to follow their seeds, minerals, birds, butterflies or reptiles wherever you choose to ship their crates," he wrote pettishly. "I do not know if they wish to have themselves stuffed for the purpose, but I can assure you that if the idea should appeal to them, I shall not prevent them."

The scientists then threatened to burn their specimens if there was a chance they would lose

them. Saint-Hilaire was explicit: "Without us this material is a dead language that neither you nor your scientists can understand. . . . Sooner than permit this iniquitous and vandalous spoliation we will destroy our property, we will scatter it amid the Libyan sands or throw it into the sea. We shall burn our riches ourselves. It is celebrity you are aiming for. Very well, you can count on the long memory of history: You also will have burnt a library in Alexandria."

Fortunately General Hutchinson was a man of some vision and imagination, sufficiently impressed by the savants' eloquence to allow the scientists to keep their collections. But he insisted on retaining the Rosetta Stone. Menon yielded the stone without grace. "You can have it," he wrote, "since you are the stronger of us two." Fortunately for the French, however, the expedition staff had made wax copies of the stone. The copies were shipped to France and formed the basis for comprehensive studies of hieroglyphs by a generation of dedicated scholars, among them the great Jean François Champollion, who, twenty-three years later, provided the literary key to the Egyptian past when he deciphered the mysterious writing of the Ancient Egyptians.

Neither the French nor the British were much concerned with moral issues. The entire collection of antiquities extracted from the sands of the Nile floodplain by the Institute was simply shipped to Europe without any recourse or reference to the Egyptian government at all. The Rosetta Stone was already regarded as a find of preeminent importance. So, by order of King George III, it was housed in the British Museum. It was only in the year 1973 that it became possible for the Louvre to borrow the original Rosetta Stone for exhibition in its galleries. No one has ever thought of exhibiting it in Egypt.

The British chose to leave Egypt to the Turks rather than annex it in the name of George III. A desultory occupation by the British army under

"The Island of Elephantine and its environs." A series of sketches and a map from La Description.

81

The savants measure the Sphinx. A drawing by Vivant Denon.

Bas-reliefs from Karnak. A series of finely executed drawings from *La Description*.

the Earl of Cavan lasted a year, during which the reins of government were handed back to the emissaries of the Turkish Empire. The sultan himself had little interest in Egypt, provided his annual taxes were paid on time. The Nile Valley was dominated by powerful landlords who harshly ground the poor in search of taxes. Egypt was desperately in need of leadership and strong government.

The hour produced the man, a ruler who had a catastrophic effect on the archaeology of Ancient Egypt. Mohammed 'Ali was a Macedonian orphan who rose to powerful commands in the Turkish army in Egypt through sheer ability. In 1805 he took the government of Egypt into his own hands, was named pasha, and became to all intents and purposes the independent ruler of the Nile Valley. This capable and ruthless man governed the

82

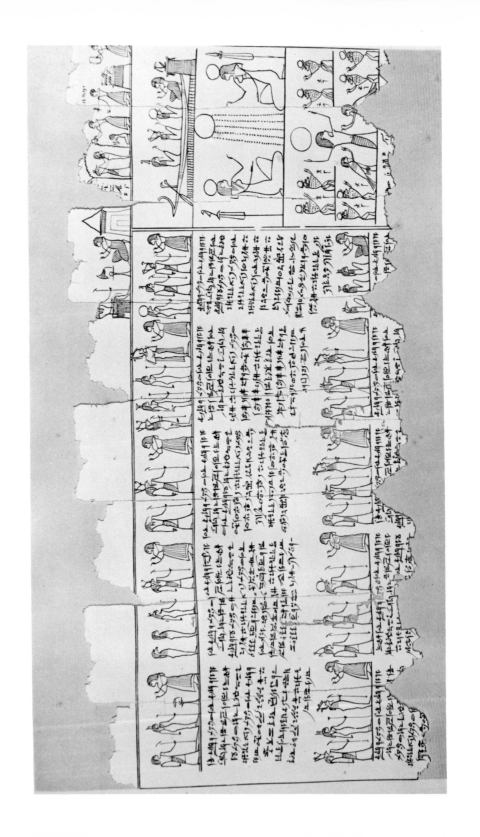

affairs of Egypt from 1805 to 1849. A well-built and intelligent-looking ruler, 'Ali provided Egypt with a firmer government than it had enjoyed in centuries, although his rule was far from benevolent toward his humble subjects. His thirst for power and international influence was tempered with a desire to bring Western technology to the Nile, to harness the river for agriculture, and to introduce industrial manufactures to Egypt. Competent foreigners with new ideas were welcomed in Cairo, and many of them were put to work developing factories, encouraging industry, and designing irrigation schemes. Unfortunately, many of 'Ali's most ambitious schemes foundered in a sea of bureaucratic inefficiency and the innate conservatism of the peasants and his ministers.

But the pasha was friendly toward foreigners and did a great deal to open up the Nile Valley not only to merchants and diplomats but also to the casual tourist and dealer. And what matter if many of the visitors were interested in antiquities and ransacking ancient tombs? To a despotic ruler interested in international power and foreign capital, the monuments of Ancient Egypt were of little interest except as a diplomatic lever or a way of keeping powerful visitors with strange hobbies interested in Egypt.

Soon Egypt was being stripped of thousands of portable antiquities by a steady stream of collectors, dealers, tourists, and just plain shady characters who saw a chance for a quick profit from the antiquities trade.

The British occupation force arrived early on the scene. The Earl of Cavan took a fancy to one of the obelisks of Alexandria and obtained a permit from the Turkish authorities to remove it to London as a memorial to the British victories in Egypt. The soldiers themselves were enthusiastic about the scheme, subscribed money for a ship, and volunteered their labor to transport the obelisk. But London was unenthusiastic, and the obelisk remained in the squalor of Alexandria

Drawing of a papyrus from a tomb at Thebes, with attempts to copy hieroglyphs. From *La Description.*

85

"Arts and Crafts. A view of a waterwheel and a lifting device." From *La Description*. A typical example of the savants' work on Egyptian life.

until 1877, when it was finally transported to London on the initiative of Erasmus Wilson, a wealthy businessman. The seventy-year delay was entirely due to British government disinterest, despite renewed invitations from both Mohammed 'Ali and his successor, the Khedive Ismail. Only when a Greek landowner threatened to cut up the obelisk for building stone did private initiative save from destruction what is now known as Cleopatra's Needle.

Then there were the diplomats, for both Britain and France, as well as other powers, maintained a diplomatic presence in Cairo and Alexandria during the early nineteenth century. In the early years of Mohammed 'Ali's rule the political functions of the consuls were minimal and the diplomats had a great deal of spare time for travel and the collection of antiquities, always an occupational hobby of early diplomats in the Nile Valley.

The first French consul general after Napoleon's expedition was Bernardino Drovetti, a Piedmontese born in Barbaria in 1776. Drovetti later

86

became a Frenchman and served with distinction as a colonel in Napoleon's Egyptian army. After the campaign he became French consul general in Egypt until 1814 and then again under the Restoration, 1820–1829. He finally retired from his diplomatic post for health reasons, but not before he had made a large fortune from Egyptian antiquities. Drovetti strongly influenced Mohammed 'Ali in matters of governmental policy. He also enjoyed enormous prestige with the Egyptians themselves. His interest in antiquities appears to have been strictly commercial, and pursued with a ruthless intensity that caused him to be hated by his rivals.

The first British consul after the campaign was Colonel Missett, a well-known and influential diplomat, who retired on grounds of ill health in 1816. He was not particularly interested in archaeology, but his successor, Henry Salt, certainly was. Salt was born in Lichfield, England, in 1780. Henry Salt's early education was at best desultory

Bernardino Drovetti

Mohammed 'Ali, ruler of Egypt (1818)

Henry Salt, British consul general in Egypt. Portrait by J. J. Halls.

until his teens, when he was sent to London to study landscape and portrait painting. He enrolled as a student at the Royal Academy and made a very casual living as a portrait painter, a career that at least brought him in contact with a wide range of people. One of these was Lord Valentia, later to become Lord Mountnorris, a wealthy aristocrat with a penchant for leisured travel to remote parts of the world. In 1802 Lord Valentia planned a journey to India and the East and accepted Salt's application for the post of secretary and draftsman to the expedition. Valentia's journey lasted four and a half years and culminated in a voyage of exploration along the Red Sea coast of Africa on board the cruiser H.M.S. *Panther,* a side trip that provided Salt with his first taste of exploration.

The young secretary was charged with the leadership of a small party sent to the uplands of Ethiopia. At this time Ethiopia was a little-known and mysterious country, almost closed to Europeans. Its diplomatic and commercial potential was still unrealized, although many people were curious about the caliber and ambitions of its rulers. Salt and his party penetrated some distance inland and were hospitably entertained by the ruler, or ras, of Tigre, who even gave them letters and presents for the king of England purporting to come from the emperor of Ethiopia. This small expedition brought Salt to the attention of the Foreign Office, which sent him out on a second mission to Ethiopia with instructions to obtain details about the state of trade in the country. The new mission failed, for Salt was unable to go farther inland than Tigre owing to disturbed political conditions in the far interior. Nevertheless, Salt published a book, *A Voyage to Abyssinia* (1814), a publication that brought his name to public notice at an opportune moment.

Salt had spent some time in Egypt in 1807 where he had indulged his antiquarian interests whetted by the discovery of a Greek inscription at

Axum in Ethiopia. The Nile Valley attracted him
enormously, and he was determined to return.
Then, in early 1816, he heard that Colonel Missett,
the British consul general in Alexandria, had resigned. He immediately lobbied for the appointment, getting his influential friends to write to the
foreign secretary in his support. Lord Castlereagh
was glad to confirm his appointment at very short
notice, and Henry Salt found himself an influential figure in Egyptian affairs at the age of thirty-
five.

The duties of the British and French consuls
general were far from arduous. Both enjoyed considerable influence with the pasha, but the political issues were hardly of major importance. Relatively few foreigners resided permanently in Cairo.
The British colony was tiny, and maritime affairs
were handled by a representative in Alexandria. It

is quite clear, however, that Salt's sponsors had other ideas as to how he might best employ his time. The elderly Sir Joseph Banks, who had accompanied Captain Cook to Tahiti in 1769 and acquired an international reputation as a scientist as a result, was now a trustee of the British Museum and saw Salt as a potential source of Egyptian antiquities for the national collections. Sir William Hamilton, already notorious for his involvement in the Elgin Marbles controversy, was now undersecretary of state at the Foreign Office. He was much more explicit and urged Salt to collect antiquities and to search for another Rosetta Stone. "Whatever the expense of the undertaking," he wrote to Salt in an official memorandum, "it would be most cheerfully supported by an enlightened nation, eager to anticipate its rivals in the prosecution of the best interests of science and literature."

Salt himself had a firm belief in his skills as an Egyptologist and developed a deep interest in hieroglyphs. His character was a moody one. He alternated between intense optimism and deep depression, and had a tendency to procrastinate and be irresolute at times when quick decisions were needed, qualities that were dangerous when confronted with Drovetti's mercurial passion and the pasha's sudden changes of direction and humor. Nevertheless, he enjoyed considerable influence with the Egyptian government, and many privileges and concessions were extended to him, a range of opportunities that provoked an intense rivalry between the British and French consuls general, Drovetti with his restless energy and deep bonds of affection with headmen and villages, and Salt, a more remote person, with money to spend and considerable political prestige.

The pasha himself theoretically controlled excavations in the Nile Valley. Any potential excavation required a firman, or permit, to search for antiquities and to remove them from Egypt. Drovetti and Salt were able to obtain as many

The French army disembarking
at Alexandria. From *La
Description.*

firmans as they wanted. Their greed and rivalry
became so intense that they reached an unspoken
gentlemen's agreement, if that is an appropriate
description, to carve up the Nile Valley into
"spheres of influence." Other acquisitive visitors
were forced to beware, for both Salt and Drovetti
were so influential that they could arrange for the
denial of firmans and ensure that local headmen
would warn off potential excavators or refuse
them laborers.

The Nile Valley was now a hive of activity, as
the search for antiquities accelerated under the
consuls' aegis. Some remarkable characters took
up residence in Egypt. The Marseillais Jean
Jacques Rifaud was one longtime resident who
went to Egypt in 1805 with the express intention
of excavating and selling portable antiquities. This
temperamental man ended up working for
Drovetti for some years, accompanying the consul
on a trip to the Second Cataract in 1816. An Armenian merchant named Giovanni Anastasi was
another well-known character. His father had
been a major supplier of Napoleon's commissariat
who went bankrupt after the French defeat. After
great effort Anastasi became a successful merchant
and subsequently Swedish-Norwegian consul gen-

91

"The ascent of the Great
Pyramid is rather a laborious
task"

eral in Egypt, as well as a highly successful dealer
in antiquities and especially papyri, bought
through agents from tomb robbers at Sakkareh.
These were but two of the many who flocked to
the Nile in search of the past. No qualifications
were needed to become a dealer or excavator,
simply a tough constitution to cope with the harsh
Nile environment, an ability with bribery and gunpowder, and the political finesse which enabled
successful applications for permits and delicate
negotiations with other interested parties. As
Howard Carter, the discoverer of the tomb of
Tut-ankh-Amun, wrote: "Those were the great
days of excavating. Anything to which a fancy
was taken, from a scarab to an obelisk, was just
appropriated, and if there was a difference with a

92

brother excavator, one laid for him with a gun."
One of the main characters of these far from
heroic years of pillage and destruction was a giant
and circus strongman, Giovanni Battista Belzoni,
one of the most fascinating personalities ever to
become involved in archaeology.

PART
TWO: THE GREATEST
        PLUNDERER
        OF THEM ALL

Sig Belzoni. the Patagonian Sampson as he appeared at Sadlers Wells
Theatre on Easter Monday 1803 carrying Eleven Persons the Iron Apparatus Weighing

6 The Patagonian Sampson

Giovanni Battista Belzoni was born in Padua, Italy, on November 5, 1778. He was one of the four children of one Gaicomo Belzoni, a barber of limited ambition who wanted his son to become a barber's assistant. The young Giovanni never left Padua until he was thirteen years old, but three years later he left for Rome on the first of a series of lifelong wanderings. The limited and narrow world of Padua does not seem to have appealed to the strapping young man. It gave him a sketchy education and some rudimentary understanding of mechanical things, but certainly no ambitions to become a barber. For four years the young Paduan tarried in Rome, apparently striving to improve his education. Some biographers talk of his studying for the priesthood and acquiring a

Belzoni's act at Sadler's Wells

97

basic knowledge of hydraulics, but his education can hardly have been an intensive one, even by eighteenth-century standards.

Political conditions in Italy were very unsettled during Belzoni's youth, for Napoleon's armies were in the process of conquering and annexing Italy for the Republic. In 1798 the French armies entered Rome in triumph, while the young Belzoni fled northward, perhaps to avoid conscription, loaded with an itinerant merchant's pack of rosaries, religious images, and relics.

The first trading venture seems to have been successful, for three years later the young Italian set out again, this time with his brother Francesco. Soon both brothers were engaged in petty trading around Amsterdam in Holland, where their imposing physiques and strength must have attracted attention. We do not know whether Belzoni was actually performing on the stage in Amsterdam, for in his later years and in his own biography he drew a complete veil over the early years of his life. The activities of a minor trader and acrobat were hardly a respectable background for a man who considered he was the stuff of which history is made.

"Aquatic Theatre, Sadler's Wells." A view dating from 1813.

Belzoni first came to public view in 1803, when he and his brother crossed to London. Whatever restless urge brought Belzoni to England, his stay in London was the first turning point in a remarkably varied life. London in 1803 was a rollicking capital city, full of lively spectacles and bawdy theatrical performances. There were many opportunities for acrobats and gymnasts, for jugglers and strongmen as well as straight actors. The London theatrical public demanded diversity and got it. Producers were forced to change their variety shows and individual acts at frequent intervals to cater to a lively and very critical audience. A wide choice of theatrical events flourished in London during the summer months. Handbills and newspapers proclaimed the sensational and spectacular, each theater vying with the others to catch the interest of the volatile Londoner.

One of the greatest London impresarios of the early nineteenth century was Charles Dibdin, Jr., owner of Sadler's Wells Theatre. Dibdin had just acquired Sadler's Wells in 1803 and was embarking on an entrepreneurial career, combining the offices of author, producer, and stage manager with great success. His permanent company was bolstered with numerous contract players, engaged to play a single act or for an entire season.

Dibdin's prompter was an Italian named Morelli, a popular actor and theatrical personality to whom "all the Italian minstrels and gymnastical performers used to apply, on their arrival in England," wrote Dibdin in his memoirs. It was to this well-known agent that Giovanni Belzoni applied for work at Sadler's Wells Theatre. One does not know what qualifications Belzoni brought to his application, and we can only assume that he had gained some experience with theatrical work on the Continent. But he must have been an imposing figure, standing more than 6 feet 6 inches high, with a handsome face—well portrayed in the pictures of Belzoni that have come down to us—and immense strength. Charles Dibdin was certainly

The Patagonian Sampson

99

SADLER'S WELLS.

Under the Patronage of His Royal Highness the DUKE of CLARENCE. The Public are respectfully informed, that this Theatre having been transferred to new Proprietors, has undergone a thorough alteration, been materially improved, decorated in a style entirely new, and will open

TO-MORROW, Easter Monday, April 11, 1803, with a new Musical Prelude, called NEW BROOMS. Principal Characters, Mr. Grimaldi, Mr. Smith (his first appearance here), Master Menage (his first appearance), Mr. Jacobs (his first appearance), and Mr. Davis; Miss Smith, and Mrs. Davis. After which a new Serio-Comic Pantomime, called JACK THE GIANT-KILLER. Principal Characters, Mr. Bologna, jun. Mr. Grimaldi, Master Menage, Signor Belzoni (his first appearance in England), and Mad. St. Amand. In the course of the piece, various Combats by Messrs. Bologna, jun. Grimaldi, &c. a Combat Dance, composed by Mr. Bologna, jun. A new Burletta Spectacle, called EDWARD and SUSAN. Principal Characters, Mr. King (his first appearance these five years), Mr. Smith, Mr. Townsend, late of the Theatre Royal, in Covent-Garden, (his first appearance at this Theatre,) and Mrs. C. Dibdin. In the course of the piece an incidental Ballet, (composed by Mr. King,) in which Mr. King and Mad. will dance a Pas Deux, accompanied on the Harp; Mr. L. Bologna and Mr. Banks will dance a comic Pas Deux, accompanied on the Union Pipes by Mr. Fitzmaurice (his first appearance in London), and Miss Gayton, pupil of Mr. Jackson, late of Covent-Garden Theatre, only nine years of age, will dance a Hornpipe with a skipping-rope (her first appearance in public). Signor Giovanni Baptista Belzoni, the Patagonian Sampson, will present most extraordinary specimens of the Gymnastic Art, perfectly foreign to any former exhibition (his first appearance in England.) The Evening's Entertainments to conclude with a new Comic Pantomime, called FIRE AND SPIRIT; or, A HARLEQUIN. Including, among other views, the following scenes of holiday resort, viz. Chalk Farm, Horns at Kennington, Paddington Canal and Passageboat, Hornsey House, Blackwall Wet Docks, Richmond Hill and Bridge, Greenwich Park and Hospital, &c. beginning with the Bower of Spring, and concluding with a Magical Cataract. Harlequin, Mr. King; Clown, Mr. Cipriani, (his first appearance at this Theatre); Pantaloon, Mr. Hartland; Marquis, Mr. Powers; Old Woman, Mr. Smith; and Columbine, Mad. St. Amand; other numerous characters incidental to Pantomime, by the rest of the Company. The Entertainments, music, scenery, dresses, and decorations of the evening entirely new. Leader of the Band, Mr. T. Ware. The Prelude, Burletta, Spectacle, Serio-Comic, and Comic Pantomime, written, invented, and produced by Mr. C. Dibdin, jun. the Overture and Music composed by Mr. Reeve, who superintends the musical department, and will preside at the pianoforte. The scenery and decorations designed by Mr. Andrews, and painted by him with assistants; the machinery executed by Mr. Garland, the dresses by Mr. Smythies, Mrs. Robinson, and assistants. The Theatre will be entirely lighted with wax.

The Public are respectfully informed, that any person admitted to the performance, on paying 1s. only, will receive a Pint of White or Red Foreign UNADULTERATED WINE, which custom the new Proprietors have revived for the accommodation of the Public, as they will lose considerably upon every pipe of Wine thus consumed.

N. B. The private boxes in the lower part of the Theatre have been totally altered from last season, and are now perfectly calculated to accommodate the Nobility, Gentry, and families in the most eligible manner; and for the convenience of the Public, the Proprietors have put on additional Patrols in the field leading from the Wells to town, also a quantity of additional lamps in the said field, and in the avenues to the Theatre, by permission of the New River Company.

Boxes 4s. Pit 2s. Gallery 1s. Doors to be opened at half past five, to begin at half past six. Places for the boxes may be taken of Mr. D'Cleve, at the Box-office at the Wells, every day from eleven till two, who will give every information to the repeated inquiries for free admission for the season.

Shortly after the opening, the Proprietors mean to give a Benefit, the profits of which will be appropriated towards the Subscription for the Beauty of Buttermere. Particulars in a few days.

SADLERS WELLS.—Under the patronage of His Royal Highness the Duke of CLARENCE.— On MONDAY next, July 4, and five following Evenings, a Comic Dance, composed by Mr. King, called HEY FOR THE HIGHLANDS, Music by Mr. Reeve. Principal Dancers, Mr. King, Mr. Cipriani, and Mad. St. Amand. The PATAGONIAN SAMPSON will perform (being positively the last week of his appearing) Mr. Bologna, jun. will present a Grand Hydraulical Exhibition, called, FIRE AND WATER. Also will be performed the favourite Burletta of THE RECRUITING SERJEANT, Music by Mr. Dibdin, sen. Serjeant, Mr. Townsend, who will sing (for the last week the song of Mammoth and Bonaparte, written by Mr. C. Dibdin, jun. Miss Dennet will sing an admired harp song called The Welch Harper, accompanied on the Harp by Mr. Platts. The Serious Pantomime of PHILIP QUARLL, Music by Mr. Reeve; and the New Harlequinade of GOODY TWO SHOES, Music by Mr. Reeve; with a touch at French Ballooning, or Aerial Invasion. The serious and comic Pantomimes written and produced by Mr. C. Dibdin, jun. and the Scenery of the whole designed and executed by Mr. Andrews with Assistants.

Boxes 4s. Pit 2s. Gal. 1s. with unadulterated Wine 2s. 6d. per bottle. Doors open at half past five, and begin at half past six. Places kept till half past seven. Places to be taken of Mr. De Cleve, at the Box-Office, from Eleven till Two. Books of the Songs to be had at the Wells.

Various playbills and advertisements for Sadler's Wells that feature Belzoni's appearances

impressed enough to engage Belzoni as a weight lifter and a player of minor parts.

So in the summer of 1803 the London theatergoer was treated to a startling act by the "Patagonian Sampson," a weight lifter of great prowess and skill. His act consisted of a series of weight-lifting feats which culminated in a human-pyramid display. The gaily dressed Belzoni would shoulder a massive iron frame weighing 127 pounds and fitted with ledges. Twelve members of the Sadler's Wells Company then perched on the frame and the Patagonian Sampson strode around the stage without any apparent effort, waving two flags in his hands. This tour de force was deservedly popular with the theatrical public, so much so that Dibdin ran it for three months, also using the huge Italian in small plays and charades which were featured between major acts in the program. Many of these were small dramas, like the saga of Philip Quarll, an imaginative story of "an Englishman who lived a solitary life on an Island inhabited only by Monkies."

SADLER's WELLS.

Under Patronage of his *Royal HIGHNESS* the Duke of Clarence,

The Public are respectfully informed that this Theatre having been transferred to

NEW PROPRIETORS;

Has undergone a thorough alteration, been materially improved, decorated in a style entirely new, and will open on

EASTER MONDAY, APRIL, 11th, 1803.

With a new Musical Prelude called

NEW BROOMS.

Principal Characters, Mr. GRIMALDI, Mr. SMITH, (his first Appearance here) Master MENAGE, (his first Appearance) Mr. JACOBS, (his first Appearance) and Mr. DAVIS, Miss SMITH, and Mrs. DAVIS, After wich a new Serio Comic Pantomime called

Fee! Faw! Fum!

Or, JACK the GIANT KILLER.

Principal Characters Mr. BOLOGNA, Junr. Mr. GRIMALDI, Master MENAGE, Signor BELZONI, (his first Appearance in ENGLAND; And Mad. St. AMAND.
In the course of the Piece various Combats by Messrs BOLOGNA, Junr. GRIMALDI, &c. a Combat Dance composed by Mr. BOLOGNA, Junr.
A new Burletta Spectacle called

EDWARD AND SUSAN;
OR THE
VILLAGE FETE.

Principal Characters, Mr. KING, (his first Appearance here these Years) Mr. SMITH,

Mr. TOWNSEND,

Late of the Theatre Royal Covent Garden,
(His first Appearance at this Theatre) and Mrs. C. DIBDIN.
In the course of the Piece an incidental Ballet (composed by Mr. KING), in which Mr. KING and Mad. St. AMAND, will Dance a Pas Deux, accompanied on the Harp—Mr. L. BOLOGNA, and Mr. BANKS, will Dance a Comic Pas Deux, accompanied on the Union Pipes, by Mr. FITZMAURICE, (His first Appearance in LONDON) And Miss GAYTON, Pupil of Mr. Jackson, late of Covent Garden Theatre, only 9 Years of Age, will Dance a Hornpipe, with a Skipping Rope, (Her first Appearance in Public)

Signor Giovanni Batista Belzoni,
THE
PATAGONIAN SAMPSON;

Will present most extraordinary Specimens of the GYMNASTIC Art, perfectly Foreign to any former exhibition (His first Appearance in England)
The Evenings Entertainments to conclude with a new Comic Pantomime called

FIRE and SPIRIT;
OR A
HOLIDAY HARLEQUIN.

Including, among other views, the following Scenes of Holiday Resort, viz. Chalk Farm—Horns at Kennington—Paddington Canal and Passage Boat—Hornsey House—Blackwall Wet Docks—Richmond Hill and Bridge—Greenwich Park and Hospital, &c.—beginning with the Bower of Spring, and concluding with a Magical

CATARACT,

Harlequin, Mr. KING—Clown, Mr. CIPRIANI. (His first Appearance at this Theatre) Pantaloon, Mr. HARTLAND, Marquis, Mr. POWERS, Old Woman, Mr. SMITH, and Colombine, Mad. St. AMAND, other numerous Characters incidental to Pantomime, by the rest of the Company.
The Entertainments, Music, Scenery, Dresses, and Decorations, of the Evening entirely new. Leader of the Band Mr. T. WARE. The Prelude, Burletta, Spectacle, Serio Comic, and Comic Pantomime, written, invented and produced by Mr. C. Dibdin Junr. the Overture and Music composed by Mr. Reeve, who superintends the Musical department, and will preside at the Piano Forte. The Scenery and Decorations designed by Mr. Andrews, and painted by him with Assistants, the Machinery executed by Mr. Garland, the Dresses by Mr. Smythies, Mrs. Robinson, and Assistants,—The Theatre will be entirely lighted with Wax.
The Public are respectfully informed that any Person admitted to the Performance, on paying 1s 0d *only* will receive a Pint of White or Red Foreign

Unadulterated Wine,

Which custom the New Proprietors have revived for the accommodation of the Public, as they will lose considerably upon every Pipe of Wine thus consumed.

N. B. The Private Boxes in the lower part of the Theatre have been totally altered from last Season, and are now perfectly calculated to accommodate the Nobility, Gentry, and Families in the most eligible manner.
And for the convenience of the Public, the Proprietors have put on additional Patrols in the Field leading from the Wells to Town, also a quantity of additional Lamps in the said Field, and in the Avenues to the Theatre by Permission of the NEW RIVER COMPANY.

Boxes 4s—Pit 2s—Gallery 1s—Doors to be opened at half past Five—to begin at half past Six—Places to be kept till Seven—Places for the Boxes may be taken of Mr. D'Cleve, at the Box Office of the Wells every Day from 11 till 2, who will give every Information to the repeated Inquiries for free Admissions for the Season.
Shortly after the opening, the Proprietors mean to give a BENEFIT, the profits of which will be appropriated towards the Subscription for the BEAUTY of BUTTERMERE, Particulars advertised in a few Days.

B. HUGHES, Printer, 156 White-Cross-Street, St. Lukes.

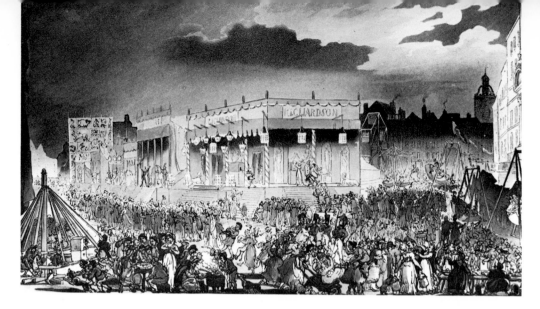

Bartholomew's Fair, after Rowlandson, 1809

In July 1803, Belzoni's three-month contract with Sadler's Wells expired and was not renewed. The reasons are not known, but the nonrenewal is surprising, for Belzoni's act was popular with Londoners and Sadler's Wells had enjoyed its best season for some years.

Two months later Belzoni was performing in very different surroundings, appearing in a human-pyramid act at Bartholomew's Fair, a popular annual event in the City of London. Bartholomew's Fair, a far cry from Sadler's Wells, was a bawdy and thoroughly hearty carnival with rides, numerous sideshows, stalls displaying everything from hurdy-gurdies to writing baboons, and, at one booth, the "French Hercules."

Fortunately, we have an eyewitness account of Belzoni's act at the fair, from John Thomas Smith, at the time the keeper of drawings and prints at the British Museum, and a well-known and garrulous commentator on the London scene. Smith and a friend visited the fair with some trepidation, for there was a real danger of robbery or mugging.

The two of them stopped at Belzoni's stall and watched him lift a series of heavy weights. Then the French Hercules asked for volunteers to form

102

a human pyramid on his shoulders. Smith and four others stepped forward and climbed onto chairs to reach Belzoni's massive shoulders. "Sampson performed his task with an ease of step most stately," remarked Smith. Belzoni was carrying quite a weight, for the fourth member of the pyramid was a "heavy dumpling, whose chops, I will answer for it, relished many an inch thick steak from the once far-famed Honey Lane market."

Giovanni Belzoni went on to become a familiar figure in London and the provinces during the next few years, traveling from fair to fair throughout the British Isles, performing acts of strength, and doomed, as the *Gentleman's Magazine* put it, "to bear on his colossal frame, not fewer, if we mistake not, than 20 or 22 persons . . . moving across the stage as stately as the elephant with the Persian warriors." This theatrical repertoire was soon expanded to include some trick effects and

Cruikshank's drawing of Belzoni's act at Bartholomew's Fair

displays with waterworks and stage hydraulics. He was soon billed as "The Great Belzoni," a title that assured him bookings all over Britain over the next eight years, a period when his wanderlust was at its most intense and when he acquired a working knowledge of weight lifting, the use of levers and rollers, and balancing techniques, useful skills for any tomb robber.

At about this time, Belzoni met and married his wife, Sarah. We know very little about Sarah, except that she was about twenty years old when she met her husband. She is variously described as being of English or Irish birth. The marriage was childless and one of perennial wandering in Europe and, later, Egypt. In the twenty-odd years of the Belzonis' marriage, they never had a permanent home or strong family ties. Yet the marriage was apparently a happy one, although Sarah did not hesitate to go off on her own or remain behind if her husband's activities bored her. She endured discomfort, hardship, and long separations with a remarkable equanimity. Her "Trifling Account" in Belzoni's biography is an insight into an observant and basically shrewd woman who had a wry sense of humor and was respected by Turk and Egyptian alike. Sarah outlived Belzoni by almost fifty years, eventually dying in dignified obscurity in the Channel Islands in 1870, long forgotten by the general public.

Accompanied by his new wife, Belzoni became a familiar figure on the circus and fair circuit, performing in Scotland and Ireland as well as London and the provinces at all manner of entertainments. The Belzonis wandered the length and breadth of the British Isles, caged in by Napoleon's campaigns and severe restrictions on foreign travel. But in 1812 Wellington liberated the southern ports of Spain, including Madrid, and Belzoni ventured abroad. His travel document has survived, showing that he was accompanied by his faithful Irish servant James Curtin but not by Sarah.

104

The pair visited Lisbon—where Belzoni may have performed in the São Carlos Theatre—Gibraltar, and Malaga before returning to England in time for a well-publicized series of performances in Oxford, Belzoni's last recorded show business appearances in England. The handbill of the first performance, at the Blue Boar Tavern, St. Aldate's, Oxford, on Monday, February 22, 1813, offered an impressive bill of fare. A conjuring turn was followed by a performance on the musical glasses. The "French Hercules" demonstrated "several striking Attitudes, from the most admired antique statues . . . uniting Grace and Expression with Muscular strength." A "Grand and Brilliant Display of Optical Illusions entitled the Aggrescopius" completed the performance.

Before leaving England, Belzoni called on Charles Dibdin and told him that he had returned to recruit performers for theaters in Lisbon. Whether he took any actors to Lisbon with him we do not know, but in mid-1813 the Belzoni family and James Curtin were in Lisbon and Madrid. After performing at various centers, the Belzonis traveled in Sicily, where we find them in November 1814 exchanging letters with the family in Padua.

But Belzoni made no effort to visit his hometown. His wanderlust was turning him in the direction of Constantinople, one of the great centers of popular entertainment in the Western world. The sultan of Turkey was forever laying on vast popular festivals which often lasted for several weeks. Conjurers and wrestlers, acrobats and jugglers, were in constant demand. Fireworks and illuminations were designed by Italians from Bologna, a town close to Belzoni's home community. The sultan made considerable use of foreign artists in entertainments and spectacles, a fact that seems to have encouraged Belzoni to try his fortune in the heart of the Ottoman Empire. At any rate, instead of returning home, the Belzonis crossed to Malta on their leisurely way to the

435. Persons coming to be registered. *Thebes.*

436. 5 4 3 2 1 Brought before the scribes. *Thebes.*

Egyptian bureaucracy. Illustrations from John Gardner Wilkinson's *Manners and Customs of the Ancient Egyptians* **(1835).**

Turkish capital. They lodged in Valletta for nearly six months, enjoying a respite from the constant strain of traveling and performing in strange places. It was here that Belzoni had a chance encounter with Captain Ishmail Gibraltar, an agent of Mohammed 'Ali, the ruler of Egypt, an event that changed his life.

Mohammed 'Ali's thirty years of rule produced

extraordinary changes, many of them far from permanent, for their ultimate success depended on the strong leadership of 'Ali himself. "When I came to Egypt," he once said, "it was really barbarous, utterly barbarous. Barbarous it remains to this day. Still I hope that my labors have rendered its condition to be somewhat better than it was. You must not, however, be shocked if you do not find in these countries the civilization that prevails in Europe." Much of government was in the hands of Turks, but the reins of official expenditure were tightly controlled by Mohammed 'Ali himself. His trusted Armenian minister Boghoz Bey was ordered to implement a European style of budget mechanism, with detailed accounts and a public audit system, that was successful in keeping 'Ali's government out of the hands of European moneylenders, even if much corruption still remained. The pasha turned to Europe for expert advice on agricultural improvement, industry, and economic development.

Unfortunately, many of his most ambitious schemes were failures. The French engineer Linant designed a barrage across the Nile which was supposed to permit complete irrigation of the delta even in poor flood years. When it was completed, water seeped under the inadequate foundations. Vast sums were invested in cotton mills, a tannery, and other commercial ventures. The more elaborate factories were a failure. Machinery was neglected and never oiled, management sporadic. Peasant farmers were unused to the monotony and regularity of factory work and were soon recruited by force. All the same, 'Ali transformed many aspects of Egyptian life, with the help of European experts, some of them genuine, others pure renegades or dregs of European society.

Most of the experts were recruited either through chance encounter or with the help of the pasha's numerous agents. Ishmail Gibraltar, a sea captain, was one such agent, employed to search out engineers and industrial experts who would

107

Cairo in the early nineteenth century. From *La Description de l'Egypte.*

Giovanni Belzoni by W. Brockendon. Date unknown.

introduce new products and agricultural methods to replace those that were still in use almost unchanged from the days of the pharaohs.

Captain Gibraltar seems to have encountered Belzoni at a time when the latter was contemplating the commercial value of his various talents in the relative peace of Malta. Belzoni and Gibraltar quickly became fast friends, a friendship that soon had the Italian talking of his idea for a new design of waterwheel that would revolutionize the Egyptian economy. The new water pump would be powered by one ox instead of many, of simple and robust design, and cheap to manufacture.

Gibraltar was sufficiently impressed by Belzoni's enthusiasm and apparent expertise to arrange for him to visit Cairo and build a prototype for the pasha. Soon afterward, on May 19, 1815, Belzoni, Sarah, and James Curtin took ship for Alexandria, where they arrived three weeks later, only to be greeted by the news that the plague was raging in the town. Soon the Belzonis made their way

108

ashore, stepping gingerly over the piles of garbage
and through narrow streets. They sought lodging
in a French house where they were isolated from
the rest of the town in a state of quarantine, at
that time about the only preventive measure
against plague that seemed to work.

The Belzonis' introduction to Egypt was hardly
auspicious. They began by succumbing to a stomach disorder which they carefully concealed from
the other lodgers for fear that panic would ensue,
for several Europeans had died of plague in recent days. Then there was the isolation in a new
and strange land. The Belzonis were thrown on
the company of their neighbors in the quarantine
house. But the plague eased by the end of June,
and Belzoni was able to get about the town. He
called on the British and French consuls, who received him with interest. Colonel Missett, the British representative, was crippled by ill health and
about to retire from his post. Apparently he
showed less interest in Belzoni than did Bernardino Drovetti, himself of Italian birth, who seems

to have taken to the visitor and given him a great deal of assistance.

The French consul gave Belzoni some letters of introduction to useful people in Cairo and seemed interested in the Italian's hydraulic designs. One suspects that his motives were partly political, for he had already learned that the British planned to give the pasha a steam engine and pumping machine, gifts that had arrived in Alexandria in the company of a mechanic at about the time that Belzoni came on the scene. Belzoni must also have seen some of Drovetti's antiquities and heard firsthand stories of the excitement and profits of archaeological discovery.

Colonel Missett's residence was an important rendezvous for travelers to the Nile, even in times of pestilence and plague. When Belzoni called on the consul, he was introduced to William Turner, a young gentleman-diplomat who was in the middle of a leisurely tour through the Near East. This charming and intelligent young traveler took an immediate liking to the Belzonis and left an engag-

Sailing up the Nile

ing description of their journey to Cairo, for they joined company in hiring a boat to carry them up the Nile.

The journey was a fascinating experience for the newcomers, who took five days to make the trip across the Nile bar at the Rosetta mouth and journey through the lush delta country. After the heat and dust of Alexandria, the green oasis of Rosetta and the slow-moving Nile were a revelation, for the travelers were able to observe a way of life along its banks that had not changed for centuries. Then, on the morning of the fifth day, their small sailing boat came to Bulak, the principal port of Cairo. Turner lodged at a convent, while the Belzonis hastened to set up house in a residence provided them by Boghoz Bey.

"Cairo: View of the Port and of the Great Mosque of Bulak." From *La Description*.

111

7   "A Connaisseur in Hydrauliks"

Cairo was an imposing sight for the arriving traveler accustomed to the flat monotony of the Nile Delta. The domes and minarets of its many mosques rose above a pall of smoke from innumerable household fires. The city was a bustling, cosmopolitan metropolis, lying a little distance from the right bank of the Nile under the Mukattam hills. Palm trees and cultivated fields bordered the river, while the pyramids could be seen in the distance. For more than a thousand years a city had flourished on this spot. The walls and citadel had been rebuilt several times by important leaders, among them the mighty Saladin. According to William Turner, at least 250,000 people inhabited the streets and bazaars of the busy city, after Constantinople probably the most influential political and economic center in the Near East.

112

View of Cairo from the Citadel, with Turkish soldiers

This sprawling commercial center was the terminus of long-distance caravan routes throughout North Africa and the Near East. Timbuktu, the Niger, Damascus, Aleppo, India, and possibly even the Far East could be reached by caravan. No one dreamed of traveling alone through the hostile desert, where drought, marauding raiders, and the crosscurrents of political intrigue could halt a caravan for weeks or even years. Thousands of merchants and their families spent their entire lives wandering over enormous distances, following trading opportunities and bartering all manner of commodities for other merchandise in kind. The bazaars of Cairo thrived on the caravan trade. Cotton, flax, grain, and a thousand and one useful and useless products of Near East craftsmen were disseminated along the caravan routes, in exchange for raw materials and exotic objects from Africa and Asia: slaves, gold, ivory, salt, spices, rhinoceros horn (a well-known aphrodisiac), ostrich shells, fine clothes, and china.

The city was a maze of narrow streets and dilapidated houses. The streets were thronged with peddlers and street vendors boasting of their wares. Small shops housed the many craftsmen for which Cairo was famous; goldsmiths and silversmiths lived in one quarter, while potters and leatherworkers had their own streets. One could buy, or experience, anything in Cairo—at a price. At night the city was quieter, for many of the streets were blocked off by wooden doors and the great gates were locked for the night. The architecture of Cairo was dominated by the huge mosques—among them al-Azhar, a major center of Islamic learning for more than a millennium, and the oldest foundation of all, the mosque built by ibn Tulun in the ninth century.

The more imposing buildings and mosques were built from blocks of granite quarried from the pyramids and temples of the Ancient Egyptians. Beyond the grand square of Ezbekiya, flooded each August when the Nile rose above its banks, there were few open spaces. Much of Cairo consisted of decaying slums, where new shacks and hovels were simply built on the ruins of old ones, and piles of garbage strewed both streets and courtyards, the home of countless scavenging animals.

Few Europeans lived in Cairo except for some consular representatives, a handful of French merchants who had stayed on after Napoleon's occu-

A view of Cairo with a caravan in process of formation. From *La Description*.

pation, and a small community of government advisers and travelers. The European quarter was isolated from the rest of the city by great wooden doors, which closed off the residences at sunset and in times of plague, riot, or political hostility. A visitor would lodge in the European quarter or, if space were not available, would take up residence at Bulak, the main port for Cairo, a mile to the northwest of the city. It was here that the pasha and other wealthy Cairenes built luxurious summer palaces with cool gardens. Of the French occupation, little remained. Napoleon's grand plans for great boulevards and impressive buildings had come to nothing. A tiny French community preserved some French interests in the city, which continued to flourish in a decaying, hothouse atmosphere of fast-flowing trade and constant political instability and intrigue. No one

116

with any taste for the Eastern life could resist the
tawdry charm of Cairo.

The Belzoni family disembarked at Bulak and
took up lodgings in a house allocated them by
Boghoz Bey. While his kind gesture was much appreciated, their first residence was hardly inspiring,
for the windows were boarded up, there was no
lock on the front door, and the roof was in danger
of collapse. Sarah laid out their sheets and mat-
tresses on the floor of one of the least ruinous and
cleaner rooms. They took their meals sitting on
the floor and waited for an audience with the
pasha.

Boghoz Bey arranged the interview for a week
later, but the encounter never took place. On the
way to the citadel Belzoni was viciously kicked
by a disgruntled Turkish soldier. The gash on his
leg laid him up for several weeks. When the in-

117

A villa and garden near Cairo

terview eventually did materialize, Belzoni was
politely received. He described his invention and
undertook to build a prototype "which would
raise as much water with one ox, as the machines
of the country with four." Mohammed 'Ali was
"much pleased with my proposal," wrote Belzoni,
as it will save the labor and expense of many
thousands of oxen in the country."

The building of the prototype took longer than
had been anticipated. Turkish soldiers in Cairo
mutinied and attempted to storm the citadel. They
were rebuffed by the guards and embarked on a
rampage of looting and destruction. Belzoni rashly
entered the city at the height of the mutiny and

118

was robbed of all his money and his passport when attempting to return to Sarah in Bulak. The pasha remained inside the citadel for more than a month until the mutiny, over the adoption of European drills in the military, had subsided. But eventually things quieted down and life returned to normal. The Belzonis moved into a small home near the pasha's palace at Shubra, living off a small subsistence allowance from the government. The pump was to be erected in the pasha's garden nearby.

William Turner, in the meantime, was busy visiting notables in Cairo and arranging various excursions in and around the city, among them a trip to the pyramids. Belzoni was invited to accompany the party, which journeyed out to Gizeh on donkeys by moonlight. Soon after sunrise the travelers stood at the chilly summit of the Great Pyramid, admiring the fine view of Cairo and the Nile spread out at their feet. Then, after breakfast, they explored the interior of the pyramid and fired off their pistols in Cheops' burial chamber, a

"For hundreds of miles up the Nile the river is lined with these *shadoofs*, men, women, and children . . . spending their whole lives in lifting water out of the bountiful river to irrigate their fields"

119

The Nile in flood

deafening pastime which must have caused them acute discomfort. There is no record of Belzoni's exhibiting anything more than the usual curiosity about the pyramids.

The long delays in obtaining materials and parts for a pump left Belzoni with much time on his hands. So he and Sarah had time to venture on another excursion with Turner, this time to Sakkareh, where more pyramids and the famous mummy pits were to be seen. The Nile was in flood, so they were able to travel by boat across the flooded fields. After a night in the open, they mounted donkeys for the ride to the famous step pyramid. They climbed to the top of the pyramid and then breakfasted in its shadow, before deciding not to visit the mummy pits, for the local people told them that ladders and a lamp were necessary. One of the servants was dispatched to fetch a mummy of an ibis. Half an hour later he returned with a narrow jar sealed with a clay stopper, which, he assured them, was a genuine antiq-

120

uity containing a mummified bird. The Europeans
laughed at him, whereupon the furious Arab
dashed the pot to the ground and picked up a
small bundle of decaying mummy fabric from the
broken pot, indeed the remains of a mummified
bird. Such jars were commonly empty and sold to
gullible tourists as genuine antiquities.

These side trips were but intervals between
Belzoni's frantic efforts to build a prototype machine for the pasha. He was delayed on all sides.
The pasha's chief engineer was sick, good-quality
wood was not available, and permits for construction could not be obtained. Belzoni's plans
were quietly opposed by many bureaucrats,

121

A Cairo street. "Cairo is a big place, and can stand a good deal of improving"—A nineteenth-century American tourist.

strongly resistant to many of the reforms proposed by the pasha, who respected Western ways of doing business.

It took him three or four months to complete his pumping machine, and it was not until the middle of 1816 that the fateful demonstration took place. Belzoni presented himself before the pasha and "several connaisseurs in hydrauliks." The demonstration took place in the palace gardens, where his prototype machine had been set up alongside six sakiehs, the traditional waterwheels used for thousands of years on the banks of the Nile. An ox was driven into the treadmill drum, and water began to flow down the irrigation channels in the pasha's garden. The owners of the six sakiehs frantically lashed their oxen into a frenzy, trying to emulate the flood of water cascading

122

from Belzoni's waterwheel. The pasha was impressed, conferred with his advisers, and pronounced that Belzoni's machine was as good as four sakiehs. But his advisers, who sensed reduced manpower and profits, were unimpressed at the efficiency of yet another European invention, and the pasha hesitated. To stall for time, he asked what would happen if men replaced the ox in the treadmill. A crowd of excited Arabs jumped into the wheel and were joined by James Curtin, Belzoni's young servant. The wheel moved merrily and the water flooded, until the Arabs jumped out, leaving the young boy by himself as a counterweight to the mass of water. He was flung out of the wheel and broke a leg. Belzoni's machine was doomed to failure after that. 'Ali's Turkish admirers were relieved. No pasha in his right mind would adopt a pumping machine so lethal as this sinister new device. Belzoni's hopes and ambitions as a hydraulic engineer collapsed around his head in a few minutes.

8 The Young Memnon

John Lewis Burkhardt in Arab dress

It was at about this time that Henry Salt, the new British consul general, arrived in Cairo. Salt had traveled out with Hamilton's fateful Foreign Office memorandum about antiquities in his baggage and was anxious to find a new Rosetta Stone as soon as possible. When he arrived at Bulak, the plague season had enveloped Cairo and he was obliged to lodge in the same dilapidated house that the Belzonis had camped in a year before. There he met Sheik Ibrahim, a tall and prematurely old man who looked and behaved like an Arab, although he was in fact a Swiss native—Johann Ludwig Burckhardt.

Burckhardt was a remarkable scholar, an expert linguist and chemist, with a passion for travel. After his family was ruined in the Napoleonic

124

wars, Burckhardt emigrated to England, where he studied Arabic at Cambridge.

A palace in Cairo. *La Description de l'Egypte.*

He then presented himself to Sir Joseph Banks, the president of the newly formed African Association, and offered to explore the sources of the Niger River, at that time a point of some geographic controversy. The Association gave him an exiguous allowance and agreed that he could spend two years in Syria perfecting his Arabic before leaving by caravan for Central Africa. Burckhardt promptly steeped himself in Arab life and became so proficient in Arabic and the Koran that Islamic scholars proclaimed him an authority on Islamic law. In 1812 he turned up in Cairo, having adopted the name Sheik Ibrahim ibn Abdullah. His vague objective was to join a caravan journeying across the Sahara to the Fezzan and West Africa. But few caravans were to be found, so he filled in the time by journeying up the Nile as far as Dongola deep in Nubia and then making a side trip to the Red Sea. At this point, he was so close to Mecca that it seemed logical to make the pilgrimage and to visit the tomb of the Prophet at Medina. Burckhardt had returned to Cairo at about the same time as Turner and the Belzonis.

This emaciated and weary traveler had an extraordinary knowledge of Islam and the Nile. His surviving letters and notes, which were later converted into splendid books, reveal him as a superlative observer of the trivial and of the important, a man who was totally wrapped up in the world of Islam. He was the first educated man in modern times to visit the magnificent Abu Simbel temples.

Burkhardt had not been impressed by Abu Simbel at first, for he came on the façade from above, looking down from the cliffs above the temple. It was only when he turned upstream a little way that he caught sight of one of the four colossal statues which formed the façade of Ramesses II's largest temple. The statues were almost completely buried in sand, so he had to guess what lay underneath. "Could the sand be cleared away, a vast temple would be discovered," he remarked prophetically. And he was vastly impressed by the single exposed head, which had, he wrote, "a most expressive, youthful countenance, approaching nearer to the Grecian model of beauty than that of any ancient Egyptian figure I have seen."

Burckhardt's journeys and observations made him a fascinating and perceptive companion in an alien city, one whom Belzoni seems to have been at some pains to cultivate. It was from Burckhardt that Belzoni heard of the Abu Simbel temples and the great statues buried in sand. But it was another observation of Burckhardt's which excited Belzoni the most. While spending a few days near Thebes, Burckhardt had come across a colossal granite head of singular beauty, known as "the Young Memnon," lying abandoned in a temple named the Memnonium on the west bank of the Nile. The head—in fact depicting Ramesses II—was well known to antiquarians, for it had been described by diplomat William Hamilton in an authoritative but extraordinarily dull book on Egyptian archaeology as "certainly the most beautiful and perfect piece of Egyptian sculpture that can

The facade of Abu Simbel as depicted by the French artist Franz Gau in 1822. This view shows the newly cleared temple and statues.

be seen throughout the whole country." The
French had also appreciated its worth and had
tried to remove it, without success.

Burckhardt heard of these attempts from the
local people and had even thought vaguely of removing the head himself. He suggested that the
pasha might give the head to the Prince Regent as
a gift, but Mohammed 'Ali had scoffed at the idea.
What monarch, he asked, would want a mere
block of stone? Burckhardt seems to have mentioned the head to Belzoni, but the latter showed
little interest in the statue until the sudden crisis
in his affairs precipitated by the accident at the
pasha's palace forced him to look elsewhere for
employment.

With all his plans dashed to the ground, Belzoni
was in a perilous financial position. Then he remembered the head and went to see Burckhardt.
The traveler was sympathetic, but certainly did
not have the money to pay for the transportation
of the Memnon all the way to England. But Henry
Salt was much more amenable. "This is a god-
send, indeed," he is alleged to have exclaimed,
and he immediately obtained the necessary firman
from the pasha. Belzoni was given a letter of instructions, which charged him with the responsibility of bringing the head down the Nile. Salt
now wrote to Belzoni requesting him "to prepare
the necessary implements, at Bulak, for the purpose of carrying the head of the statue of the
younger Memnon, and carrying it down the Nile."
The letter gave instructions about recruitment of
labor and a boat crew, information on expendi-
tures, and specific guidance on how to identify
the head. "It must not be mistaken for another,
lying in that neighborhood, which is *much mutilated*," the letter cautioned.

Belzoni threw himself into a fever of preparations, hiring a boat and scouring Bulak and Cairo
for suitable lifting materials. All he was able to
obtain were a few poles and some palm fiber
ropes. It was clear he would have to rely on local

128

materials. On June 30, 1816, the Belzonis left by boat for Thebes, accompanied by James Curtin and a Copt interpreter.

This was the first time that Belzoni had been any distance upstream of Cairo, so he paused at intervals to look at places on the way. The party took six days to reach Manfalut, where they met the pasha's son Ibrahim on his way to Cairo. Drovetti was with Ibrahim's party, laden with antiquities he had collected near Thebes. He seems to have welcomed Belzoni warmly, although he had heard that he was on his way upstream to remove the great head. But Drovetti warned that the Arabs at Thebes were refusing to work, and—one suspects rather cynically—presented Belzoni with a beautiful granite sarcophagus cover, which was, however, still firmly embedded in a rock-cut tomb near Thebes, all efforts to remove it having failed.

At Asyut, Belzoni called on the local bey and presented his credentials, but he had great difficulty in obtaining boats, materials, and carpenters. Excuses were made—the stone was useless, permission to obtain workmen would not be granted. Then he became more explicit. "He plainly recommended to me not to meddle in this business, for I should meet with many disagreeable things, and have many obstacles to encounter." Quite obviously Drovetti had been at work, hoping to secure the head for himself. But he had sadly underestimated the determination of Belzoni.

On July 18 they were at Dendereh and paused to admire the magnificent temple so ably described by Vivant Denon. They examined the famous zodiac in the temple ceiling and found an abandoned village on the roof. The local people seemed to have little respect for the monuments of antiquity. Four days later the expedition arrived at Thebes and wandered among the ruins of Luxor and Karnak, transported with wonder. Belzoni waxed lyrical over the temples and statuary. "It appeared to me like entering a city of giants, who, after a long conflict, were all destroyed, leav-

Edward de Montulé's rendering of the Memnonium with the Young Memnon still in position. "The palace of Memnon is a stupendous monument, supported by columns and caryatids; but it is in a ruinous state, and its ensemble is somewhat confused."

ing the ruins of their former temples as the only proof of their former existence."

Belzoni's first thought was to identify and examine the head of Memnon that was the objective of his expedition. "I found it near the remains of its body and chair, with its face upwards, and apparently smiling on me, at the thought of being taken to England," he wrote. Belzoni was slightly daunted by the size of the head, for it was larger than he had been led to believe. All he had at his disposal were fourteen poles, four palm ropes, and four rollers. There were no tackles, nor could he obtain more timber in a treeless environment. The task seemed almost impossible. But a base camp was soon prepared in a small and comfortable stone hut constructed from loose boulders from the temple. While his carpenter made a crude car out of eight of the Cairo poles, Belzoni examined the flood level of the river, which would be lapping at the edge of the temple within a month. Unless the head was dragged to the river bank before the flood, it would have to remain for another year, a delay that would be fatal, for others were also after the trophy.

It was soon obvious that Drovetti had been at work. The local Turkish headman received Belzoni politely, even effusively, but was far from helpful. He stated that all the local peasants were busy in the fields, which was untrue. Furthermore, it was Ramadan, and Belzoni should wait until after the flood. In any case, he added, the local people would rather starve than undertake such an arduous task. Eventually the headman promised to find men on the morrow, and Belzoni departed well satisfied. But several frustrating days and many bribes were needed before work could actually begin.

The first step was to place the head on the carpenter's car, a task that Belzoni achieved in short order by placing four levers under the bust, heaving up the dead weight of the stone, and pushing the car underneath. Two large rollers were then

The portico of the temple of Dendereh in the 1870s

133

trundled under the loaded car, by lifting it at one end. The men were convinced the head would never be moved and gave a great shout when the levers shifted it. "Though it was the effect of their own efforts, it was the devil, they said, that did it; and as they saw me taking notes, they concluded it was done by means of a charm," Belzoni remarked with satisfaction.

The long haul to the riverbank now began. A day later the head was out of the temple, although Belzoni had to break the bases of two columns to get it out. Despite great suffering from the heat, Belzoni saw the head move 200 yards in the next two days. Then the ground became sandy and the head sunk into the soil; so they had to make a detour of 300 extra yards.

All went well until August 5, when the head reached an area of low-lying floodplain which would soon be inundated by the Nile. Early in the morning Belzoni arrived at the car to find only the guards and the carpenter, but no workmen. The headman had forbidden the laborers to work for a Christian dog any longer. Belzoni confronted

The triumphal progress of the Young Memnon. From the watercolor by Giovanni Belzoni.

The temple of Amun at Karnak: detail of the pillars

135

the chief. An angry interview ensued at which Belzoni received insolent treatment and lost his temper. He "then became more violent, and drew his sword. . . . There was no time to be lost; . . . I gave him no leisure to execute his purpose. I instantly seized and disarmed him, placing my hands on his stomach, and making him sensible of my superiority, at least in point of strength, by keeping him firm in a corner of the room." After giving the fellow a good shaking, Belzoni told him that he would report his behavior to the pasha. The next morning the head was moving again.

Five days later Belzoni was able to write,

"Thank God, the young Memnon arrived on the
bank of the Nile." He gave the laborers a bonus
payment of sixpence each in addition to their
wages, "with which they were exceedingly pleased."

The next requirement was a boat, but all available rivercraft were in the service of the pasha.
So a letter was sent to Cairo asking Salt to send
one to Thebes. In the meantime, two guards were
posted at the site and an earth bank built around
the loaded car.

Belzoni now turned his energetic thoughts toward the sarcophagus which Drovetti had given
him. It lay inside a burial cave in the hills behind
Kurneh, one of the sepulchers that were famous
for the fine mummies they contained. Accompanied by two Arab guides and interpreters, Belzoni
removed most of his clothes, lit candles, and
squeezed his way into a narrow cavity in the
rock, which extended a fair distance into the hill.
The party passed through various burial passages

**The pasha's state barge
off Luxor**

137

until they appeared completely lost as the Arabs tried to trick Belzoni into paying for directions to the lid. Fortunately, he stumbled onto it by accident and thwarted them.

Belzoni set the men to work cleaning the passage to the sarcophagus, only to discover three days later that the headman of Erment had imprisoned his workmen "bound like thieves." Drovetti's agents had arrived from Alexandria and become alarmed at Belzoni's success and determination. The headman informed Belzoni that the lid had been sold to Drovetti and that was the end of the matter. "I feigned to be quite unconcerned about the matter, as well as about the Arabs he had put in prison," he records. Playing for time, he promised to write to Cairo about the matter, and turned his attention to other sites.

9 A Nubian Journey

Having time to kill, Belzoni decided to venture farther upstream, both out of curiosity and also with a view to purchasing more antiquities. His boat could go wherever he wished it to proceed without further cost, and it seemed logical, with the Young Memnon stuck on the bank of the Nile and the matter of the sarcophagus unresolved, to see what lay upstream of well-exploited and highly suspicious Thebes.

The boat trip upstream from Luxor to the First Cataract is normally an uneventful one, for the traveler passes through intensively cultivated countryside, with small villages clustered on the higher ground which escapes inundation each August. For the Belzonis every bend in the river was a new adventure, enlivened by night stops in small

The temple of Horus at Edfu

towns and villages where they called on the local headmen or entertained them aboard their boat.

Kom Ombo, Aswan, and the island of Elephantine were pleasant interludes in the monotony of river travel, where the travelers visited temples and Coptic chapels. Elephantine was disappointing to Belzoni, who had read the rapturous accounts of it penned by earlier travelers. Perhaps his disappointment was due to the hazardous ferry crossing. Nine people—one of them the mas-

140

sive Belzoni—crammed themselves into a matting and palm fiber boat only 10 feet long and 5 feet wide. "It cost, when new, twelve piasters, or six shillings," calmly observed Belzoni.

The First Cataract breaks the serenity of the river at Aswan, and Belzoni there sought to hire a boat to take him upstream to the island of Philae and into Nubia. The local aga made the mistake of trying to bargain with Belzoni, who argued with such determination that the aga eventually let him have a boat "at the price a Nubian paid." The agreed price for the return trip to the Second Cataract was 20 dollars, a lot less than the aga's original asking price of 120 dollars.

On August 27 they came to Philae. "Long before

The island of Philae with a dahabeah at the tourist landing

the rising of the sun, I stood at the stern, waiting for the light to unveil that goodly sight, the beautiful island of Philae," Belzoni recalled. "When I beheld them, they surpassed everything that imagination could anticipate." The wind was so favorable that they paused for the briefest of visits, resolving to return for a more leisurely inspection on the downstream passage.

The Belzonis soon found out they were in foreign territory where the pasha was less powerful. The day after they left Philae a group of natives appeared while some of the party were ashore. Soon armed warriors with spears were swarming around the boat. Only the Belzonis and their interpreter were on board. They all grabbed pistols, and Belzoni gestured at the natives to keep away. "I then stepped forward, and with my right hand prevented the first of them from entering the boat, while I held the pistol in my left. . . . At last I pointed a pistol at him, making signs, that, if he did not retire, I would shoot at him." Once again Belzoni's decisive behavior had prevented trouble.

They were now in less well-known country, where Belzoni relied on notes given him by Burckhardt. A search for antiquities took them to Kalabsha, where they inspected a temple near the river. A large crowd of armed locals blocked the entrance as they turned to leave and demanded money. Belzoni drew himself up to his full and imposing height, told them he would not give them money under duress, stared them in the

Afloat in Nubia

face, and walked through the crowd unmolested. Later he was able to buy some tombstones with Greek inscriptions.

Leaving Kalabsha they came to Derr, the capital of Lower Nubia, a village consisting of "several groups of houses, built of earth intermingled with stones." Here, Hassan Kachif, one of three brothers who ruled this area of Nubia among them, greeted Belzoni with great suspicion. It was impossible for the travelers to venture farther, he said, for the people upstream were at war with each other. Fortunately, Belzoni had made inquiries in Cairo about Nubian tastes and found out that they valued looking glasses and glass beads above all other possessions. So, in a moment of inspiration, he took a stock of mirrors with him just in case.

A handsome looking glass was solemnly presented to Hassan, a gift that produced a letter of safe passage addressed to Hassan's brother upstream in record time. "The Kachif was never tired of admiring his bear-like face; and all his attendants behind him strove to get a peep at their own chocolate beauty," exulted Belzoni. Two days later the party reached Abu Simbel, which was the real objective of Belzoni's trip. Ever since he had learned of the huge and beautiful figures that Burckhardt had seen three years before, Belzoni had planned to visit the vast statues and to uncover the great temple that lay behind them.

Having admired the great frieze and the six colossal figures from a distance, Belzoni clambered up the steep, sandy slope to a point where a likeness of the hawk-headed god Hor-akhty projected out of the sand. This he judged to be above the lintel of the temple doorway. Even Belzoni was daunted by the size of the undertaking. He estimated that the door lay 35 feet below the surface of the soft sand, which poured into his foot imprints as fast as he made them.

After a rapid inspection of the site, the Belzonis landed at the village of Abu Simbel some short

distance away, where they found a group of
armed men assembled under some trees, among
them Daud Kachif, the local headman. Daud was
a man of about fifty, "clad in a light blue gown,
with a white rag on his head as a turban." Somewhat surprised to see a stranger, the ragged assembly greeted Belzoni roughly and inquired as to his
business. When he explained that he had come in
search of ancient stones and wished to open the
buried temple, the kachif laughed scornfully. He
had heard that story before, for some months pre-
viously another European had passed by and
taken away a lot of gold. Did Belzoni not want
the stones to take gold from them? Patiently, the
Italian explained that he was interested in the
people who had made the stones, not gold. Besides, asked the kachif, what use was money to
his people, who never used it? Undaunted, Belzoni
gave a piaster to a bystander and told him to give
it to the carefully briefed *reis* of the boat, who
would give him a measure of corn in exchange.
The people were suitably impressed when the
man returned with three days' ration of grain.

Eventually Belzoni was able to strike a bargain
of two piasters a day per man, a bargain which
pleased him when he learned that no less a visitor
than Consul Drovetti had left 300 piasters with the
kachif as a fee for opening the temple—a fee that
was returned, for the people had no use for cash.

Having settled matters at Abu Simbel, Belzoni
journeyed on to Ashkit, a day and a half's sailing
upstream, to get permission for the work from
Hussein Kachif, brother of Hassan Kachif.
The Belzonis landed on some islands immediately
below the Second Cataract inhabited by
primitive people whose total wordly possessions
were a "baking stove and a mat to sleep on."
There they obtained two pilots who took
them right up to the cataract. The party nar-
rowly escaped shipwreck when the boat was
driven against a rock by a strong current. Soon afterward they landed and climbed a high rock

144

which provided a magnificent view of the cataract. "The blackness of the stones, the green of the trees on the islands, intermixed with the white froth of the water, form a fine picture, which can scarcely be described or delineated," wrote Belzoni.

Hussein Kachif, a majestic ruler in his seventies, was waiting for them at Ashkit with a fierce bodyguard. He questioned Belzoni minutely, expressed little surprise at his wish to open the temple, a task he clearly considered impossible, and gave permission provided that he received half of

Abu Simbel, from a watercolor by Giovanni Belzoni. "Could the sand be cleared away, a vast temple would be discovered."

145

all the treasure. Belzoni readily agreed, for he suspected—rightly as it turned out—that he would find nothing except statuary.

He hastened back to Abu Simbel, only to find that the people had decided they did not want to work. Exasperated, Belzoni pretended to lose interest and leave. The kachif saw a useful source of revenue evaporating, and, after prolonged arguments, it was agreed that forty men would report for work the next day. No one turned up on the morrow, so Belzoni made the kachif send soldiers to round up the men. Eventually a group of workers began digging in pairs, using long sticks with crosspieces of wood at the ends to drag away the sand down the slope from the façade of the temple. The work went quite well, for the men's thoughts were on the treasure they would find. But the pace soon slacked off. It was becoming clear that the kachif was out to extort every piaster he could from visitors, and Belzoni only got his way by bribing the kachif's brother, who arranged for a bonus of grain to satisfy the workmen's demands.

When the work resumed, a palisade of palm leaves and saplings was placed upslope of the suspected temple entrance so that new sand did not cascade into the excavation. So many men arrived on the third day of digging that eighty men worked for the wages of forty. At the end of the day the kachif's brother took everyone's wages. Belzoni sarcastically observed that his magic for obtaining money seemed to be more effective than his own.

There were other incidents too. Two of the laborers made to plunder the boat with only Sarah Belzoni and a young girl on board. "They were rather impertinent to her," observed Belzoni. "At last she presented a pistol to them, on which they immediately retired, and ran up the hill." It was impossible to identify the culprits, for "they were all like so many lumps of chocolate seated on the sand at work."

146

By this time the Belzonis' money was running out. Obviously the clearing of the temple entrance would have to wait for another visit, for they had underestimated the dramatic effect that the introduction of money would have on the avarice of the local people. The workmen had now uncovered 25 feet of the front of the temple and of the two colossal statues in front of the door. There were at least 15 feet to go, if Belzoni's calculations were correct. So Belzoni marked the spot carefully and extracted a promise from the kachif that he would let no one touch the place until he returned in a few months. Not that he had much faith in the kachif, but he gambled on the apparent indolence of the local people.

With that, the Belzonis made tracks for home and headed downstream. This time Belzoni was able to spend more time at Philae and lingered among the small but magnificent temples on the island. "I took particular notice of a small obelisk . . . which, if brought to England, might serve as a monument in some particular place, or as an embellishment to the Metropolis," he wrote. This delightful monument, 22 feet long and 2 feet wide at the base, could readily be transported to Cairo in a large boat when the waters of the First Cataract were high. Belzoni sent for the aga of Aswan and made him agree that he was taking possession of the obelisk "in the name of his Britannic Majesty's Consul-General in Cairo."

A small temple at the south end of the island yielded a series of twelve exquisitely carved stone blocks that could be pieced together to show the "god Osiris seated on his chair, with an altar before him, receiving offerings from priests and female figures." The blocks were 30 inches thick, far too bulky to be shipped on Belzoni's boat. So he arranged for them to be sawed down for later shipping and moved his headquarters to Aswan, where he sought another boat.

No boats were to be had, for the aga had hidden them all to delay the travelers in the town.

147

Approaches to Aswan

But as Belzoni was about to hire camels, the aga himself rented him one of the hidden boats for an exorbitant price. This was one of the rare occasions when Belzoni's tactics did not prevail. He had no option but to press on, for the river was falling rapidly and Young Memnon had to be moved before the flood receded.

There were no boats at Luxor either, for the pasha had commandeered most rivercraft. Fortunately, a large boat appeared on October 7 carrying two of Drovetti's agents on their way to Aswan, and Belzoni was able to engage it for the return journey. The agents moored their boat close to the carefully guarded head of Memnon and were moved to observe in their jealousy that "the French invaders did not take it away, because they thought it was not worth taking."

The agents went over to Kurneh with Belzoni, had the local people assembled, and told them in Belzoni's presence that if they sold any antiquities to the English, they, the agents, would arrange for them to be flogged by the kachif of Erment. Another member of their crew went so far as to warn Belzoni that if he persisted, his throat would be cut by the orders of his enemies. Undeterred,

148

Belzoni went on with his arrangements, at the same time setting twenty men to work digging for antiquities at a likely spot near Karnak.

The great temples of Karnak were such powerful political and religious institutions that they were richly endowed with magnificent statues and other works of art by generations of wealthy pharaohs. The precincts of the temples were a gold mine for any excavator two centuries ago. We cannot be sure where Belzoni dug, but it was probably somewhere within the precinct of the temple of Mut, the vulture goddess, well away from where the French had been digging. In the course of a few days he found a cache of black granite statues of the goddess Sakhmet, the lion-headed wife of the god Ptah, and other valuable pieces. The extent of his finds was limited only by the money at his disposal, for in those days one could dig practically anywhere at Karnak and still find plenty of antiquities.

Nevertheless, Belzoni's discoveries caused even greater jealousy among Drovetti's agents, who could do nothing to stop him. It was quite clear that the hard-driving Italian would return for more digging, and their efforts to prevent his recruiting labor were to no avail, for the people of Karnak, unlike those of Kurneh, were anxious for work. Fortunately, also, Calil Bey, the ruler of the province and a relative of the pasha, was in Luxor. Belzoni dined with the bey on a dish of mutton spiced with green peppercorns, onions, and garlic dropped onto the metal serving dish by careless servants with a noise "like a drumhead." The bey expressed surprise that Europeans would want more stones, when presumably they had plenty of their own. Belzoni gravely assured him that "we had plenty of stones, but we thought those of Egypt were of a better sort." With that more than adequate response, he was given his firman.

While waiting for money from the British consul and the boat, Belzoni crossed the Nile to the

A seated statue of the lion-headed goddess Sakhmet in black granite. Found by Belzoni in the temple of Mut, now in the British Museum.

149

western bank and wandered around the desolate Valley of Kings behind Kurneh. He admired the temples at Deir el Medineh, and examined the royal tombs that were open, some of which had been visited since Roman times. However, his examination was more thorough than earlier searches, and he visited every recess of the valley. At its western end he came across a heap of stones. The gaps between the boulders were filled with sand and rubbish. A stick thrust through the pile met no resistance, so the next day he returned with several laborers. Within two hours all the stones had been removed and Belzoni was able to enter a palatial tomb, which contained part of a sarcophagus and "several curious and singular painted figures on the walls." This was the tomb of Ai, a priest who briefly annexed the throne of Egypt on the death of Tut-ankh-Amun in the fourteenth century B.C. Belzoni ascribed this find to luck rather than deliberate search, but it was enough to whet his appetite for another visit later on, a stay that yielded much more important results.

The boat from Aswan now arrived without the

The Avenue of Sphinxes at the temple of Amun at Karnak

Another view of the Sphinxes
at Karnak

stones from Philae and loaded with a cargo of
dates. The owners stopped to return the money
and break the agreement. "I had much to say to
them, as may be imagined in such a case," remarked Belzoni with commendable understatement. Drovetti's agents had succeeded in cowing
the captain with stories of shipwreck. Belzoni's
situation was desperate, for the Nile was falling
rapidly and the head of Memnon was still on the
bank. At this critical moment, fortune played into
Belzoni's hand. A soldier arrived with a gift of
anchovies and olives and an invitation to dinner
from his old enemy, the kachif of Erment, a most

unlikely gesture. The messenger provided enlighten-ment. The French consul had made the mistake of sending the kachif an insulting present, namely the olives and anchovies now in Belzoni's hands, instead of the sizable gifts he was expecting. "Strange as it may appear, it will be seen that the effects of a few salted little fish contributed the greatest share towards the removal of the colos-sus," wrote Belzoni gleefully. Determined to strike while the iron was hot, he hastened to Erment and "set off alertly to my anchovy and olive man." He found the kachif in a pliable mood, pro-vided gifts, and the next day obtained a judgment in his favor.

The boat owners were forced to unload their dates, take on Belzoni's cargo, and hire a boat of the kachif's to carry their fruit downstream at such an exorbitant rate that there was almost no profit for them.

Armed with an order from the kachif, Belzoni hastened to Kurneh to load the Young Memnon. After the usual labor troubles, Belzoni built a large earth causeway from the top of the bank to the water's edge, for the Nile was now 100 feet from the head and 18 feet below the bank. This prodigious labor was executed with 130 men, but was far easier than the loading itself, for the great weight of the head had to be placed right in the middle of the boat to prevent it from tipping over.

The boat was maneuvered to the end of the causeway, and a bridge of four large poles was constructed from the slope to the center of the craft, so that the weight of the head bore down fairly amidships. A sack of sand was placed in the middle of the bridge to stop the head if it ran away during loading. The boat itself was carefully padded to prevent damage to the head. Large palm fiber ropes secured to stout posts were passed around the colossus to check its descent, while great levers were used to shift the seven tons of the head from the causeway. The opera-tion was entirely successful, much to the surprise

153

of the boat owners, who were in a frenzy of despair and apprehension. It was not for nothing that Belzoni had been a circus strongman.

Belzoni now rejoined Sarah in Luxor, where she had been lodging uncomfortably with an Arab family for the past six weeks, and loaded the rest of his Karnak finds onto his heavily laden vessel. On November 21 they set off downstream. Twenty-four days later, they arrived in Cairo with probably the most spectacular load of antiquities ever to be shipped down the Nile, after an arduous journey of five and a half months.

Henry Salt was away in Alexandria when the Belzonis arrived, but he had left instructions that all the antiquities were to be unloaded at the British Consulate, except for the head of Memnon, which Belzoni was to take on to Alexandria. Belzoni obeyed this rather strange instruction without question, although he was under the impression that everything was to go to the British Museum. Early in the new year, 1817, Belzoni took the Memnon to Rosetta, transshipped it to a larger vessel, this time with proper tackle, and soon reached his destination in Alexandria, where the head was deposited in the pasha's warehouse awaiting a ship to England.

Thus ended a remarkable and exceptionally arduous archaeological expedition. Belzoni had achieved more in a short time than any of his rivals. His unique qualifications derived from circus and theater gave him an advantage in moving large antiquities which even Napoleon's armies had failed to shift. His determination and ruthlessness were matched by a shrewdness in bargaining and political intrigue that enabled him—most of the time—to get his way and outmaneuver his rivals. And rivals they were. From the moment he entered Nubia, Belzoni had become a marked man whose life was in danger because he dared challenge a comfortable monopoly on antiquities and excite the greed of others for wealth from the Egyptian soil.

154

10 "The Most Magnificent of Temples"

Belzoni found himself greeted with enthusiasm in English quarters. Henry Salt, delighted with Belzoni's success and hard work, paid the Italian 50 pounds in addition to the sum of 25 pounds against the Young Memnon which Burckhardt and he had advanced when the expedition was mooted. These payments were intended to cover Belzoni's expenses. Whether they were also wages is unclear. Certainly Belzoni was unhappy about the arrangement, for he received neither public credit nor financial gain from the sale of the antiquities he had labored so hard on his own initiative to obtain at Luxor and Karnak. But he immediately proposed to the British consul a second journey, this time with the objective of finishing the work at Abu Simbel.

Henry Salt had other ideas: he was watching
with interest the activities of a Genovese sea captain named Giovanni Battista Caviglia who was
digging in the depths of the pyramid of Cheops
and in tombs near the Sphinx. By great determination, Caviglia succeeded in penetrating to the
bottom of the so-called Well in the pyramid, and
had made other important discoveries. Salt suggested that Belzoni join the mercurial Caviglia,
but the Italian declined, knowing full well that he
worked better on his own. He was also worried
about the activities of Drovetti's agents at Thebes.
Instead he pressed for a second journey to Upper
Egypt and Nubia, this time to last six months.
Eventually Salt fell in with the revised plan, and
Belzoni and a small party left Bulak on February
20, 1817. This time Sarah and the Irish servant,
James Curtin, stayed behind. Belzoni was accompanied by a Turkish soldier, a cook, and two em-
ployees from the British consulate—Henry William
Beechey, Salt's secretary, and an interpreter
named Yanni Athanasiou, who was soon to be-
come a bitter enemy.

The journey started slowly, for a strong contrary wind was blowing. Progress was so leisurely
that they were able to witness Arab dances, the
last of which "fully compensated for the extraordinary modesty of the first." Belzoni called on
the "Admiral of the Nile," Hamet Bey, and presented him with two bottles of rum, a necessary
precaution to prevent their boat from being requisitioned by the pasha. Next he visited a Dr.
Valsomaky, a druggist and distiller of "aqua vita"
who also collected and sold antiquities. Two Copt
interpreters in Drovetti's pay were already at his
house, so Belzoni shied off rather than interfere
with their business.

The next day they called on a Mr. Brine, who
had set up a sugar factory for the pasha near Ash-
munain. Here they learned that Drovetti's Copts
were now on their way to Karnak posthaste, presumably to stake out a claim on Belzoni's excava-

Luxor: the temple of Amun-
Mut-Chons. Queen Nefertity
at the side of the statue of
Ramesses II in the forecourt.

157

tion and to buy up all the antiquities which had been found in the area since the last travelers came through. Belzoni was in action immediately. Leaving Beechey to come on by river, he hired a horse and a donkey and, accompanied by Yanni, left in the middle of the night on a forced march of 280 miles to Karnak. During the next five and a half days, they had but eleven hours of sleep, stopping at Coptic monasteries or Arab rest houses for a brief nap or a meal of bread and onions.

But Belzoni found the Daftardar Bey at Asyut totally unsympathetic to his activities, on account of a mistake by Salt's secretary, who had failed to reply to letters or send the bey a present. In retaliation, the bey had ordered a Piedmontese doctor named Marucchi to dig in the area where Belzoni had found his lion-headed statues. Officially the bey was forming his own collection of antiquities, but in practice he had transferred his favor to the French, and he sold all the finds to Drovetti's agents. It was some consolation to Belzoni that the excavations yielded only four statues in good condition.

Fortunately the kachif of Erment (he of the anchovies and olives) was still friendly and promised every cooperation. Belzoni immediately set small gangs of workmen to dig on both banks of the Nile and concentrated his efforts on a large seated figure almost 30 feet high, which sat in the forecourt of the Great Temple of Amun. He found a 7-foot seated statue at the foot of the huge figure, conveniently divided in two at the waist. So the bust was removed at once and put under guard, while the chair in which the seated king was ensconced was left in the ground until a boat could be found to transport it.

Drovetti's agents had already turned up and were hard at work. With the connivance of the bey, they promptly engaged nearly all the available labor, leaving Belzoni with only a few men. So he was forced to work near Kurneh on the

158

west bank, where the headmen were more friendly.

While awaiting Beechey and more funds, Belzoni found time to wander alone among the ruins of the vast Karnak temples. Although not a particularly romantic man, he was uplifted by the magnificent architecture: "I was lost in contemplation of so many objects . . . for a time I was unconscious whether I were on terrestrial ground, or in some other planet." The palimpsest of columns, walls, and friezes transported Belzoni into a state of ecstasy, "as to separate me in imagination from the rest of mortals, exalt me on high over all, and cause me to forget entirely the trifles and follies of life." Belzoni was happy for a whole day, until the gathering darkness caused him to stumble over a stone block and nearly break his nose. The pain brought him abruptly back to earth.

Not that there was much time for reflection. Beechey was so long in arriving that Belzoni took a boat downstream in search of him. When the party returned to Thebes, Belzoni concentrated his work at Kurneh, whose people "were superior to any other Arabs in cunning and deceit, and the most independent of any in Egypt." They boasted of being the last people that the French had been able to subdue, and even then they had forced the invaders to pay for their services. Many hiding places abounded in rocks to the west of Thebes, a place of refuge in times of stress and a rich and apparently inexhaustible source of mummies and papyri, which the people of Kurneh sold to consuls, travelers, and antiquities merchants indiscriminately, but always at the highest prices they could extort.

Belzoni seems to have got on with these inveterate tomb robbers well enough to embark on a busy search for papyri. He penetrated deep into the tiny burial chambers and caves behind Kurneh, where "a vast quantity of dust rises, so fine that it enters into the throat and nostrils, and chokes the nose and mouth to such a degree, that

Temple of Amun at Karnak: "At times I was unconscious whether I were on terrestrial ground"

Asyut. From *La Description de l'Egypte.*

it requires a great power of lungs to resist it and the strong effluvia of the mummies. In some places there is not more than a vacancy of a foot left, which you must contrive to pass through in a creeping posture like a snail, on pointed and keen stones, that cut like glass." One can imagine the problems that the huge Belzoni had in squeezing through such narrow defiles.

After struggling through the passages, some of them up to 200 or 300 yards long, the archaeologist could sometimes find a place to sit down and rest.

But what a place of rest! surrounded by bodies, by heaps of mummies in all directions . . . the blackness of the wall, the faint light given by the candles or torches for want of air, the different objects that surrounded

162

me, seeming to converse with each other, and the
Arabs with the candles or torches in their hands, naked
and covered with dust, themselves resembling living
mummies, absolutely formed a scene that cannot be
described.

One eventually became inured to the dust and
mummies. It helped if, like Belzoni, one had no
sense of smell, but even then one "could taste that
the mummies were rather unpleasant to swallow."
On one occasion, Belzoni

sought a resting place, found one, and contrived to sit;
but when my weight bore on the body of an Egyptian,
it crushed like a band-box. I naturally had recourse to
my hands to sustain my weight, but they found no better support; so that I sunk altogether among the broken

163

mummies, with a crash of bones, rags, and wooden
cases, which raised such a dust as kept me motionless
for a quarter of an hour, waiting till it subsided again.

"My purpose," he openly admitted, "was to rob
the Egyptians of their papyri; of which I found a
few hidden in their breasts, under their arms, in
the space above the knees, or on the legs, and
covered by the numerous folds of cloth."

The inhabitants of Kurneh lived in the mouths
of the burial caves they had despoiled. They neglected their agriculture, finding tomb robbing a
more profitable venture than farming. "This is the
fault of travellers," wrote Belzoni rather senten-
tiously, "who are so pleased the moment they are
presented with any piece of antiquity, that, without thinking of the injury resulting from the example to their successors, they give a great deal more
than the people really expect." The result was
high prices, especially for papyri, arising in part
from a firm, and probably correct, conviction on
the part of the tomb robbers that the antiquities
were worth ten times more than they sold them
for.

The dwellings of the Kurnese were built in the
passages between the tomb entrances and lit by
small fat-oil lamps set in niches in the walls.
Black soot covered the walls, and the bleating of
sheep accompanied the constant murmur of
human voices. Belzoni was warmly welcomed. "I
was sure of a supper of milk and bread served in
a wooden bowl," he recalled, "but whenever they
supposed I should stay all night, they always
killed a couple of fowls for me, which were
baked in a small oven heated with pieces of
mummy cases, and sometimes with the bone and
rags of the mummies themselves."

At first Belzoni was astonished by the casual
way the people of Kurneh could live among
"hands, feet, or sculls," which littered the floors of
their caves. They thought no more of it than if the
human remains had been cattle bones. Soon Bel-

zoni himself was indifferent to the constant presence of fragmentary ancient Egyptians. "I would
have slept in a mummy pit as readily as out of
it," he casually remarks. This offhand attitude to
archaeological remains contrasts sharply with the
sedulous care with which he purchased and
looted the past.

Mummies were one of Belzoni's primary targets
at Kurneh. His objective was quite simply to obtain as many mummies as he could in the shortest
time possible. So he paid the mummy robbers of
Kurneh a regular wage as well as a bonus for the
mummies they found. This made it possible for
him to look as well, and no one was suspicious or
out to conceal important discoveries. Finding
tombs or burial pits was a matter of luck, for
there were few surface indications to go by. Mummies of less wealthy people were stacked in rows
in large burial pits, some embedded in a form of
cement. Many corpses were wrapped in coarse
linen without much ornamentation, their bodies
stacked in dense layers right up to the entrance of
the burial cave. Such burials were hardly worth

165

the tomb robbers' time, as few ornaments or papyri were to be found in their wrappings.

The more richly adorned burials were eagerly sought, for the heavily bandaged and embalmed body was often deposited in a richly painted sycamore mummy case. Belzoni described some of the cased mummies he found, the garlands of well-preserved flowers still lying on the breasts of the burials, the carefully wrapped packages of entrails, and the fine colors and varnish of the decorative casing. Such finds were popular with tourists and museums and had commanded a ready market for at least a century.

The burials of the most important people were much more carefully laid out in tombs with several painted chambers bearing fine friezes of funeral processions and everyday life. Belzoni was particularly interested in the smaller objects buried with the wealthy—vases containing embalmed viscera, alabaster vessels, clay ornaments, carvings, gold leaf, and scarabs.

By this time Belzoni had accumulated a larger boatload of antiquities than he had acquired the year before, including a magnificent red granite monument bearing the figures of Hat-Hor and other gods from the little temple of Montu-hotpe at the northeast corner of Karnak. This fine antiquity was moved from the temple and hauled up a steep cliff from a narrow defile to the accompaniment of much ingenuity and clouds of fine dust, under the very noses of Drovetti's Copts. Belzoni's stockpile already contained the fine granite sarcophagus that Drovetti had given Belzoni on his first journey, now safely removed from its apparently impregnable resting place.

Belzoni had been so successful and energetic that his opponents were now seriously concerned. His finds were arousing lively jealousy among Consul Drovetti's lethargic agents. So they bribed the bey to issue an order forbidding Belzoni to employ laborers or acquire any antiquities. Their pretext was simply that they were unable to pur-

Ti watches his men armed with harpoons and ropes engaged in a hippopotamus hunt in front of a papyrus thicket. V Dynasty tomb at Sakkareh.

167

Agricultural laborers leading cattle and domestic birds. Tomb of Ptah-hotpe, VI Dynasty, Sakkareh.

chase anything because Belzoni had such good relations with the people of Kurneh that they sold him everything, which was probably true. As was his normal practice, Belzoni promptly called on the bey, who was visiting a village a few miles from Thebes. The bey was evasive. Whenever the Italian steered the conversation toward antiquities, the bey talked of other matters. Belzoni's firman from the pasha was greeted with indifference. The bey then called for horses and the audience shifted to Kurneh, where he summoned the kachif and told him to produce an unopened mummy within an hour. Knowing that the kachif was friendly to Belzoni, the bey was looking for an excuse to justify his conduct. But when an unopened burial was produced, he flew into a tantrum of rage and ordered the kachif beaten on the spot.

Belzoni stood silently by, powerless, realizing that a loss of temper would be fatal, while the soldiers inflicted a savage beating on the unfortunate kachif. Eventually the kachif was carried off, practically insensible. Belzoni now calmly stated he would complain to the pasha. The bey then realized he had gone too far. The next day an order arrived authorizing Belzoni to employ twenty men for eight days. After some difficulty, for the local people were now afraid even to talk to foreigners, he succeeded in getting enough men to stockpile all his finds on the quay at Luxor and to build a mud wall around them.

Just as the cache was completed, the bey appeared and inspected the collection, apparently in a more pliable mood. Belzoni pressed his case, complaining that his party was being treated unfairly. All he wanted was a chance to buy antiquities on an equal basis with others. The bey apparently relented, leaving orders that he might buy antiquities, as well as a firman addressed to the kachif of Aswan, for Belzoni still had his sights on Abu Simbel.

He quietly prepared to resume work at Kurneh,

168

seeking to convince the kachif that it was now
safe for him to work in the mummy pits without
incurring the bey's displeasure. A public assembly
was convened, at which the bey's order was read
aloud. To Belzoni's horror, the famous order,
which, through some strange oversight, he had
never had translated, turned out to be instructions
forbidding the locals to sell any antiquities to anyone but Consul Drovetti. It was clearly impractica-
ble to continue, so Belzoni placed a guard on his
cached antiquities and took a boat upstream for
Nubia in disgust.

The first lengthy stop was at lovely Philae,
where Belzoni paused to await dispatches from
Henry Salt. He spent his time wandering through
the magnificent ruins and making a wax impression of the portico of the temple of Isis, a difficult

170

The island of Philae from the northwest. From *La Description.*

task since the thermometer mercury registered over 124° F. in the shade!

Some days before, Belzoni had been joined by two young and adventurous English naval officers on half pay, Captains Charles Irby and James Mangles, who were in the middle of a long and leisurely journey through Europe and the Near East in search of adventure and excitement. These enterprising and engaging travelers joined forces with Belzoni, for they were bent on visiting the Second Cataract. Irby and Mangles were delighted to be traveling in company with an experienced Nubian hand and added considerable strength to the party of seven who were now preparing to leave Philae.

On June 5 Sarah Belzoni turned up, accompanied by the servant James Curtin. Belzoni gives no reason for her arrival, but he was obliged to leave her behind encamped on the roof of the temple of Isis in solitary splendor, accompanied by Curtin and a brace of firearms.

On June 16 the travelers left on a boat whose five-man crew was to be a constant headache in the weeks ahead. The chief villain was a blue-shirted gentleman called Hassan, who was promptly nicknamed the "Blue Devil" by the two sea captains. Thirteen days later they arrived at Abu Simbel, only to find that the kachif was absent. So they sent complimentary messages and took the opportunity to visit the Second Cataract. At this point the crew decided to mutiny. The local people demanded gifts, and the situation became serious when loaded guns were produced. Belzoni remained calm, distinterested, and apparently good-humored. Mangles reasoned with them: admittedly the foreigners had seen the cataract without paying, but "they had seen us without giving us anything as a recompense, though we were as novel a sight to them as their cataract was to us, and therefore we were quits."

The kachif had still not returned to Abu Simbel when the travelers returned on July 5. But two days later a messenger came from Daud Kachif asking if they were the Englishmen to whom Hassan Kachif had made promises. Fortunately Belzoni had sent turbans from Cairo as gifts, which had not been forgotten. Further gifts were presented when the kachif arrived a week later—a gun, a turban, and smaller items.

The digging went slowly at first, for the fifty men spent much of their time singing a Nubian song which proclaimed that they were going to get as much Christian money as they could. "This song, though cheering to them," remarked Mangles, "was not much so to us." A bargain was struck with the kachifs "to open the temple for three hundred piastres," a task that Belzoni calculated would take four days. It was soon clear that the temple would never be opened by this means.

172

The kachifs demanded their money, they spent a day plundering a caravan, and Ramadan began. Both the kachifs and the crew bombarded everyone with demands for presents; food was in short supply and could not be purchased.

So Belzoni determined to dig for himself. At three o'clock in the afternoon of July 16 the Europeans quietly slipped up to the temple and stripped to the waist. An hour later some of the crew turned up and were astonished to find the Christians working. They sheepishly joined in, and by nightfall the small party had done as much digging as forty locals would have accomplished in an entire day, at the cost of many blisters.

For the next fortnight, the work continued from before dawn until the hot sun became intolerable at nine o'clock. Six hours later, the small group of diggers returned to labor again until sunset. For the most part they made steady progress, sometimes joined by their troublesome boat crew, at others by local people. The kachifs made repeated efforts to strip them of their firearms and equipment. Two headmen from the other side of the Nile came to threaten and offer assistance—at a price. The cook threw a pot of water over a man demanding money, a "truly cook-like mode of assault" that resulted in drawn swords and near-bloodshed. Food again ran short, and they were unable to buy more. A foreman tried to cheat them by withholding wage tickets. But persistence was rewarded. On the last day of July, the diggers came on a broken upper corner of a doorway. By dusk they had made a hole large enough to admit a man's body but decided not to enter the temple until the next morning, for they were uncertain how much sand lay inside and the air was probably foul.

Before daybreak on the following day, Belzoni and his companions hastened to the entrance with a good supply of candles. The crew stayed behind, but soon an uproar broke out led by Hassan, the

173

**Belzoni's own watercolor of
the interior of Abu Simbel**

Blue Devil. Loud complaints about wages and
threats to leave at once were ignored by Belzoni,
whereupon the crew arrived on the site, armed
with long sticks, swords, and rusty pistols. The
uproar continued amid a litany of farcical and
often-repeated complaints until someone noticed
that the Armenian interpreter, Giovanni Finati,
had quietly slipped into the temple during the argument. Immediately everyone was agog to follow
him, and arguments were forgotten.

Quickly a wall was built to barricade the door
against drifting stones, and, as the sun rose and
shone briefly through the entrance of the temple
for the first time in more than a thousand years,

174

Belzoni was able to gaze on one of his most important discoveries. He found himself in a lofty, pillared hall where eight huge Osiris-like figures of Ramesses II faced one another across a central aisle. The square pillars behind the statues were decorated with brilliantly painted reliefs of the pharaoh in the presence of the gods. A smaller chamber, an antechamber, and a sanctuary opened up beyond the great hall. The rising sun's rays briefly lit up the seated figures of the gods—Amun-Re, Hor-akhty, Ptah, and Ramesses himself—in the sanctuary.

The visitors gazed wonderingly at the mighty figures and the battle scenes, painted on the walls of

The interior of Abu Simbel in the 1870s

175

the great chamber, in which Ramesses conquers the Hittites at Kadesh. Belzoni made a thorough search for portable antiquities, but there was little to be found, except for "two lions with hawks' heads, the body as large as life, a small sitting figure, and some copper work belonging to the doors."

The naval men sat down to make a plan of the temple on a scale of $\frac{1}{25}$ inch to the foot. Meanwhile Beechey and Belzoni collected portable items and tried to record the essence of the drawings in the temple. Beechey's drawing book was soon spoiled by perspiration, for the air in the temple was like the hottest of steam baths. But they had enough time to write lengthy descriptions of the battle scenes and the executions of prisoners. "The expression of agony and despair in their several features is admirable," recorded Mangles, who was excited and fascinated by the costumes of some of the "perfectly black" prisoners shown in the paintings.

After a last admiring look at the statues, and having further strengthened the barrier at the temple door, the explorers carried their finds down to the boat and loaded them on board despite more vigorous expostulations from Hassan. On August 4, 1817, they set off downstream. It was not until eighteen months later that the interior of the temple was fully recorded for the outside world. Adventurer William Bankes, Beechey, and a French draftsman named Louis Linant—later famous as an engineer—worked for some weeks at Abu Simbel, recording the inscriptions and paintings and clearing the sand away from the most southerly statue of the façade. Future visitors were then able to appreciate Ramesses II's largest temple more fully. The monument became so famous that it was moved to higher ground by international effort in the 1960s when Lake Nasser was rising to flood it forever.

The return trip to Philae was uneventful except for another furious argument with the crew when

Seated figure of Pa-ser, the governor of Nubia under Ramesses II. Found by Belzoni in the Abu Simbel temple.

176

Hassan tried to stab Belzoni and Irby cut his hand during the fracas. Sarah was waiting patiently at the temple of Isis, but the beautiful stone sculptures that Belzoni had carefully marked down the year before lay in mutilated fragments. Someone had deliberately smashed the carvings and scribbled the scornful words *operation manquée* (operation canceled) in charcoal on the stones. Belzoni was furious and suspected Drovetti's agents. But the damage was done, and he turned his attention to other projects.

11 "This Beautiful and Invaluable Piece of Antiquity"

Belzoni was now anxious to resume work near Thebes, but he found that two of Drovetti's most hated agents had moved in on Kurneh during his absence and were "digging the ground in all directions" and finding plenty of mummies. Since one of them, the Piedmontese Rosignano, had already threatened to cut his throat, he decided to concentrate his efforts on the desolate Valley of Kings, where he had already obtained promising results a few months before.

The Valley of Kings, separated from Kurneh by a range of stony hills, has been known as the burial place of pharaohs since Classical times. Belzoni knew of ancient reports that the valley contained at least eighteen royal tombs. Napoleon's savants had recorded eleven and found a twelfth, while the Italian himself had discovered the modest tomb of Ai in the previous year. There were persistent rumors of more royal tombs—perhaps up to forty—lying within the confines of the valley. By this time Belzoni had developed an instinct for discovery, a "nose" for new sites based on wide field experience and that intangible instinct that leads archaeologists to contemplate an area in detail over a considerable period of time in the knowledge that persistence and experience will yield dividends. He retired by himself into the Valley of Kings, and after considerable thought chose to work in the western part.

Belzoni set a group of twenty men to work in about a hundred yards from the entrance to the tomb of Ai. A few feet below the surface the men came across several large boulders, apparently the entrance of a rock-cut passage. The next day Belzoni made a crude battering ram from a palm trunk rigged on a cross-pole. "The walls resisted the blows of the Arabs for some time, as they were not Romans, nor had the pole the ram's head of bronze at its end." But a breach was made at last and a staircase revealed. Eight mummies in painted cases covered with a large cloth lay at the bottom of the stairs.

The nineteenth-century tourist's view of the Valley of Kings

179

He was not satisfied with this undisturbed find and was even more determined to find a royal burial. On October 6 the laborers were digging in several places at once. Three days later they came across the entrance of a huge but unfurnished tomb, with "painted figures on the wall so perfect, that they are the best adapted of any I ever saw to give a correct and clear idea of the Egyptian taste." We now know that this was the tomb of Prince Montuherkhepeshef, the eldest son of a late Ramesses. The same day, October 9, another large but unpainted tomb came to light not a hundred yards from the painted sepulcher. It had been robbed in antiquity and contained two completely naked female corpses with long hair that was "easily separated from the head by pulling it a little."

This unidentified royal tomb had just been discovered when Belzoni had to break off his researches to conduct three important English visitors around the temples of Thebes. The visitors were greatly excited by the royal tombs and were lucky enough to witness the discovery of another sepulcher, that of Ramesses I. The burial chamber still contained a red granite sarcophagus and two mummies, neither of which was that of the pharaoh. A huge wooden figure of the king dominated the chamber, one of a pair that had guarded the sarcophagus. This tomb lies only 60 feet from that of Tut-ankh-Amun, which Belzoni fortunately missed.

On October 16, Belzoni was on his own again. He put his men to work at a spot where he had noticed some likely surface indications, where rainwater washed down a bare slope into the floor of the valley. He does not tell us exactly why he chose this spot; indeed his men, experienced in the ways of ancient tomb builders, thought he was on a wild goose chase. Just before the end of work the following day, an artificial cut in the rock appeared, and Belzoni's suspicions were confirmed. Eighteen feet below, the entrance of the

Ramesses II in his chariot at the Battle of Kadesh (*opposite*)

Wooden *Ka* of Ramesses I found by Belzoni in his tomb in 1817

tomb came to light, choked with huge stones and
rainwater from the slope above. Eventually a
small hole was made, through which one could
wriggle into a half-choked passage behind, which
turned out to be more than 36 feet long. The walls
and ceiling were decorated with magnificent
paintings. A staircase at the end of the passage led
to another long and finely decorated corridor.
Both passages had sloping floors so that rainwater
could drain into a huge pit, 30 feet deep and 14
feet wide at the end, which blocked further progress. Some fragments of wood and rope, which
crumbled to dust at a touch, showed how some
earlier visitors had crossed the pit to get at the
plastered and decorated wall at the other side of
the hole.

Next day Belzoni and Beechey returned with
stout beams to bridge the pit and inspected a
jagged aperture at the other side. It turned out to
have been made by tomb robbers who had not
been deceived by the attractive false wall. Belzoni
squeezed through the tiny aperture and found
himself in a magnificent hall with four beautifully
decorated pillars adorned with "figures of Pharaoh
embracing or being embraced by the gods." Three
steps led into another chamber decorated with unfinished paintings, another device to convince
tomb robbers that the sepulcher was never completed. But they had tapped the walls and exposed a hidden entrance to a lower passage beyond. At the end of this corridor, again
beautifully painted with even finer figures and
gods, Belzoni came on an even larger hall with six
richly painted pillars and a dark blue ceiling,
gleaming with fresh paint.

By the glittering light of candles, Beechey and
Belzoni now gazed on an unbelievable sight, a
translucent alabaster sarcophagus more than 9 feet
long, but only two inches thick. The magnificently
decorated sarcophagus glowed softly when a light
was placed in it and was shaped to accommodate
the body and headdress of the pharaoh. The exte-

182

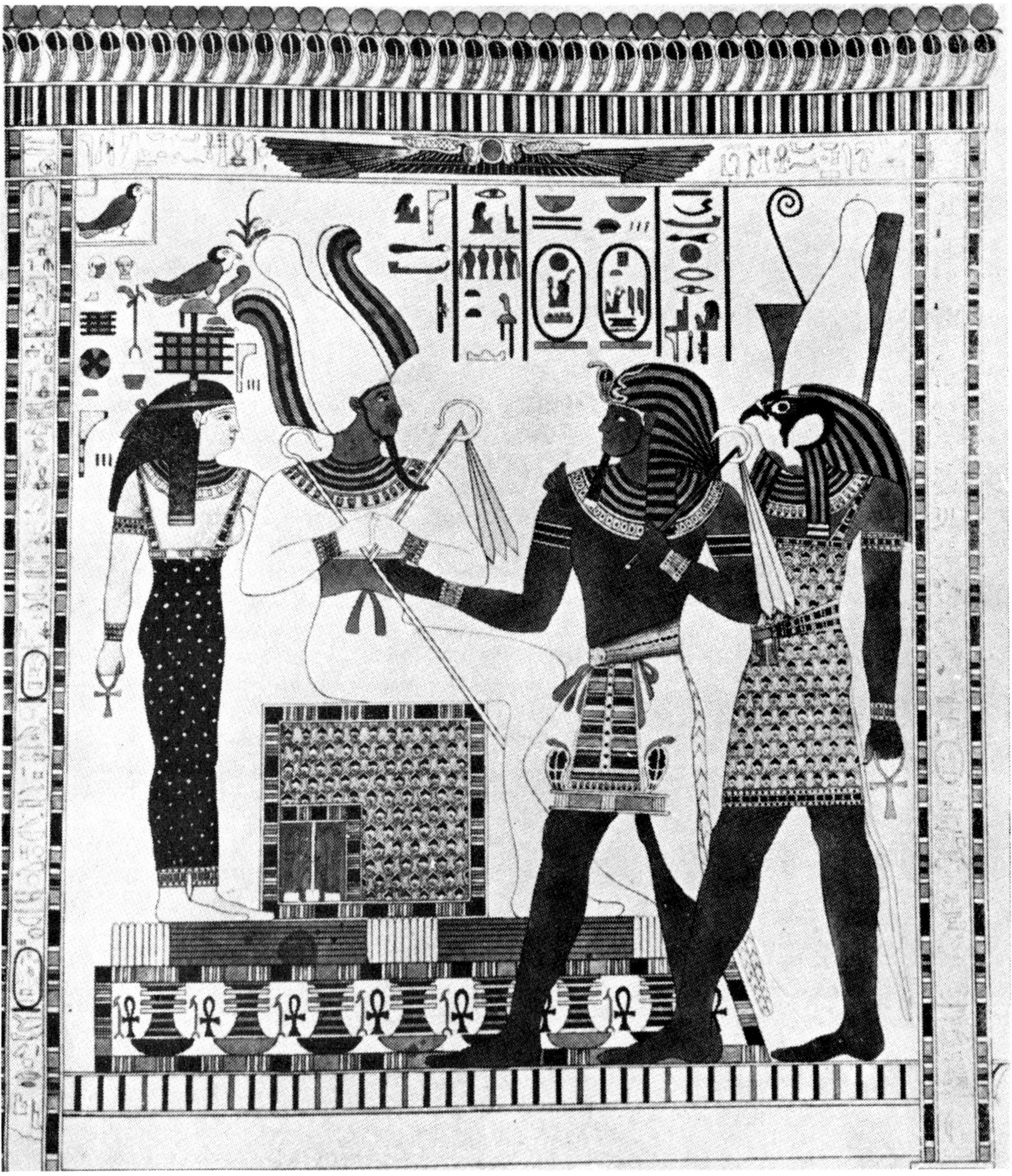

rior was decorated with hundreds of tiny, delicately inlaid figures. The bare-breasted female goddess Neith was depicted on the bottom of the sarcophagus, waiting to receive the dead king. Unfortunately the sarcophagus was empty, for tomb robbers had carried off the body and the lid. Belzoni found fragments of the lid in the debris near the entrance of the tomb.

Five chambers opened off the burial area, the largest of which contained a mummified bull and a large number of *ushabti* figures as well as several large wooden statues "with a circular hollow inside, as if to contain a roll of papyrus, which I have no doubt they did." The sarcophagus disguised the entrance of a walled-up subterranean passage, which extended 300 feet under the mountain in the upper part of the valley.

What Belzoni had found was the magnificent tomb of Sethy I, the father of Ramesses II, who died in about 1300 B.C. Sethy's tomb was entered at least twice by royal priests, who first placed the mummy of Ramesses II in the sepulcher for safety and subsequently removed both the bodies to Queen Anhapu's tomb, where they were recovered in modern times.

The tomb itself had been gutted by robbers, who left few portable items for Belzoni to remove, except for many *ushabtis* and, of course, the alabaster sarcophagus, which Belzoni claimed, with reason, was unlike anything else ever removed from Egypt to Europe. But the paintings and bas-reliefs on the walls of the tomb remained in all their pristine freshness.

In Belzoni's time, no one could read the thousands of hieroglyphs on the walls, but they could admire the scenes of the pharaoh being embraced by the gods, the vultures hovering on the blue ceiling of the tomb, and the figures of the king and the godess Hat-Hor dressed in magnificent costumes. It is everlastingly to Belzoni's credit that he recognized the vital importance of recording the magnificent and delicate artwork in the

184

tomb. He realized that the tomb was his finest discovery, the one that would bring him fame and success, if properly displayed.

News of Belzoni's spectacular discovery spread rapidly. Soon there was a crackle of firearms, and a large party of Turks on horseback galloped into the valley. It turned out to be Hamid Aga from Keneh, who had heard rumors of great treasure and leaped to his horse to claim his share, completing a two-day journey in a scant thirty-six hours. Belzoni was mildly alarmed at such a display of force, but the aga was all smiles. The aga and his soldiers barely glanced at the paintings, but they searched every corner of the chamber and passages "like hounds." They found nothing, and at length the aga turned to Belzoni and asked where he had put the treasure, "a large golden cock, filled with diamonds and pearls." Belzoni, barely concealing his laughter, drew the aga's attention to the glorious paintings on the walls of the empty tomb. The aga just glanced at them and remarked that "this would be a good place for a harem, as the women would have something to look at." With that, he left in a state of what Belzoni called "much vexation."

The three weeks after the discovery were busy ones, for the tomb had to be secured and the extensive operations in the valley run down. As Belzoni was busy with his preparations, three large and luxurious boats of English visitors arrived at Thebes. The party was led by the British consul himself, who was accompanied by an English peer, Lord Belmore, his wife and family, and various functionaries including the earl's private chaplain. Their goal was the Second Cataract, and His Lordship was out to acquire a private collection of fine antiquities on his travels. The travelers were entranced with the paintings. Belzoni was soon conducting the distinguished visitors all around Thebes and the Valley of Kings. Lord Belmore, with Belzoni's help and contacts, was able to acquire a large collection of papyri, mummies,

185

The temple of Karnak photographed by Maxine Du Camp, a famous early photographer of the Nile Valley

and other objects which soon found their way to England. Henry Salt was so excited by Sethy's tomb that he immediately began to dig for a royal tomb on his own account. But he failed to find another major burial.

Another visitor was the French traveler Edward de Montulé, who was making a journey up the Nile. He had paused at Kurneh, where he was fascinated by the tomb robbers and their nefarious trade. The scenes of destruction surprised de Montulé but did not deter him from acquiring "the mummy of a female, wound around with broad bands of linen, and enclosed in a double case, the paintings of which are pretty well preserved." Soon the Frenchman was wandering through Sethy's tomb, accompanied by the voluble Belzoni. The paintings were entrancing, but de Montulé's conscience seems to have been troubled by the looting and destruction, if not by Belzoni's rather drastic methods. "If any perfect tombs still exist," he subsequently wrote, "I sincerely wish they may escape the research of the curious antiquary; to them the learned are become objects to be dreaded as Cambyses, for the sarcophagus's

186

and mummies which they contained, would inevitably take the road to London or Paris." He bemoaned the lack of an Egyptian national museum to house all the consular loot, a notion that was several decades ahead of its time.

Belzoni was now riding the crest of a wave. He had found no less than four new tombs in the Valley of Kings in twelve days, after years of failure. The sarcophagus itself was a symbol of his success, but it was doubtful whether he was getting all the credit—or financial gain—he deserved. The trouble was that his business relationship with the British consul had never been exactly clarified. He had originally undertaken to bring the Young Memnon to Cairo and to collect other antiquities for Salt, but had received no salary or remuneration for his latest trip beyond funds for food and excavation.

Relations between the two men were soon strained, despite Salt's promising to pay Belzoni a thousand piasters a month for his services retroactively from the day he left Alexandria ten months before. Belzoni could not understand a relationship that had him doing the work while the credit and antiquities went elsewhere. But the ever restless Italian loaded his precious cache of antiquities on his boat and arrived in Cairo with his spectacular cargo December 21, 1817. He had at least one belated consolation. The Belmore party fell in with Consul Drovetti on their return visit to Thebes as they journeyed downstream. They showed him Sethy's tomb, where he "completely ran out of the small change of compliment and admiration. He was so lavish of his civilities on entering the tomb, and every thing was so superb, magnifique, superlative and astounding, that when he came to something which really called for epithets of applause and admiration, his magazine of stuff was expended, and he stood in speechless astonishment, to the great entertainment of the beholders." For once, Drovetti did not have the last word.

12 "Pyramidical Brains"

Belzoni's immediate concern was to return to the Valley of Kings as soon as possible. But he was short of money and unable to leave Cairo in the immediate future. Sarah had finally grown tired of the Nile and wanted to go to the Holy Land. A few weeks after Christmas, she left for Jerusalem in the company of James Curtin and the interpreter Giovanni Finati, who was going to Jerusalem to join William John Bankes in Acre. The party set off dressed in young men's clothes, and it was arranged that Belzoni would join them in Jerusalem once the work in the tomb was completed.

One piece of tragic news awaited the Belzonis in Cairo. Burckhardt had died of dysentery during their absence, leaving his mission to West Africa uncompleted. At least he had had the satisfaction

Cairo: the citadel gate known as Bab el Gebel. From *La Description de l'Egypte.*

188

The pyramids of Gizeh

of knowing that the Young Memnon was on its way to England. Belzoni had lost a valuable and influential friend at a critical moment in his career. Casting around for funds, Belzoni realized that about his only source of revenue was the few antiquities that Salt had allocated him. Among them were two lion-headed statues of the goddess Sakhmet, which he managed to sell to Count de Forbin, director general of the French Royal Collections, for 7,000 piasters.

By this time, Belzoni was lodging at the British Consulate and entertaining many of the European visitors who were always passing through Cairo. His collection of antiquities—or rather Salt's—had become a tourist attraction in Cairo. His discoveries were being discussed, often with considerable heat, in the French and English press. A letter from Belzoni to a friend at the Louvre was published in a French journal in 1818. His claims and discoveries were promptly castigated by the great Edmé Jomard, the talented editor of the *Description de l'Egypte*. He flatly disbelieved Belzoni's description of Sethy's sarcophagus. But both Salt and Burckhardt had warmly praised Belzoni in the *Quarterly Review* and other influential London

190

periodicals, both for his discoveries and for his
mechanical talents, which, to quote Henry Salt,
"had enabled him, with singular success, both at
Thebes and other places, to discover objects of
the rarest value in antiquity, that had long baffled
the researches of the learned." Whether the
French liked it or not, Belzoni was rapidly acquiring a reputation as an archaeologist of genius.

Belzoni had now laid definite plans for displaying the tomb of Sethy in European capitals. Such
an exhibition would bring him both fame and social success, as well as financial reward. With the
funds derived from the statues of Sakhmet, he
engaged the services of a fellow Italian, Alessandro Ricci, a young doctor with a talent for drawing and recording hieroglyphs. Belzoni's ultimate
plan was to make wax impressions of the bas-
reliefs and tomb ornaments so that he could erect
a complete reproduction of the tomb in London.
Belzoni dispatched Ricci to Thebes, but remained
behind to raise more funds and collect copying
materials.

Belzoni now met a certain Major Edward
Moore, who was passing through Cairo on his
way to England with dispatches from India.

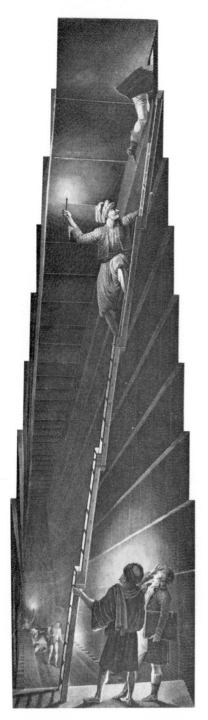

Moore was a member of the Society of Antiquaries of London, then, as now, an influential archaeological society in Britain. His journey to Alexandria was delayed by strong winds, so the courier accompanied Belzoni on a visit to the pyramids. The two antiquarians speculated idly about the interior of the Second Pyramid, which had never been opened, although there had been talk among French and British savants of trying.

Captain Caviglia, the latest digger to work at the pyramid, whom Belzoni had met at the end of his first journey, had now left Egypt, and both Drovetti and Salt were in Upper Egypt. The field was clear, and a second visit to Gizeh with another party of Europeans some days after Moore's departure further convinced Belzoni that the Second Pyramid could be opened. While his companion visited the First Pyramid, Belzoni wandered off by himself and sat down in the shadow of a boulder contemplating "that enormous mass, which for so many ages has baffled the conjectures of ancient and modern writers." He walked around the pyramid, looking for telltale traces of an entrance with an eye honed by months of work on Kurneh and the Valley of Kings.

On the north side, he noticed that sand and rubble were piled up at the foot of the pyramid to a greater elevation than the lintel of any door. His instinct suggested that an inconspicuous doorway lay below the modern ground surface.

The next day, he returned to Cairo without telling anyone of his plans, and with good reason. There had been much talk of starting a public subscription in Europe to open the pyramid, if necessary with gunpowder. Drovetti's name had been mentioned as a possible leader for the enterprise. Influential people might well have blocked Belzoni's plans. Fortunately Belzoni was able to use backdoor contacts to obtain a firman from the pasha's deputy.

Taking a small tent and some food, Belzoni slipped away from Cairo, ostensibly on an expedi-

192

tion to the mountains of Mukattam. He had but
200 pounds in his pocket and was afraid that his
French rivals would try to stop his excavations, or
at any rate ridicule them in public. A large labor
force of eighty men was hired to dig in two spots,
one on the north side of the pyramid and the
other on the east, where the remains of Che-
phren's mortuary temple, which stood in front of
the pyramid, could still be seen.

The diggings went slowly at first, for hard deposits of stone and mortar bent the workmen's
hoes on the north side. But the temple party was
soon digging 40 feet below the surface, where the
workmen uncovered a stone pavement which is
now known to have run all around the pyramid.
But after sixteen days of hard digging, uncovering
the original surface of the pyramid, and removing
many large stones, the workmen found a small
chink between two stones. A long palm stick
could be inserted into the crack for 6 feet without
interference. The next day a loose stone was removed, revealing a small choked-up entrance that
led nowhere. So Belzoni gave his workmen the
day off and retreated to brood over the pyramid.

Now Belzoni's incredible "nose" for the past
came into full play. He wandered back to the pyramid of Cheops and suddenly noticed that the entrance was offset from the center to the east side
of the base. Hastening back to the unopened pyramid, he measured off the same distance and found
a telltale clue—the deposits were apparently less
well compacted and there was a slight concavity
in the surface of the pyramid where he estimated
the entrance might lie. "Hope," he remarked, "returned to cherish my pyramidical brains."

Renewed excavations made slow progress, for
the ground was very hard. Soon three huge boulders, "two on each side and one on the top," sloping toward the center of the pyramid, came to
light. Then, on March 2, Belzoni saw the entrance
for the first time. The inclined passageway leading
into the pyramid proved to be 4 feet high and

Belzoni's diagram of the Second Pyramid

formed of huge blocks of granite. It took two days to unblock the passage, whereupon Belzoni found the now level defile obstructed by a huge granite boulder fitted in grooves in the walls.

Fortunately, there was a small gap at the base between the stone and a groove in the floor, which enabled Belzoni to measure the thickness of the portcullis stone. He found it was 15 inches thick, while probings with a barley stalk revealed an empty space ready to receive the stone in the ceiling. Slowly and laboriously the stone was raised with levers and propped up with small boulders. A small Arab slipped in with a candle and reported the passage was clear. It was not long before Belzoni had raised the portcullis high enough to admit his large frame.

A month after starting work, Belzoni was now able to penetrate the interior of the burial chamber. He found that the floor dropped away to a

194

low passage that ran back and downward under the first one toward the north face. The walls of the passage were salt-encrusted and ended in a huge burial chamber, 46 feet long, 16 feet wide, and 23 feet high. It had been carved from solid rock, and a large decorated sarcophagus was sunk into the floor. The sarcophagus had been broken into and was half full of rubbish. An Arabic inscription translated by a Copt brought out from Cairo confirmed that others had been there before Belzoni.

Belzoni now cleared the lower passage, which sloped back toward the north face. He found another burial chamber as well as a second portcullis, and established that the actual entrance lay outside the base. In the meantime, a visitor rummaging in the rubbish in the sarcophagus had found a bone fragment. Belzoni excitedly dispatched it to the curator of the Hunterian Museum of Anatomy in Glasgow, who pronounced it to be from a bull. The bovine identification seems to have vexed Belzoni and caused quiet chortling in some quarters, for Belzoni described the jokers rather pettily as having "little taste in antiquity."

By this time Henry Salt, who had been digging unsuccessfully for royal burials in the Valley of Kings, wrote to say that he was returning to Cairo. He was closely followed by Lieutenant Colonel Fitzclarence, an aristocratic officer carrying dispatches to London from the governor general of India, Lord Hastings. He had traveled overland to the Nile from the Red Sea and arrived at the consulate, dead tired and after dark, where he was startled by the "extraordinary figures against the walls around me." He imagined he was in the catacombs, "had I not recollected that I was in the sanctum sanctotum of an inveterate and most successful antiquarian." Salt was having dinner when the colonel arrived, and their meeting was overshadowed by the appearance of Belzoni, who presented a striking appearance in Turkish costume, "the handsomest man I ever saw."

The entrance of the pyramid

Two days later, Fitzclarence and Salt accompanied the Italian on an excursion to the Second Pyramid. Fitzclarence was very impressed by Belzoni's achievements and the man himself. "I have had a long conversation with Belzoni," he wrote. "He professes that his greatest anxiety is to become known to the various antiquarians of Europe. . . . He said he looked upon it as a fortunate circumstance I had passed through Egypt, and trusted I should be able to speak of him in England, so as to bring his merits before a nation to which he declares himself to be most devotedly attached." Soon Fitzclarence was promising to publish an account of the entry of the Second Pyramid written in Belzoni's own hand.

Belzoni's personal relationships with Salt were not so happy. The consul had immediately offered to pay the full expenses of the pyramid excava-

196

tions, some 150 pounds. But Belzoni refused and jealously guarded his latest discovery in a fit of deep resentment against the eager antiquarian. The consulate was now full of exciting and unique statuary and hundreds of smaller antiquities, many of them of great rarity. Belzoni's only reward had been the money for the Young Memnon and the price of the two statues he had sold to the French. He felt that he had gained no personal credit for his remarkable discoveries and that the fame he craved so greatly had eluded him.

A series of long and protracted arguments dragged on, for neither Belzoni nor Salt seemed to be able to communicate with each other. Eventu-

Belzoni's sketch of the same entrance

A trading vessel on the Nile

Medinet Habu: the first pylon of the temple, depicting Ramesses II hunting bulls

ally, an agreement was drawn up, under which Belzoni was to receive 500 pounds during the next year, half the price of the alabaster sarcophagus when it was sold, and assistance in gathering a collection for himself in Thebes. Belzoni undertook to assist the consul to remove some sarcophagi still at Thebes and to help Beechey, his agent there, in any way possible. The agreement was signed in Cairo on April 20, 1818, and the two men parted on good terms. With that, Belzoni set off for Thebes on his third and last journey up the Nile.

Only pausing to renew his firman with the Daftardar Bey, who had given him so much trouble on his earlier journey, Belzoni joined Alessandro Ricci in the Valley of Kings, where the diligent artist had been busy at work in Sethy's tomb

for more than two months. The copying work was well advanced, and Belzoni now began the laborious task of making wax impressions of the major bas-reliefs. Belzoni and Ricci lived in the tomb for most of the summer, a rather cooler base than the searing floor of the Valley of Kings, but nevertheless a hot and uncomfortable place to copy hieroglyphs and work with soft wax. Wax alone melted too readily and had to be mixed with resin and fine dust to form a workable compound. The hardest task was to make the wax impression without damaging the paint on the walls. Enormous numbers of castings were needed.

"The figures as large as life I found to be in all a hundred and eighty two: those of a smaller size, from one to three feet, I did not count, but they cannot be less than eight hundred. The hieroglyphics in this tomb are nearly five hundred." The copying operation was an astonishing feat of patience and skill under very trying conditions.

Sethy's tomb, now protected with a stout wooden door, preoccupied Belzoni for most of the summer of 1818. He had little time for excavation, although his firman allowed him full access to both banks of the Nile at Kurneh. The trouble was that both banks had been staked out by Drovetti's agents or Salt, who had quietly marked down extensive claims of promising ground before leaving for Cairo. Rather than risk a confrontation, Belzoni had retired to "his tomb," in the extraordinary position of being at Thebes at his own expense for the first time and yet unable to dig for himself. "If I pointed out any spot in any place whatsoever, one of the parties, I mean the agents of Mr. Drovetti or those of Mr. Salt, would consider it was valuable ground, and protest that it was taken by them long before. I verily believe, if I had pointed out one of the sandbanks or the solid rocks, they would have said they just intended to have broken into it the next day."

Belzoni's competitors had taken effective steps to see that the most successful archaeologist

Seated statue of Sethy II, holding a small shrine surmounted by a ram's head, discovered by Belzoni at Thebes

200

among them was frozen out. After some abortive excavation at localities he had already found unproductive and which had not been claimed by the others, Belzoni defied Beechey's protests on behalf of Salt and worked over a spot behind the two great Colossi on the Nile floodplain marked out by the British consul. Drovetti had already dug there and found only a few broken statues. But Belzoni had his usual luck. On the second day of excavations, he uncovered a magnificent seated black granite statue of Amun-hotpe III, in almost perfect condition. With admirable restraint he ceded the rights of ownership to Henry Salt and merely contented himself with carving his initials on the base. This beautiful statue can be seen in the British Museum.

After this chance discovery, Belzoni abandoned excavation and concentrated on his tomb. But he did manage to accumulate what he modestly called "a little collection of my own, in which I can boast of having a few good articles, particularly in manuscript, &c." His friends among the tomb robbers of Kurneh were only too glad to sell him some of their choicest discoveries, for he, of all the excavators of the time, seems to have made a real effort to understand their society and way of life—partly, of course, in strict self-interest.

13 "In Search of Old Berenice"

The copying of Sethy I's burial chamber was practically complete when a chance encounter with a visitor sent Belzoni off on a new and remarkable journey. Some time before, two Copts had called on the pasha after an arduous desert crossing from the Red Sea to the Nile. They told him that they had seen some old sulfur mines in the mountains near Kosseir, overlooking the Red Sea. Eventually the pasha looked around for an experienced European traveler to inspect the mines and, on the recommendation of Consul Drovetti, gave the job to Frédéric Cailliaud, a young French minerologist and antiquarian who had arrived in Egypt just before Belzoni and had worked for Drovetti on several occasions.

Cailliaud was soon on the road with an escort of soldiers. He confirmed that the sulfur mines

"The overflowing of the Nile."
Belzoni's sketch of the disaster near Thebes.

were useless, but also visited Mount Zabara, the famed site of emerald workings described by Classical writers and hitherto uninvestigated in recent times. The young Frenchman returned two months later with glowing reports of the emerald deposits. Soon the pasha provided another military escort and a party of Syrian miners for a return expedition.

Cailliaud himself came back in a few months with ten pounds of rough emeralds and tantalizing stories of a ruined city with eight hundred houses and several temples lying near the emerald mines. Although the ruins were at least eight miles from the sea, the armchair antiquarians of Cairo immediately claimed that they were the remains of the ancient city of Berenice. Berenice had long been Ancient Egypt's main trading port on the Red Sea, a center of vigorous commerce with Arabia, India, and the Persian Gulf, especially under the Ptolemies, and was obviously a rich prize for the first archaeologist to dig there. Visions of a new Pompeii rose before the eyes of Cairo's antiquaries, for Cailliaud, before he quietly slipped away from the mines, had written a glowing report of his discoveries.

It so happened that a few months later one of the Syrian miners became ill while visiting the

203

Nile to buy provisions. Hearing that a Christian doctor was living in the Valley of Kings, he called on Belzoni and Ricci and begged for treatment. Belzoni had heard rumors of Cailliaud's discovery and questioned the man closely. The miner soon offered to guide him to the place. Since the work at Sethy's tomb was now almost complete and there seemed to be little going on at Thebes, Belzoni leaped at the chance of a new expedition. Within a few days, on September 16, a small expedition was ready to move. The party of eight included the miner, Ricci, whose artistic talents might prove useful, Beechey, and several servants.

The expedition hired a small boat to take them upstream to Edfu, where they were to cut across the desert toward the Red Sea. It was a year of record flood, and the Nile rose three and a half feet above the previous year, inundating several villages and drowning several hundred people. Every available boat was engaged in carrying precious grain to higher ground. One village they called at was already four feet below river level. Day and night vigils at the barricades were the only hope for survival, for there were no boats in the village or palm trees to climb if the dikes broke. Farther upstream, the situation was even more critical. Whole villages had been washed away, and the people were clustered on patches of higher ground with their grain and stock. There was danger of starvation, for the flood would not recede for at least two weeks and there were few boats. Some people had fled to safety on the backs of water buffalo or on bundles of reeds. Belzoni was unable to do anything to help, for his small boat would have been swamped by a great press of people. But at Erment, farther upstream, they spent the best part of a day ferrying people to safety across the river. The fourth and last trip across the flooded stream brought the women to safety, "the last and most insignificant of their property, whose loss would have been less regretted than that of the cattle."

204

A Bedouin camp, by Belzoni

At Esneh, they called on Ibrahim Bey, the governor, who received Belzoni very civilly and readily granted them a firman, but with strict instructions that they were not to mine for emeralds. As always, the Turks could not understand why anyone should be interested in ruins or stones and suspected some more mercenary motives. These suspicions were shared by the chief miner, Mohammed Aga, who turned up at Edfu just after Belzoni's arrival. By this time, the local kachif had arranged for camels and drivers with Sheik Abeda, the leader of the desert tribe through whose territory the route to the mines passed. A good bargain had been struck, which cost Belzoni a piaster a day for the camels and a small wage for the drivers. But the next day he found the sheik less cooperative. Obviously the chief miner had aired his suspicions, for he had pressed Belzoni to wait on his journey until his own return. Belzoni countered by insisting that the camels depart the same day, before the sheik had time to delay him further, and on the afternoon of September 22 the caravan of sixteen camels, six of them laden with provisions, set out on a well-trodden road which had been in use for centuries.

Berenice had first come into prominence in the third century B.C., when Ptolemy II built the port in a small, sheltered bay protected from the prevailing northerly winds. From the sea captain's point of view, the journey up the Red Sea was cut short by offloading at Berenice, although the port

205

Travel in the desert

itself was more than 250 miles from the Nile. Ptolemy II also caused a road to be built from Berenice to Koptos on the Nile. A southern branch route joined the Nile at Edfu. This was the route Belzoni had chosen. The highway ran through desert country, but the government maintained rest stations and wells along the road and levied a regular scale of tolls along the way. Many of the precious metals, stones, and spices of the eastern desert and the East traveled along this ancient highway to the comfortable world of the Nile.

The first part of Belzoni's journey lay through level but arid countryside covered with stunted sycamore trees and thickets of camel thorn. Soon the expedition came across traces of ancient settlement, abandoned caravan stations for early

206

travelers on the road, identified by scattered boulders and filled-up wells. At the end of the second day they camped at the entrance to the Wady Hiah, near a small rock-cut temple. The remains of a guard station with a camel enclosure and accommodation for travelers lay nearby.

They resumed their journey before daybreak on September 25 and came to more desertic country where little vegetation was to be seen. The same evening Dr. Ricci was taken violently ill, and it was decided to send him back to the Nile before he got any worse. So the caravan split up into three detachments, the heavy baggage going to the east along the main road, while Belzoni and Beechey took a side trip to look at some ruins described by the local people. They turned out to be another roadside watering place.

Belzoni was fascinated by the desert tribes scattered in small villages over a huge expanse of the eastern desert. The Ababde were independent-minded nomads who owed allegiance to no government. Some made a sketchy living by breeding and trading camels, but most were content to live at a subsistence level. With their dark complexions and black curly hair, they closely resembled the Nubians that Belzoni had met at Abu Simbel. Most Ababde walked around nearly naked, except for elaborate hairstyles which they covered with small pieces of mutton fat—when they had any. The fat melted in the hot sun, producing "an exquisite odour for those who have a good nose." Belzoni found the Ababde quite friendly and willing to sell a few sheep, although there were few to be obtained owing to a prolonged drought. He marveled at their endurance, for they were able to go for twenty-four hours without water, even in the hottest season.

About two in the afternoon of September 29, after seven days on the road, they saw the blue waters of the Red Sea at a great distance. The following day they reached the miners' encampment at the foot of Mount Zabara. Conditions in the

207

camp were appalling. Provisions were brought in by camel from the Nile and never arrived on time. There was a real danger of famine or death at the hands of the Ababde, who resented the miners' presence and their rough ways with local women. No emeralds had been found in the ancient workings, and the work of clearing the old shafts was highly dangerous. Fights were commonplace, and at least two miners had been killed in an uprising against their leaders.

Belzoni was anxious to move on. So he stopped for a brief look at the ancient mines, acquired as much (vague) information as he could from the miners, and engaged a local guide for the brief trip to Cailliaud's ancient city.

The resulting journey was a nightmare of thirst and arduous going. Their guide led them through rough, narrow valleys and a steep and craggy pass which exhausted their camels. No sign of Berenice appeared from the summit, although Cailliaud's lyrical descriptions had led Belzoni to expect "lofty columns and architecture of some magnificent edifice."

It was soon clear that Cailliaud's account was grossly exaggerated. They came across some enclosures and ruined walls, which the guide insisted were the remains of Cailliaud's city. Violent expostulations ensued, for Belzoni was determined to press on to the coast. Finally he mounted his camel again, much to the annoyance of the animal, "which would much rather have remained where he was than have gone in search of old Berenice." The rest of the caravan followed reluctantly as Belzoni spurred his camel down a south-facing valley. For more than four hours he traversed the valley in all directions looking for the ruins, but no sign of them had been seen by darkness. Camp was pitched under a large rock, and Belzoni took stock of the situation. They had now run out of water and had but twenty days' supply of biscuits. The nearest water was 15 miles away, and the camels were sent off to drink and to fetch water for the human members of the party. Meanwhile, the Europeans dined on biscuits and a three-day-old piece of mutton that made Belzoni thankful he had no sense of smell.

The next morning Belzoni and Beechey made their way over to a hill about five miles away, from the summit of which they surveyed the landscape around them. No city, no Red Sea, could be discerned, and Belzoni realized that Cailliaud's report was totally inaccurate. "It was rather provoking," he wrote, "to have taken such a journey in consequence of such a fabricated description." Bitterly disappointed, he compared Cailliaud's ruins to the "desired island of the squire of the astonishing champion of La Mancha," which never appeared.

The travelers were now practically lost, for they had no maps except D'Anville's famous map of the Red Sea, published in 1766, which was far from accurate and on too small a scale. The trend of the valley drainages seemed to be toward the south, and Belzoni conjectured that the Red Sea lay in that direction. When the weary camels returned, he gave orders to resume the journey to the south. This caused great consternation, and only promises and threats carried the day. Eventually the caravan set off in a northeasterly direction, which took them down a steep-sided valley to a narrow opening in the mountains known as Khurm el Gemal, translated by Belzoni as the "rent of the camels." There they camped at sunset. At noon the following day they sighted the blue waters of the Red Sea and soon were plunging into the ocean "like crocodiles into the Nile."

Belzoni now had but seventeen days' food left and turned southward along the coast in search of the elusive port. The drivers protested. Their protests were in vain in the face of Belzoni's determination, so the camels were watered at a well and the caravan set off along the sandy and rock-strewn coast. They soon encountered some fishermen, who caught a meal for them using a crude

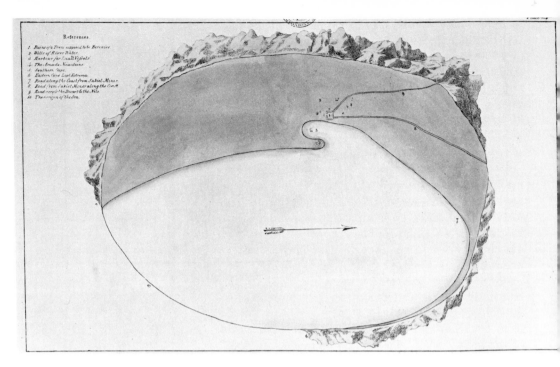

Belzoni's map of Berenice

tree-trunk boat as a base to spear large fish some distance offshore. Belzoni also feasted on shellfish taken from the rocks. Unfortunately these aggravated the travelers' thirst.

The party was now split in two. The baggage and most of the camels were sent off to a nearby spring in the mountains, while Beechey and Belzoni, with five men and two boys and five camels, pressed on to the south with as much water as they could carry. Two days later, the flying expedition was thirsty, although not hungry, for they had helped themselves to some fish cooking in a deserted fishermen's camp. Beechey scrupulously left money for the meal, for the inhabitants fled at the sight of the strangers and refused to return. On October 7, they reached Ras Banas and camped near the shore with only a little water to satisfy their raging thirst. The following day brought them to the unmistakable signs of a long-abandoned city. "We entered," recalls Belzoni,

210

"and at once we saw the regular situations of the houses; the main streets, their construction, and in the centre, a small Egyptian temple, nearly covered by the sand. . . ." The site lay inside an amphitheater of mountains and was sheltered by the mass of Ras Banas to the north. Belzoni measured the town and found it more than 2,000 feet by 1,600 feet in extent. He was convinced—and later archaeological researches have proved him right— that this was indeed the site of Berenice. But it was far less spectacular than Belzoni had hoped.

Time was very short, for their water supplies were critically short and they had eaten nothing but dry biscuits since the cooked fish of several days before. Their guides were thirsty and restless, so Belzoni had to promise that he would leave at noon the next day. Fortunately, it was full moon and they could survey and sketch at night. One of the Egyptian boys was set to work clearing sand from the temple. For some reason Belzoni had forgotten to bring a spade, so they had to use a large seashell. The boy managed to clear a hole four feet deep and unearthed a bas-relief and part of an inscription engraved on a small tablet of red breccia. They took it away then "as a memorandum of having seen an Egyptian temple on the coast of the Red Sea." We now know that the temple was dedicated to Serapis, the Apis-Osiris cult so popular through the Nile Valley in Roman times.

While the boy was excavating the temple, Beechey and Belzoni surveyed the town. They found that the homes were placed close together and were at the most 40 by 20 feet across. Many were smaller, and Belzoni estimated that there were four thousand houses at Berenice. But he cut this estimate in half to two thousand, "so that I might not be mistaken for another Cailliaud." Belzoni had just enough time to complete these calculations and to measure the temple—he found it to be 130 feet long by 43 feet wide. Berenice had been dramatic but a little disappointing. Belzoni

211

reckoned that a population of about ten thousand people had lived there at the height of its prosperity.

They were fortunate enough to find water at about midnight on the second day, at a well called Aharatret in the hills behind Berenice. Even better was the sight of a flock of sheep, but the owners promptly "drove the intended repast away." Belzoni sent his drivers in pursuit, and they stopped the two young girls tending the flock as they were slipping into hiding. "We were gallant with them, for the sake of devouring some of their lambs," remarked Belzoni circumspectly, "but the sheep prevailed above all, and took our chief attention." They were soon feasting on half-cooked but tough mutton for the first time in days. Two days later they rejoined the rest of the caravan at the spring of Amusue, where water flowed in abundance, observing traces of the ancient caravan route from Berenice to the Nile on the way.

Belzoni was now certain that he had located Berenice and that all Cailliaud had seen was a large miners' camp of small houses scattered over an arid and hilly terrain where the sun baked the soil like an oven and life was harsh and lonely. Cailliaud's imagination had been fired by these desolate ruins. He had wandered in and out of the houses for some time. "With unbounded satisfaction," he wrote, "I greeted and hailed a town, hitherto unknown to all our voyagers, which had not been inhabited, perhaps, for 2,000 years, and almost entirely standing." Belzoni was openly scornful of the place. He counted only eighty-seven houses, as opposed to Cailliaud's estimate of five hundred.

It was now time to return to the Nile, and the caravan turned for home. The homeward journey was wearisome and thirsty. By the time they reached the mountains by the Nile the camels were so tired they could hardly crawl. Four died by the roadside. The travelers were much troubled by bad well water and thirst. By the time

212

they reached the Wady Hiah temple five days later they were so thirsty that the water in the last well, which had tasted horrible on the way out, "appeared pretty good on our return."

On October 23, after an absence of little over a month, Belzoni and Beechey reboarded their boat and paid off their weary drivers, taking care to give a present of pocket pistols to the helpful local kachif. By this time the Nile flood had receded. "All the lands that were under water before were now not only dried up, but were already sown; the muddy villages carried off by the rapid current were all rebuilt; the fences opened; the Fellahs at work in the fields, and all wore a different aspect."

Belzoni had good reason for satisfaction. He had undertaken an arduous desert journey under difficult conditions and returned without losing a man. The mystery of Berenice was now cleared up and Cailliaud's discovery placed in the correct perspective. He could now return to his archaeological researches in the comfortable knowledge that he had established a credible reputation for exciting and unusual discoveries, something that Belzoni prized above all else.

"Temple on the Road to Berenice on the Red Sea" by Belzoni

14   The Obelisk of Philae

The desert is a seductive environment, one that can both attract and repel the traveler. History is full of remarkable explorers who have devoted their lives to nomadic exploration and caravan life. Belzoni's friend Burckhardt was one such man, and for a while the Italian shared the craving for desert adventure. No sooner had he reached the Nile than he began to plan a return to Berenice, or a visit to the great Khargeh oasis to the west of Thebes, which Cailliaud had also visited. Perhaps important discoveries awaited him there. But developments at Kurneh soon turned his energies in other directions.

Henry Salt, the British consul, was now in residence at Kurneh, accompanied by a large party of wealthy travelers. These included Baron Sack, an elderly Prussian nobleman who was a dedicated naturalist with long experience of tropical environments, and William John Bankes, an adventurous young antiquarian with a penchant for travel and sparkling conversation. Bankes had been at the university with the poet Lord Byron and shared some of his tastes and values. The party was traveling in high style and proposed a leisurely journey up to the First Cataract, with the general objective of removing the beautiful obelisk that Belzoni had claimed in Salt's name on his first journey.

Salt had now ceded his rights to Bankes, who was evidently delighted when Belzoni accepted a commission to transport the obelisk to Cairo. Belzoni joined the party with alacrity, for the luxury was incredible after the privations of recent months. The consul had a large boat, two smaller ones carried Bankes and the baron, while the rear of the convoy was brought up by a raucous canoe-load of "sheep, goats, fowls, geese, ducks, pigeons, turkeys, and donkeys, which . . . accompanied the fleet with a perpetual concert." Belzoni was not long impressed with the luxurious waste. "Even at table," he wrote sarcastically, "we had not ice to cool ourselves after the heavy repast, which was concluded with fruits, and only two sorts of wine. In short our lives were a bother to us from the fatigue and dangerous mode of travelling."

The stay at Kurneh gave Belzoni and Salt some time together. Belzoni complained that he had no chance to collect on his own account, so a new, and more satisfactory, agreement was made. He could now dig at Salt's expense on either bank of the Nile in the British claim areas, and a third of the finds were to be his. It is surprising that Belzoni and Salt did not reach an agreement of this type much earlier, for it was by far the fairest arrangement under the circumstances.

Soon afterward, the French consul arrived in Thebes and promptly made an offer for the purchase of the alabaster sarcophagus, which was

215

Bernardino Drovetti and his agents

immediately rejected. Belzoni and Salt accompanied Drovetti on a tour of the Karnak sites to check the various areas reserved for the British in that area. The meeting was superficially cordial, and any misunderstandings about rival claims were soon worked out. But Drovetti, while amiability itself, persisted in telling stories about a man dressed like Belzoni who was hiding in the ruins, who wished to do Drovetti harm. So he had warned the local headman about the stranger. Salt laughed at the story, but Belzoni was concerned, for he feared that "if I had happened to go among the ruins, which it was my constant practice to do, and some one had sent a ball at me, they could have said after, that they mistook me for

216

the person who had assumed my appearance in dress and figure." This incident put Belzoni on his guard, which, perhaps, was fortunate.

After the tour Drovetti regaled his guests with sherbet and lemonade in his hut among the ruins. The talk was of Berenice and of antiquities in general, until Belzoni let slip his plan to remove the obelisk of Philae, despite the lateness of the season. Immediately Drovetti feigned surprise. The rogues at Aswan had deceived him, he said, for they had promised on many occasions to bring the obelisk down for him. Belzoni pointed out that he had taken possession of it on Salt's behalf during his first trip into Nubia and had paid for guards to protect it. He quickly explained that Salt had given the obelisk to Bankes, on whose behalf he, Belzoni, was to remove it to Alexandria. Drovetti then conceded the ownership to Bankes with charming courtesy, rather in the manner that he had given the granite sarcophagus to Belzoni many months before. Presumably he assumed that the obelisk could never be moved. But he did casually ask when the English party planned to depart.

Two days later, on November 16, the large caravan left for the First Cataract. Six days later they came to the magnificent temple of Edfu, where they found Drovetti's agents hard at work. They also heard that one of the agents had just left posthaste for Philae in response to an urgent message from downstream. A little farther upstream they overtook the Piedmontese agent Antonio Lebolo traveling up the Nile at speed in a small boat. He refused to stop in answer to their hails, so Belzoni was sufficiently worried to leave the main party at Kom Ombo and charter a special vessel to take him on to Aswan as quickly as possible.

But the mischief was done by the time he reached Aswan. Lebolo had started by trying to persuade the local people not to let Belzoni have the obelisk. The aga, who had reason to be grate-

217

The temple of Horus and Sobk at Kom Ombo

ful to Belzoni, pointed out that the English had taken possession of the obelisk three years before and paid for a guard all this time. The crafty Piedmontese now resorted to bribery. He crossed over to Philae, pretended to read the inscriptions on the obelisk, and told the gullible locals that the hieroglyphs stated that the monument had belonged to Drovetti's ancestors. A bribe and an affidavit in front of the local qadi completed Lebolo's dirty tricks, after which he promptly disappeared.

Belzoni arrived too late to stop Lebolo, but he managed to convince the aga of Aswan of the legitimacy of his claim. Time was obviously of the essence. The obelisk would have to be removed immediately, or the Nile would be too low for safe transport across the cataract. So Belzoni decided to ignore Lebolo's phony document of ownership and rely on possession being nine-tenths of the law. It was fortunate for Belzoni that he enjoyed much better relations with the local people than did Drovetti's harsh agents. So the aga was given a handsome present of a watch and the boat captain presented with half his money in advance,

218

The obelisk of Philae in its final resting place in the grounds of Kingston Lacy House, Dorset, England. It stands on a site chosen by the Duke of Wellington.

a bribe for moving the obelisk through the cataract. It is an interesting reflection on Belzoni's powers of persuasion that the same captain had refused to attempt the same task for Drovetti two months earlier on the grounds that the water was already too low.

No time was wasted. A set of hauling tackle was assembled and the boat moored to the riverbank close to the obelisk. The greatest difficulty was finding suitable poles to move the monument the few critical yards to the bank, for wood was in short supply. But enough timber eventually came to hand to shift the obelisk by rather similar methods to those used with the Young Memnon. Just as operations were about to begin, the aga brought over a letter from Drovetti telling him to allow no one to remove the obelisk except himself. Salt told the aga to give his compliments to Drovetti and to tell him the English were taking it anyhow.

Meanwhile, the workmen had built a rough stone causeway out from the bank, while Belzoni went off to spy out a channel through the cataract. Then disaster struck. As the obelisk was rolled out along the causeway, the stones sank into the mud and the priceless monument slid slowly into the Nile. Belzoni was transfixed with horror. Only the tip of the obelisk could be seen above the swirling water.

The rest of the party left Belzoni alone with his problems and sailed on upstream into Nubia, although a close inspection of the obelisk convinced the Italian that two or three days should see the obelisk in safety. Fortunately the Philae workmen were both strong and very willing to work.

A large number of extra stones were hauled to the river bank, after which the recovery operations began. The boulders were laid underwater next to the obelisk. Large levers were then worked under the monument, which was gradually lifted onto dry land, a pavement of stones being piled under it as it was turned toward the shore. In two days the obelisk stood on dry land.

All this was accomplished to the accompaniment of vigorous complaints from Drovetti's agent, who put the whole town of Aswan in an uproar and brought the aga to Philae in an attempt to stop operations. But neither the aga nor the local people seemed inclined to stop Belzoni, regarding the quarrel as a matter between the English and the French. So he continued operations, loading the obelisk onto the boat with the aid of a palm-tree bridge, of the same type used to move the Young Memnon on shipboard.

The next morning, the boat and its precious cargo were brought to the edge of the steepest part of the cataract. A heavy rope was tied to a large tree upstream of the torrent and the other

220

end passed inboard so that the passage of the boat could be controlled by the five men remaining on board. A number of men stationed on the rocks on either side of the cataract held more ropes attached to the boat, designed to prevent its being stove in. Everything depended on the skill of the rivermen, for the large stern warp was incapable of stopping the boat, merely sufficient to check the breakneck pace of descent. The ship's captain was beside himself with anxiety and in tears begged Belzoni to give him his boat back. Finally he threw himself on the ground and buried his face in the sand, refusing to witness the imminent destruction of his most valuable possession.

When everything was ready and the men were in position, Belzoni gave the signal to slacken the cable.

It was one of the greatest sights I have seen. The boat took a course which may be reckoned at the rate of twelve miles an hour. Accordingly, the men on land slackened the rope; and at the distance of one hundred yards the boat came in contact with an eddy, which, beating against a rock, returned towards the vessel, and that helped much to stop its course. The men on the side pulled the boat out of the direction of that rock, and it continued its course, gradually diminishing its rate, till it reached the bottom of the cataract; and I was not a little pleased to see it out of danger.

Even the workmen were thrilled at the safe passage. The captain of the boat "came to me with joy expressed in his countenance, as may easily be imagined."

Now there were only two or three dangerous spots to be traversed. But these presented few problems, and the precious cargo reached Aswan safely the same day. One of Belzoni's most daring and tricky exploits had ended in brilliant success. Again, he was careful to pay off the local people and the aga to everyone's satisfaction, setting off downstream to Thebes as quickly as possible. Headwinds delayed the passage, so Belzoni went

221

The temple of Dendereh in an early photograph by Maxime Du Camp

on by land and took up residence again in his old home in the tomb of Sethy I. There he found Sarah waiting for him.

Sarah had had an adventurous journey to Palestine, one that rivaled Belzoni's own arduous travels in its frustrations and many dangers. Accompanied by James Curtin and Giovanni Finati, she had made her way to Jerusalem in time for Easter, bathed in the Jordan, and visited Nazareth. Most of the time she was dressed as a Mameluk youth and traveled practically by herself, a dangerous thing to do at the best of times in Palestine in the early nineteenth century. When she realized that her husband would not be joining her, Sarah returned to Alexandria on an evil-smelling packet boat. The cabin she had booked was full of melons and the deck crowded with Albanian soldiers. Soon she came down with a serious stomach fever. "I never suffered on the ocean what I suffered on this insignificant voyage," she wrote some years later. It took her ill-

222

fated packet no less than thirteen days to cross
from Jaffa to Egypt.

She engaged a boat to take her to Thebes, accompanied only by a young Mameluk. The journey was uncomfortable, for dense rains soaked
her bedding and possessions. The same storm had
washed mud into Sethy's tomb, the humidity
causing some of the walls to crack. She ordered
the mud removed and sat down to wait for her
husband. He returned on December 23, and they
spent a quiet Christmas together, "in the solitude
of these recesses, undisturbed by the folly of mankind." It was a wonderful rest and reunion.

The day after Christmas Belzoni and his Greek
interpreter mounted donkeys and, accompanied
by two Arab servants, went over to Karnak. The
obelisk had arrived safely at Thebes on Christmas
Eve. Rather tactlessly, the captain had moored the
boat under the noses of Drovetti and his agents at
Karnak. "It irritated them," recalls Belzoni, and
the irritation led to a violent confrontation, which,
according to Belzoni, was deliberately engineered
by the French.

As Belzoni made his way toward Karnak, he
met an Arab who warned him not to go near the
other Europeans. He ignored the warning and
soon came upon a party of laborers working on
one of Salt's claims. Despite the protests of the interpreter, Belzoni feigned to ignore them, recogniz-
ing the provocative strategem for what it was. So
he went on past the great temple of Karnak where
the Drovetti party were lodging and inspected
some of Salt's claims nearby. He then set off for
Luxor, passing again near the great propylaeum of
the temple where he met an Arab who cried out
that he had been beaten because he worked for
the English. Belzoni again ignored this attempt at
provocation and passed on his way.

Soon he noticed the agent Antonio Lebolo,
Guiseppe Rosignano, and about thirty armed
Arabs hurrying toward him. In a moment the
angry men had surrounded the travelers. Loudly,

**The propylons of the temple
at Karnak from the south.**
From *La Description de l'Egypte.*

Antonio Lebolo inquired why he had moved Drovetti's obelisk from Philae, an obelisk that was not
Belzoni's property. With that he seized the bridle
of Belzoni's donkey with one hand and his waist-
coat with the other. The Arabs disarmed the Italian's servants and beat them. Rosignano pointed
his double-barreled rifle at Belzoni's chest in a
rage. It was time, he said, that Belzoni should pay
for his deeds. "My situation was not pleasant, surrounded by a band of ruffians like them," remarked
Belzoni with almost casual understatement, "and
I have no doubt that if I had attempted to dismount, the cowards would have dispatched me on
the ground, and said that they did it in defense of
their lives as I had been the aggressor." So he decided to stay on his donkey and treat them with
contempt. This only inflamed their tempers.

Drovetti and another band of armed Arabs now
came on the scene. The consul angrily demanded
what Belzoni meant by stopping his men from digging and ordered him to dismount. Belzoni replied

224

that he knew of no such instance and complained
of the discourtesy shown him. "At this moment a
pistol was fired behind me, but I could not tell by
whom. I was determined to bear much, sooner
than come to blows with such people, who did
not blush to assail me all in a mass; but when I
heard the pistol fired behind my back, I thought it
was high time to sell my life as dear as I could."
So he dismounted in a fury.

But Drovetti evidently realized matters had gone
too far and attempted to smooth things over.
Among other things, the local Arabs had come to
Belzoni's aid and had surrounded Rosignano with
menacing threats. The affair ended with Belzoni's
"informing Mr. Drovetti that I had resisted many
and various sorts of attacks by his agents, but I
did not expect they would come to such a pitch,
and that it was high time for me to quit the country." He returned to the Valley of Kings in a state
of fear and agitation, where Sarah was having "a
violent bilious fever."

The savants' view of Pompey's Pillar, Alexandria, with minute sketches of details. From *La Description*.

It took a month to pack up the valuable wax impressions and records from Sethy's tomb. The fragile alabaster sarcophagus was carefully transported on rollers from its centuries-old home over three miles of uneven terrain to Belzoni's boat. Belzoni even found time to repair some of the damage to the tomb caused by the flood. Then on January 27, 1819, the Belzonis left Thebes for the last time: "I must confess," he wrote, "that I felt no small degree of sorrow to quit a place which was become so familiar to me."

The Belzonis took their valuable cargo all the way to Alexandria with the intention of taking ship for Europe immediately. But a letter from Salt caused Belzoni to delay, for the consul recommended that he institute legal proceedings against the miscreants. Indeed, Mr. Lee, the British consul in Alexandria, had already taken matters up on his behalf with the legal authorities and the French consul. Drovetti had now returned to Alexandria and intervened on behalf of his agents. So it was agreed to leave matters until Henry Salt returned from Upper Egypt. Belzoni himself was not keen on a legal battle, for he knew the political influence exercised by his opponents. Furthermore, an Italian "stranger" who had helped Belzoni during the fracas had arrived in Alexandria laden down with antiquities presented to him by Drovetti's agents for resale in Europe. He could hardly be called a potentially reliable witness by this time. Belzoni had little option but to settle Sarah into a home provided by an English merchant in Alexandria and to cast around for an outlet for his restless energy. He thought of excavating in Lower Egypt, but concluded that it was too close to the "fountain head of our opponents." Instead, he resolved on a side trip into the western desert in search of the temple of Jupiter Amun.

The temple of Jupiter Amun was located in the remote Siwa oasis in the western desert. This temple achieved notoriety when, according to Plutarch,

226

its priests addressed Alexander the Great as the "son of Zeus," an event that filled the young leader with ambitions of world conquest and godlike status. The Persian king Cambyses lost an army in the desert when searching for the Ammonites. According to Herodotus, he dispatched an army of 50,000 men across the desert, but they never returned. "The Persians . . . had reached about half way . . . when, as they were at their midday meal, a wind arose from the south, strong and deadly, bringing with it vast columns of whirling sand, which entirely covered up the troops, and caused them wholly to disappear," records Herodotus, quoting the Ammonites. So Belzoni was looking for a notorious temple.

In fact, the temple of Jupiter Amun had already been visited by an English traveler, William George Browne, who crossed to the Siwa oasis in 1792 and located extensive ancient ruins there. But he did not attribute the site to Jupiter Amun, and considerable mystery still surrounded his discovery. Belzoni, certainly unaware of the importance of Browne's discovery, searched for the temple in the Fayyum instead. As a result, he never came within a hundred miles of the Siwa oasis or the temple of Jupiter Amun, although he had a most enjoyable journey.

Belzoni's last Egyptian journey differed from his earlier travels in being a more solitary expedition. His primary interest seems to have been to discover and examine the great temple rather than to bring home another load of antiquities. We can detect a change in the Italian's interests, brought about both by the pressures at Thebes and by his most recent discoveries in the pyramids, at Berenice, and in the Valley of Kings. Belzoni's hunger for fame and visibility had now surfaced, as he sought to become known as an adventurer and traveler as much as an archaeologist. The antiquities were now secondary; his primary objective was to discover new and spectacular temples and ancient monuments as a catalyst for his travels.

228

The party was a small one, consisting of Belzoni, a Sicilian servant, and a "Moorish Hadge," a pilgrim returning from Mecca, who begged passage in the boat and proved "very useful." They left the Nile at Beni Suef, some 80 miles upstream of Cairo, on April 29, 1819, and continued their journey into the Fayyum by donkey. The journey to the great depression led them through "a vast plain of cultivated land, along the route of an ancient channel, which brings water into the Faiyum." That night they camped near the brick pyramid of Sen-Wosret II (c. 200 B.C.), after setting a careful watch. Belzoni as usual reclined on his special mattress, "thin enough to serve as a saddle when folded up, but when laid on a mat or on the ground, affording as good a bed as any traveller ought to expect."

The next day, Belzoni climbed the pyramid and gazed over the surrounding countryside, searching for the site of ancient Arsinoe and the fabulous Labyrinth, described by Herodotus as an even greater wonder than the pyramids. He found no trace of the Labyrinth, although he found signs of an ancient town near the pyramid of Hauwareh. It was not until seventy years later that Flinders Petrie found the Labyrinth, of which nothing remained except a mass of limestone chips.

The travelers were now in country famous for its rose water, used to keep the stench of Cairo from the delicate nostrils of its inhabitants. Here Belzoni obtained a firman and guides. He had avoided doing so in Alexandria or Cairo, for fear that his rivals would disrupt his plans. They passed by the ruins of ancient Arsinoe and left them to be examined on their return, pressing northward to the desolate Birket Karun, a brackish lake that lay more than 120 feet below sea level. There was some difficulty in finding a boat to carry the party westward to the far shore of the lake; when one did arrive, Belzoni was horrified and fascinated. "It was entirely out of shape," he wrote; "the outer shell or hulk was composed

230

of rough pieces of wood scarcely joined, and fastened by four other pieces, wrapped together by four more across, which formed the deck; no tar, no pitch either inside or out, and the only preventive against the water coming in was a kind of weed moistened, which had settled in the joints of the wood."

Belzoni was still in search of the Labyrinth, which he was convinced lay across the lake. It was a romantic, if crazy, journey. They camped on a deserted shore and dined off fresh fish. "The scene here was beautiful—the silence of the night, the beams of the radiant moon shining on the still water of the lake, the solitude of the place, the sight of our boat, the group of fishermen . . . put me in mind of the lake Acheron, the boat Baris, and the old ferryman of the Styx." It was a memorable night for Belzoni, who thought of it later as one of his happiest moments.

At the southwestern corner of the lake they landed to explore a complex of ruins and a temple, now known as Kasr Karun. The ruins were nothing spectacular, but Belzoni was startled out of his wits by a hyena which rushed out at him from a small temple. Fortunately the animal fled, for Belzoni was unarmed. But still no Labyrinth came to light, despite a two-day search along the northern shores of Birket Karun. Belzoni had some accounts of the lake with him, including unreliable maps, which led him to believe that it would be worth venturing into the mountains some distance from the lake. Only two miles from its shores, they came across another ruined town, consisting of "a great number of houses, and a high wall of sun-burnt bricks, which includes the ruins of a temple." Fortunately the fishermen had brought their hatchets with them, so they were able to excavate two or three of the houses. Under the collapsed roofs, the houses were choked with rubbish. One contained a fireplace. This was not the Labyrinth either, and we now know that Belzoni had stumbled on a Ptolemaic town called Nesos Sokonopaiou.

231

"The city of Bacchus on the Lake Moeris" by Belzoni

They now gave up the search for the Labyrinth and crossed to the east side of the lake. Belzoni was puzzled by the few signs of the Labyrinth. Everywhere he saw fragments of columns and ancient building stone used in the construction of Arab huts. "I have no doubt," he concluded, "that by tracing the source of these materials, the seat of the Labyrinth could be discovered, which must be most magnificent even in its ruined state." This fruitless excursion had one interesting side experience, for Belzoni was able to enjoy a meal of pelican meat, which he described as "on the whole very tender, and pleasant to the palate."

Belzoni now moved away from the lake, on his way back to Medinet el Fayyum and the rose-water factories. He passed through Fedmin el Hanaises, where he heard the legend of the three hundred Coptic churches once said to exist there. The churches were reportedly buried under the town. But, said Belzoni, "the canal cuts through the town and none of the said churches appeared in the progress of the excavation through the

232

town, which must have been the case had it been built on the said three hundred churches."

The following day Belzoni reached Medinet el Fayyum and immediately set out for Arsinoe nearby, where he admired "sculptures of most magnificent taste" and dug in the filling of an ancient reservoir in the middle of the town. But his real interest was in visiting the oasis to the west of Lake Moeris. He had some difficulty finding a guide, for the area was little known except to the Bedouin. Eventually his old friend Khalil Bey, formerly of Esneh and now stationed at Beni Suef, gave him a firman and arranged for a sheik named Grimar to guide him. Belzoni described Grimar as "a tall stout man, six feet three inches high, with a countenance that bespoke a resolute mind, and great eagerness after gain."

On May 19, the caravan of six camels set out from Grimar's camp, where Belzoni had spent several sleepless nights plagued by fleas. They traveled westward along the south side of the Fayyum, passing into the desert and through a formerly populated area, which included some large burial mounds, which Belzoni attributed to Cambyses' army. Six days later the caravan reached the Wady el Baharia, an oasis where they watered their camels and made contact with the inhabitants. The first man they met was a dwarf who threatened Belzoni with a gun. Fortunately, Grimar spoke the local dialect and averted disaster. By using coffee and tobacco, both rare luxuries in the desert, Belzoni was able to persuade the local sheik to show him the ruins near the two villages in the area.

The ruins around the oasis were far from spectacular, but included some mass burials and some terra-cotta sarcophagi whose lids bore modeled heads. Belzoni broke several and took away the heads. At the second village, the father of the qadi was a wealthy date merchant who had, it was generally believed, buried his wealth in the ruins near the settlement; so Belzoni could get only within 50 yards of the ruined Roman temple. But he promptly whipped out his pocket telescope and enjoyed a close-up view of the walls. Nearby was a wall of hot and cold water which Belzoni visited several times on the pretext of having a bath. He found that the temperature varied, a phenomenon he attributed to the wide variations in the air temperature relative to water temperature. He confused this spring with the famous Fountain of the Sun at the temple of Jupiter Amun, alluded to by Classical writers. This led him to believe that he had located the temple when in fact it lay in the Siwa oasis, to the south.

Despite many pleas, the Bedouin Sheik Grimar refused to take Belzoni on to Siwa, where he had heard of Browne's and others' discoveries of ruins that might be, and in fact were, the elusive temple. It later transpired that the sheik was well known at Siwa for his prowess as a raider. Reprisals might have resulted if the chief had visited the area without his people. So Belzoni was forced to visit el Farafra, an oasis only three days' journey away to the southwest. All that was to be seen there was a ruined Coptic church and a few suspicious villagers. At one point, the party was obliged to make a forced march by night to avoid an attack.

Belzoni now turned for home, but was detained at Wady el Baharia by the qadi, who told him that the sheik and his father agreed with the qadi that Belzoni should turn Muslim and stay with them. They would give him land for new agricultural products and four wives from their daughters, and "I should be happy there without getting about so much after stones." It was with difficulty that Belzoni extracted himself from this situation, by promising to return when he had settled his affairs in Cairo.

The journey home was uneventful, except for a nasty fall from a camel. The animal stumbled on a rock and rolled about 20 feet down a steep slope. Belzoni fell heavily and was badly bruised,

234

perhaps breaking a few ribs. In great pain, he laid up at the home of the sheik of Zabu. His bed was set up in a narrow passage by the house, which was constantly in use by people, "cows, buffaloes, donkeys, sheeps, goats and dogs." Passers-by accidentally kicked him on the head. When animals passed, "I had reason to fear the consequence of my being thus situated." A funeral was in progress, and the lamentations and comings and goings disturbed his slumbers. All in all, it was an uncomfortable visit, capped by the widow of the dead man begging Belzoni for two pieces of his "magic paper" for the purposes of obtaining a new husband and protecting him from death. Belzoni tried to persuade her that he was not a magician. "I could not help reflecting, that if I had the art of procuring husbands to widows, I could have obtained employment enough in Europe, without travelling in strange lands for such a purpose."

Three days later Belzoni was well enough to travel, and the camels set off across the desert on what proved to be an arduous journey. They drank some rather salty water, which caused agonies of thirst in the final stages of the crossing, so much so that a crust of salt formed on Belzoni's mouth. Thankfully, the travelers reached the Nile on May 14, and a day later Belzoni embarked for Cairo.

By this time Henry Salt had returned to base, and the two men met at night to avoid a new plague raging. They settled their accounts and parted on excellent terms. There only remained

A bridge near Alexandria.
From *La Description.*

the matter of the Karnak incident to settle. But in Alexandria the legal situation was full of confusion and intrigue. Drovetti had exercised his influence with the new French consul, Foussel, who had replaced Drovetti some years before. When the consul was recalled to France, the vice-consul took over. Belzoni was required to put down a deposit of 1,200 dollars in advance to cover the expenses of the lawyer's travel to Thebes. When this requirement was got around Lebolo and Rosignano turned up in Alexandria and were openly boasting of their achievement. In the end, the matter was closed when the vice-consul ruled that the two accused were Piedmontese, not Frenchmen, and could be tried only in Turin.

Belzoni was disgusted and still in pain from his Zabu fall. He was convinced that Drovetti had acted in jealousy and malice. By mid-September he had had enough and put his affairs in order. Giovanni and Sarah sailed for Europe with considerable thankfulness. "Not because I disliked the country I was in, for, on the contrary, I had reason to be grateful; nor do I complain of the Turks or Arabs in general, but of some Europeans who are in that country, whose conduct and mode of thinking are a disgrace to human nature."

236

15 "A Multitude of Collateral Curiosities"

Giovanni Belzoni left Egypt at a moment when interest in Ancient Egypt was at an all-time high. The *Description de l'Egypte* would soon be digested by European antiquaries and gentlemen of leisure. Mohammed 'Ali was favorably disposed to foreigners, and the British and French consuls enjoyed powerful influence with the pasha. As a result it was easier for the wealthy tourist to visit the Nile and sites that hitherto had been accessible only to the adventurous or to official visitors. But few people could emulate the exploits and achievements of the tall Italian. In three short years he had opened up the Second Pyramid and Abu Simbel, discovered a magnificent royal tomb, and recovered both the Young Memnon and a host of fine antiquities for the British consul and on his own account.

Belzoni paused only briefly in Italy before going on to London, where he arrived by the end of March 1820. On the last day of that month the mighty London *Times* announced: "The celebrated traveller Mr. Belzoni has arrived in this metropolis after an absence of ten years, five of which he has employed in arduous researches after the curious remains of antiquity in Egypt and Nubia." The newspaper report went on to announce that Belzoni planned an exhibition of his "beautiful tomb" from Thebes as soon as a convenient hall could be found.

The newcomer was a welcome visitor in London and was lionized by various social hostesses. But his first objective was to publish a book on his travels. The obvious publisher was John Murray of Albemarle Street, probably the most influential English bookman of the nineteenth century, who specialized in travel books written by explorers returning from remote places. (He later published the works of David Livingstone and other African explorers.) It was an opportune time for a book on Egypt. Belzoni's exploits had been widely publicized in the influential *Quarterly Review*. The Young Memnon was being admired in the British Museum, and interest in Egyptian antiquities was running at a high pitch. Belzoni seems to have written his book with extraordinary rapidity, for it appeared before the end of 1820, in two volumes.

Narrative of the Operations and Recent Discoveries within the Pyramids, Temples, Tombs, and Excavations, in Egypt and Nubia; and of a Journey to the Coast of the Red Sea, in Search of the Ancient Berenice; and Another to the Oasis of Jupiter Ammon was an immediate and widely read success. Yet it is a verbose and clumsy book, full of contradictions and curious stylistic usages. Belzoni refused all editorial help, basing the book on his extensive journals. "The public will, perhaps, gain in the fidelity of my narration what it loses in elegance," he wrote in the preface. At

Giovanni Battista Belzoni. The portrait that appears as the frontispiece to his *Narrative*.

238

The Egyptian Hall, Piccadilly, London

times the *Narrative* is fiercely polemical, especially against his French rivals. But the story moves along convincingly, as if the reader was at Belzoni's side, sharing in his extraordinary experiences and supplied with the same nervous energy.

The *Narrative* and the expensive—and now rare—folio of plates that went along with it were well received by the reviewers, who admired the author's courage and devotion to the English cause. The poet Lord Byron was sent a copy by John Murray; he was moved to remark that "Belzoni *is* a grand traveller, but his English is very prettily broken." The *Quarterly Review* was especially polite and discussed the book in a thirty-page article. "But though no scholar himself," the *Review* wrote, "he may justly be considered as a pioneer, and a most powerful and useful one, of antiquarian researches; he points out the road and makes it easy for others to travel over." This was a prophetic statement. The *Narrative* was soon translated into French, German, and Italian, and a second English edition was hastily ordered from the printer.

Belzoni's exhibition was displayed in the Egyptian Hall in Piccadilly, a building that had been designed as an exhibition hall in 1812. By a curious coincidence, the façade of the hall was decorated with moldings in the Egyptian style. The exhibition opened on May 1, 1821, and was an immediate success. Nineteen hundred people paid half a crown each to visit the displays on the first day alone. With a superb touch of showmanship, Belzoni asked a crowd of leading doctors to witness the unwrapping of a fine mummy of a young man "perfect in every part" just before the show opened.

The displays themselves were dominated by two full-sized models of the two most beautiful rooms in the tomb, the pillared hall and another showing five human figures. The plaster of Paris models were taken from Belzoni's wax impressions and colored accurately from Ricci's fine paintings. Here the visitor could witness all the splendor of a royal tomb. The magnificent figures of Osiris, Sethy himself, Horus, Anubis, and other gods were grouped in the halls, together with vivid depictions of the terrible underworld of the dead. Abu Simbel was also reproduced in model form, and a cross section of the Second Pyramid revealed the mysteries of one of the greatest monuments of the Nile. Lion-headed statues of Sakhmet, mummies, papyri, and what the *Times* called "a multitude of collateral curiosities" accompanied the models.

The exhibition placed Belzoni in the forefront of the travelers of his day, largely because he had

240

THE NEW & THE WONDERFUL!

PROFESSOR PEPPER

ALWAYS AT THE

EGYPTIAN HALL

BY
PROFESSOR J. H. PEPPER AND THOS. WM. TOBIN.
Every Evening at 8.   Wednesdays and Saturdays at 3 and 8.

the tangible results of his travels to display in a new and alien environment many thousands of miles from their original and exotic homeland. So great was the success of the show that Belzoni began to lay plans for displays in Paris and St. Petersburg in Russia as well. The London exhibition lasted until 1822, when its contents, including the models, were auctioned off to eager buyers. One client paid 490 pounds for the facsimiles of the tomb and some additional models.

Much of Belzoni's time was taken up in frustrating negotiations with the British Museum over the

241

alabaster sarcophagus from Sethy's tomb. The situation was complicated by Henry Salt, who during 1820 and 1821 was forwarding his magnificent first collection of Egyptian antiquities to the British Museum, in the hope that the trustees would purchase it. He did this in the context of the encouragement he had received from both Sir William Hamilton and Sir Joseph Banks, still a trustee of the museum. But he found the museum lukewarm and the trustees outraged at the price he placed on the collection—around 8,000 pounds. It was obvious, even to the casual bystander, that he was out for a handsome profit by any standards.

The trustees had just paid 35,000 pounds for the Elgin Marbles from the Parthenon, a transaction that had been greeted with outrage and horror in

The main exhibit area of Belzoni's show

The Egyptian Room at the British Museum

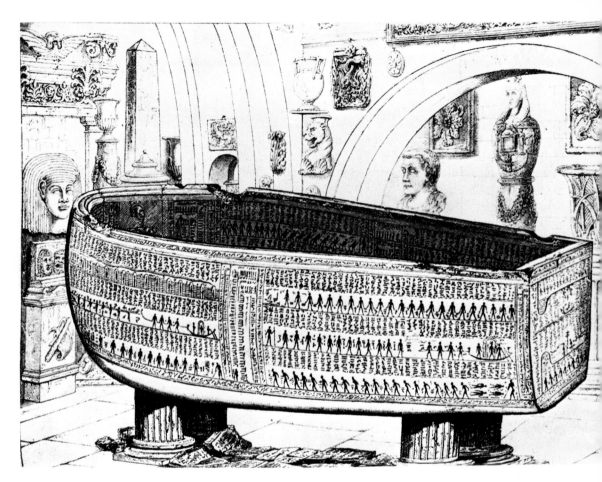

The alabaster sarcophagus from Sethy I's tomb on display in Sir John Soane's house in London

some circles, and they were in no mood to spend more money on foreign antiquities. It was not until the alabaster sarcophagus arrived in London on board the frigate H.M.S. *Diana* that negotiations were reopened. Belzoni now intervened on his own behalf and pointed out that Salt had made over to him half of whatever the sarcophagus raised above a base price of 2,000 pounds. The arguments and memoranda flowed desultorily across the trustees' meeting table for many months, much to Belzoni's frustration and Salt's disgust, for the consul was now in need of money to continue his collecting. He was anxious to re-

244

cover his outlay and make some money to enable him to retire within a reasonable time; "otherwise," he wrote to William Hamilton, "I must be for ever condemned to remain here, which you will allow is no very desirable lot."

Salt ended up spending the rest of his career collecting antiquities and selling them for a profit, practically to the exclusion of his consular duties. In the end, however, he was obliged to sell his first collection to the British Museum for a paltry 2,000 pounds. The trustees flatly rejected the offer of the sarcophagus, sensing both legal difficulties and inflated prices, despite protestations by both Salt and Belzoni that they had received higher offers from Drovetti and other buyers. Eventually the sarcophagus was sold for 2,000 pounds to John Soane, the wealthy London architect and art collector. All the money went to Salt and not a penny to the Belzonis.

The sarcophagus was placed on exhibition in Soane's house, after a wall was breached to admit it to the basement. Three open-house evenings were attended by "the rank and talent of this country, to an immense number," who viewed the sarcophagus as it glowed softly in the light of a solitary candle placed inside it. Sarah attended the receptions and received "every attention from the guests." By this time she was a widow; Belzoni had died miserably some time earlier at the outset of his final and most ambitious journey.

The curious restlessness that afflicted Giovanni Belzoni had caused an abrupt shift in his interests and fortunes. Exasperated with the British Museum, tired of city life and of being a celebrity, he seems to have hankered for a change. Sometime in early 1822 he decided to leave Europe and search for the sources of the river Niger in West Africa. The Niger problem was still one of the great controversies of African exploration and one of more than passing concern to the British government. Several enterprising explorers had been robbed or murdered in their search, and the

Head of an unknown Egyptian found by Henry Salt

government was now resolved to attach individual travelers to trans-Saharan caravans.

Belzoni planned to set out across the Sahara from Morocco on his own account, a venture that failed when the shifting sands of Arab politics left him deprived of critical firmans at the last minute. Eventually he traveled to West Africa, hitching a ride for the last stage of the journey to the Gold Coast on the warship H.M.S. *Singer.* On October 15, 1822, he arrived on the coast and was at the mouth of the Benin River a month later. The journey to the interior began in the company of a merchant named Houston. The pair soon reached Benin itself, where they were kindly received. But Belzoni came down with a severe attack of dysentery. A week later the intrepid traveler was dead.

Belzoni was quickly buried under a large tree. A wooden notice on his grave recorded the date and circumstances of his death and expressed the wish that the grave be kept cleared and fenced. But forty years later, the great traveler Sir Richard Burton could find no trace of the grave, although the local people still remembered the large, bearded explorer who had died among them. It was a pathetic ending to a life that packed more experience and energy into it than most men would into twenty lifetimes. An era in Egyptology had ended with a whimper.

Although Belzoni's work in Egypt had been much admired by both collectors and serious antiquarians, it was difficult for them to break the monopoly over excavations held by the British and French consuls. Henry Salt continued to collect antiquities, writing to a friend that he spent most of his consular time "ransaking tombs, poring over old inscriptions, and learning to decypher monograms, in which I assure you I am become very expert." He remained bitter toward Belzoni to the end, feeling that the remarkable Italian had taken all the credit for the discoveries he, Salt, had financed, and that the British Museum had treated him badly over his collection. His extraor-

dinary bitterness was aggravated by the death of
his young wife of puerperal fever and by his own
poor health. "I have but one wish," he wrote to
his London agent, "never to have my name cou-
pled with his." To cap it all, much of Salt's original work on hieroglyphs was anticipated by the
work of Champollion.

Salt's later collecting activities were managed
by the Greek Yanni Athanasiou, who had worked
with Belzoni and became deeply embittered
against the Italian. Two other major collections
found ready buyers in Europe. The first was assembled between 1819 and 1824 and was sold to
the king of France for 10,000 pounds. It was purchased on the advice of none other than Jean
François Champollion himself, the scholar whom
Salt admired above all others. The last collection
was Salt's largest and auctioned at Sotheby's in
London eight years after his death, in 1835. A total
of 1,083 lots fetched more than 7,000 pounds. In
eleven years of consular work, Salt had made a
collection at a low cost to him from which he had
netted over 20,000 pounds. He did not live to
enjoy his profits, for he died of an intestinal infec-
tion in October 1827, still a lonely consul without
the pension and scholarly recognition he had
craved all his diplomatic life.

Drovetti lived on for many more years and was
reappointed French consul general in Egypt in
1821. He retired for reasons of health in 1829,
after twenty-seven years of residence and collecting in the Nile Valley. Over the years, he sold antiquities to all manner of travelers and assembled
a remarkable collection, which he tried to sell to
the French government. Like Salt, he had considerable difficulty disposing of his antiquities. The
French government procrastinated, largely because
of clerical opposition on fundamentalist grounds.
It was believed that Drovetti's collection would
show that Egyptian civilization was older than
4004 B.C., the established date of the creation, calculated from the scriptures by Archbishop James

247

Ussher in the seventeenth century and accepted as theological dogma. While the clerics and bureaucrats argued and both the English and the Germans made bids, Drovetti finally sold his finds to the king of Sardinia for 13,000 pounds. The French consul also assembled two later collections, the first of which he sold to Charles X of France for a quarter of a million francs. It now graces the Louvre, while Drovetti's last antiquities were bought by the German scholar Richard Lepsius for the Berlin Museum.

Drovetti, who finally died in a lunatic asylum in 1852, was never a great pioneer or expert on Egyptology. His excavation and collecting methods and those of his agents were quite ruthless. The pettiness of his unscrupulous dealings with Arabs, tourists, and colleagues alike made him notorious. But the fruits of his labors, and those of his diplomatic colleagues, grace the museums of Europe and caused a dramatically heightened interest in Ancient Egypt among educated Europeans.

Yet, by a curious twist of fate, the three rival collectors of antiquities—Belzoni, Drovetti, and Salt—whose fierce nationalistic competition had enlivened the burial grounds of Thebes for so long, each enriched the national collections of their rivals' homelands. Belzoni, an Italian, furnished the Egyptian gallery of the British Museum. Drovetti's antiquities formed the basis of the Turin collection, while Henry Salt's efforts greatly enhanced the collections of the Louvre. All reaped the rewards of fame, notoriety, or financial gain. The only loser was Egyptology.

PART THREE: ASSAULT ON ANTIQUITY

The temple of Hat-Hor at Dendereh from the southwest

16   "A Violent Passion"

Where Giovanni Belzoni had pioneered, others
soon followed. He and his rivals had started a
scramble for Egyptian antiquities which soon expanded to a rape of massive proportions. Literally
thousands of collectors, amateur antiquarians, and
curious tourists descended on the Nile during the
twenty years after Belzoni's departure. Many of
them were content to visit and admire, but others
were out for loot, treasure, or simply personal
profit. The names of the most active collectors
have come down to us through their collections,
remnants of which are scattered in the museums
of the world, listed in auction sale catalogs, and
held in private hands. Some of the most acquisitive, and the majority of the most famous dealers
in Egyptian antiquities, are enshrined in that ad-

mirable publication *Who Was Who in Egyptology,* an exhaustive compilation of the saints and criminals of Egyptology.

One important collector was Anthony Charles Harris (1790–1869), an English merchant who lived in Alexandria. He bought and sold fine antiquities, specializing in papyri. His own collection was acquired by the British Museum in 1872, one of hundreds of collections, large or small, assembled in the eighty years between the departure of Belzoni and the end of the nineteenth century. Papyri, mummies, scarabs, even whole temples were removed from Egypt by individuals who were anxious for a quick profit or wanted to gratify a collector's desire to acquire a tangible relic of the Egyptian past, a type of disease described by one French scholar as "a passion so violent that it is inferior to love or ambition only in the pettiness of its aims."

The trouble was that collecting was so easy. Mohammed 'Ali had no cause to legislate against the removal of antiquities, for Egypt had no national museum to keep them in. The Turkish rulers of Egypt had no interest in or identity with the ancient past. To them the antiquities of the Nile were a significant political tool, useful for gratifying eccentric but powerful visitors or diplomats with curious collecting habits. The tangible monuments of Ancient Egypt were merely a source of building stone, or perhaps the site for a modern village elevated above the annual floodwaters.

The museums of Europe were now so eager to obtain Egyptian antiquities that they were quite prepared to ship entire rooms, friezes, or tombs. Forty-five years after Belzoni's excavations the French philosopher Ernest Renan wrote:

Purveyors to museums have gone through the country like vandals; to secure a fragment of a head, a piece of inscription, precious antiquities were reduced to fragments. Nearly always provided with a consular instrument, these avid destroyers treated Egypt as their own

252

property. The worst enemy, however, of Egyptian antiquities is still the English or American traveler. The names of these idiots will go down to posterity, since they were careful to inscribe themselves on famous monuments across the most delicate drawings.

In 1859 another Frenchman, Vivien de Saint Martin, was moved to lament: "Elephantine has been stripped of its lovely temple which exists only in the great work of the Commission. Armant has yielded to a sugar refinery the most beautiful half of the portal. The small temples of Esna, el Kab, the Typhonium of Edfu, the great tomb of Onnofre at Saqqara, half of the Hypogeum of Lycopolis are lost for ever." By that time the secrets of Ancient Egypt had been unlocked by the decipherment of hieroglyphs, and some people had begun to realize the full extent of the awful damage that had been done. But it was too late. Firm government leadership and legislative action had been urgently needed and was sadly lacking even as the *Description* was published.

One of the most notorious cases of monument looting was perpetrated by a French collector, Sebastien Louis Saulnier, and his agent, Jean Baptiste Lelorrain, who removed the famous zodiac relief from the ceiling of the temple at Denderah. The zodiac is a magnificent planisphere which dates from the end of the Ptolemaic period or even later. It represents celestial Egypt, which the Egyptians thought of as a duplication of terrestrial Egypt with the same districts and features.

Saulnier and Lelorrain decided that the zodiac, which had been located by General Desaix during the French expedition, had "in a way become a national monument," and should therefore be moved from Denderah to Paris. Lelorrain arrived in Alexandria in October 1820 prepared to export the zodiac by any means possible. Carefully concealing his real intentions, Lelorrain announced that he planned to try some digging at Thebes. Even so, he had to eject an "observer" from his

boat, a spy planted by Henry Salt to keep a watch on his activities.

Some English visitors were sketching at Dendereh when Lelorrain took his first look at the zodiac. So he went on upstream to Thebes, where he bought a few mummies and other antiquities to cover his tracks. When the French returned to Dendereh the artists had left, so Lelorrain was free to begin his operations. The zodiac lay in the ceiling of the center room of three in a small building near the magnificent temple which Napoleon's soldiers had so greatly admired. The task of removal was a formidable one, for the zodiac was carved on two huge blocks three feet thick. Chisels and saws were the only hand tools available for the operation, so Lelorrain resorted to gunpowder to blow holes in the temple roof. Fortunately his carefully controlled blasts did not bring the ceiling down. Saws were inserted in the jagged holes, and a large force of well-paid Arabs worked day and night to saw through the granite.

Twenty-two days later, the zodiac was dragged down the slope of earth that still filled the building and placed on special wooden rollers for the journey to the waiting boat more than four miles away. Soon the rollers were worn out and Lelorrain had to revert to levers and brute strength to move the sledge to the Nile. At the river the precious sledge slipped off the sloping planks during loading and the zodiac plopped into the soft mud by the river's edge. By prodigious labors the Arab workmen managed to rescue the slabs and load them safely into a boat that was now leaking disastrously. Timely caulking saved the day, for Lelorrain had wisely paid his Arabs exceptionally high wages and they were as keen as he was on seeing the boat safely loaded.

Then the captain refused to cast off. A passing American had seen Lelorrain at work and told Salt, who had arranged for a timely bribe. Lelorrain promptly paid the captain a 1,000-piaster gratuity and started downstream. Halfway to Cairo

The zodiac of Dendereh, as illustrated by Napoleon's savants. From *La Description de l'Egypte*.

255

Thomas Young (1773–1829)

they were stopped by one of Salt's European agents, who presented them with an order from the pasha's grand vizier forbidding Lelorrain to remove the zodiac. Lelorrain ran up the French colors and boldly challenged the English to board his vessel. His bold stratagem worked, and the agent sailed away in ineffectual rage. Salt, who had been on the point of removing the zodiac for himself and William Bankes of obelisk fame, was furious. He pursued Lelorrain to Alexandria and interceded with the pasha, claiming he had dug at Denderah before the Frenchman had even heard of the place and therefore owned the zodiac, but to no avail.

Eventually the zodiac arrived in Paris amid scenes of great enthusiasm. Saulnier and Lelorrain made a handsome profit. They sold the zodiac to King Louis XVIII for 150,000 francs. It can now be seen in the Louvre. The visitor to Denderah must be content with a plaster replica.

The impudent tricks of Lelorrain and Salt were but typical of the antiquarian morality of the times, for people like Saulnier, Drovetti, and Athanasiou were motivated partly by curiosity, mainly by greed, and also by nationalistic concerns. The trouble was that no one had any understanding of what he was seeing or removing, because no one was able to read hieroglyphs. But the Rosetta Stone, with its bilingual inscription in Greek and demotic, and hieroglyphic Egyptian, had rightly been hailed by the savants of the Egyptian Institute, from the moment of its discovery, as a landmark find, possibly the key to decipherment. Wax impressions of the inscriptions were soon circulating in the studies of scholars in several European countries. The Greek inscription was soon translated, and there was general expectation that the hieroglyphic passage would be readily deciphered. But the "picture symbols" were quite meaningless, and no sense could be made of the hieroglyphs. It was hardly surprising, for the scholars were trying to translate the

256

hieroglyphs as individual ideas rather than sounds. The demotic inscription was considered less baffling. It was written, the experts thought, in an alphabetic script of the language of the Ancient Egyptians.

The next stage was to identify the source of the demotic script. Eminent scholars like Sylvestre de Sacy, a well-known French Orientalist, and Jean David Akerblad, a Swede, tried to work out the demotic alphabet, with mixed results. Everyone was feeling very discouraged when Thomas Young, an English doctor with broad research talents in medicine, natural philosophy, mathematics, and languages, became interested in a papyrus shown him by a friend. He obtained a copy of the Rosetta inscription and began a comparison of the demotic and Greek scripts. Eventually, by a combination of systematic comparison of Greek, hieroglyphs, and demotic, and by inspired guesswork, he concluded that demotic was a cursive form of hieroglyphs, a "running script," as it were, of hieroglyphs, bearing little resemblance to the symbolic writing.

But the real credit for the decipherment of hieroglyphs must go to that brilliant Frenchman Jean François Champollion. Champollion was born on December 23, 1790, in Figeac, France, the son of an impoverished bookseller. At the age of five he was able to read. When eleven, he was taken to visit the mathematician Jean Baptiste Fourier, who had been a member of Napoleon's Commission. Fourier seems to have inspired the young Champollion with the desire to break the secrets of hieroglyphs. By the time he was seventeen, Champollion had learned Hebrew, Arabic, Sanskrit, Persian, and other Eastern languages, as well as English, German, and Italian. Soon he was adding Coptic to his repertoire, in the belief that the language of Christian Egypt might have retained something of Ancient Egyptian speech.

In 1807 Champollion went to Paris. While living in great poverty, he studied under the Orien-

Jean François Champollion by Leon Cogniet

talist de Sacy. He pored over the Rosetta Stone
for months, apparently without result. Seven years
later he published two volumes on the geographical place names of Ancient Egypt in which he
proclaimed rather brashly that he could read the
demotic inscription on the stone. He was nearly
right, for he believed that Coptic was the closest
surviving relative of Ancient Egyptian.

In 1819 the *Encyclopaedia Britannica* published
a long article by Thomas Young on Ancient
Egypt, in which he summarized his own attempts
to read hieroglyphs. Although at the time Champollion rejected Young's view that hieroglyphs
were an alphabetic script, two years later he was
moving rapidly toward decipherment, translating
such foreign names as Ptolemy by using Young's
alphabetical approach. Then, in September 1822,
he discovered a cartouche from Abu Simbel in
which he could identify an Egyptian pharaoh's
name, that of Ramesses, and he realized that, in
the case of Egyptian kings' names, the hieroglyphs
were used phonetically, too. Champollion was so
excited that he rushed from his small apartment,
sought out his brother, cried, "I've got it," and
dropped in a dead faint. Within days he was hard
at work again on his famous *Lettre à M. Dacier,
secrétaire perpétuel de l'Académie royale des Inscriptions et Belles-Lettres, relative à l'alphabet
des hiéroglyphes phonétiques*, published on September 27, 1822, in which he announced his discovery. His theories were received both with acclaim and with scorn, depending on one's point of
view about the subject, but independent studies
soon demonstrated that the young scholar had deciphered hieroglyphs beyond all reasonable
doubt. Within two years Champollion completed
his *Précis du système hiéroglyphique*, in which he
finally showed that the script was a mixture of
ideographic and phonetic signs.

Fame and recognition came to Champollion fast.
He was soon appointed a conservator at the
Louvre. Then, in 1828, he was at last able to see

Egypt itself at first hand. Champollion's expedition was a triumph from beginning to end. A party of fourteen including his pupil Niccolo Rosellini, as well as several artists and architects, accompanied the Master on his triumphal journey. It was an electrifying experience both for Champollion and the other members of the party. For the first time they were able to read the inscriptions on the great temples and understand the significance of some of the oldest monuments in the world. Champollion's ideas and the many startlingly revolutionary hypotheses about the significance and context of Egyptian monuments which had welled up in his mind were confirmed again and again by his field observations. At that time he was the only man alive able to comprehend fully the significance of the hieroglyphs and of the magnificent temples and monuments of the Nile.

The expedition traveled upstream in two boats and penetrated far into Nubia, copying inscriptions and works of art at all manner of locations. After three months in Nubia, the enthusiastic scientists came downstream to Thebes and took up residence in the Valley of Kings, commandeering the tomb of Ramesses VI, where they spread their beds amid antiquity itself. But it was Dendereh that was the most overwhelming experience, the very Dendereh that Napoleon's soldiers had saluted in 1799.

Unable to restrain themselves, the members of the expedition rushed ashore from their boats on a brightly moonlit night and stormed the temple in a state of wild excitement. "An Egyptian would have taken us for Bedouins," recalled Champollion. After a tumultuous two-hour march they reached the magnificent temple bathed in moonlight, "a picture that made us drunk with admiration," wrote one member of the party. "On the way we had sung songs to ease our impatience, but here, in front of the propylon, flooded with a heavenly light—what a sensation! Perfect peace and mysterious magic reigned under the portico

259

Niccolo Rosellini's published copy of his drawing of Ramesses II's chariot at Abu Simbel, executed during Champollion's expedition

with its gigantic columns—and outside the moonlight was blinding! Strange and wonderful contrast!" For two glorious hours the travelers wandered through the moonlit temple, drunk with enthusiasm and rapture.

The seventeen months that Champollion spent in the Nile Valley were the climax of a remarkable and intensely productive career. It was not given to Champollion to excavate sites and recover Ancient Egypt from the ground. Rather, he was content to observe the remains themselves and put them into a true chronological perspective. Jean François Champollion had, at one

260

stroke, extended the frontiers of written history by thousands of years into unknown epochs where the origins of Egyptian civilization were to be found.

The prospects for scientific investigation were stupendous, yet all that Champollion saw was destruction and looting. Not that he was above recommending that an obelisk from Luxor be removed to Paris as a memorial to Napoleon's troops. Mohammed 'Ali eventually agreed to the request, although he had originally given the Luxor obelisks to the British. At colossal expense, one of the two obelisks in front of the temple at Luxor was transported to Paris in 1830—on a special barge named the *Dromadaire*. On October 25, 1836, it was erected in the Place de la Concorde in the presence of the king of France and 200,000 spectators.

Champollion also wrote to the Egyptian government deploring the widespread destruction of archaeological sites and the trade in antiquities. He pointed out how many tourists were now visiting the Nile simply to see the monuments and admire the marvels of the past. Tourists meant money, and in the long run a greater profit than that obtained from demolition and looting. He recommended that excavation be controlled, that quarry-

Obelisk from Luxor in the Place de la Concorde, Paris

ing stone from temples be forbidden, and that the exporting of antiquities be strictly regulated.

Champollion's strongly worded pleas had an effect on Mohammed 'Ali's thinking and led to a landmark government ordinance published on August 15, 1835. The preamble of the ordinance noted that museums and collectors were so hungry for antiquities that there was a danger that all traces of ancient monuments would vanish from Egyptian soil to enrich foreign countries. The ordinance forbade all exportation of antiquities, authorized the construction of a museum in Cairo to house antiquities owned by the government or found in excavations conducted by it, made it illegal to destroy monuments, and endorsed efforts at conservation. At the same time Mohammed 'Ali appointed an inspector of museums to travel through Upper Egypt and inspect key sites.

The ordinance was, of course, unenforceable. But it was a start in the right direction, even if the pasha's museum got off to a shaky start and most of the antiquities in it were sold or given to foreign dignitaries by 'Ali and his successors. Excavation was not forbidden, but the ownership of finds was made less certain and export of large antiquities became much harder. The feat of decipherment had given an impetus to serious research into Ancient Egypt that in time gave some credence to the need for conservation of what was, in the mid-nineteenth century, finally recognized as a finite resource. Unfortunately, Champollion himself never lived to see the fruits of his labors, for he died in Paris on March 4, 1832, felled by a stroke while preparing the results of his expedition for publication.

17 "There Is One More Powerful Than I"

While the serious study of Egyptology began with
Champollion and the decipherment of hieroglyphs,
the move toward better records and more careful
analysis rather than destruction and rape of the
past had been gaining impetus since Belzoni's departure. Serious travelers now came to the Nile
alongside treasure hunters, men like the Englishman John Gardner Wilkinson, later to become one
of the founders of Egyptology in Britain. Wilkinson first arrived in Egypt in 1821, where he remained for no fewer than twelve years recording
archaeological sites and studying Arabic and Coptic. Soon he was working on problems of decipherment and correcting Champollion's results.
His first stay in Egypt ended in 1833, by which
year he had completed the first really systematic

**Sir John Gardner Wilkinson
(1797–1875)**

survey of the major archaeological sites of Egypt and Nubia.

Wilkinson, who worked almost single-handed, deciphered dozens of inscriptions and recognized many royal cartouches correctly for the first time. We owe to Wilkinson the first attempts to put the royal dynasties and kings of Egypt into proper order. He made exact drawings of the tomb paintings at Beni Hasan before Champollion and Niccolo Rosellini worked there, identified the long-lost site of the Labyrinth at Hauwareh, and covered the pages of many notebooks with minute and exact records far in advance of those of his contemporaries. Unlike Champollion, Wilkinson worked without government support and achieved miracles with minimal resources.

Wilkinson remains a shadowy figure, for much of his work is still unpublished and no one has written a biography of a man who exercised a pervasive influence on Egyptology for much of the nineteenth century. The educated public at large knew Wilkinson for his famous and monumental work *The Manners and Customs of the Ancient Egyptians,* first published in three volumes in 1837. This was one of the first attempts to write a comprehensive account of the Ancient Egyptians, and it brought the inhabitants of the Nile Valley to life in a wealth of detail never possible before, through their sites, and particularly from their paintings, papyri, and inscriptions. The emphasis was on the religion, culture, and daily life of the Ancient Egyptians rather than on their political history. It was the first study in centuries to look beyond Herodotus and the traditional legends to the Egyptian sources themselves. John Gardner Wilkinson was one of those rare but highly influential scholars with the ability to carry out enormously important basic research while simultaneously possessing the knack of fascinating the general public with more popular accounts of his discoveries.

Wilkinson was not alone in the field. Robert

264

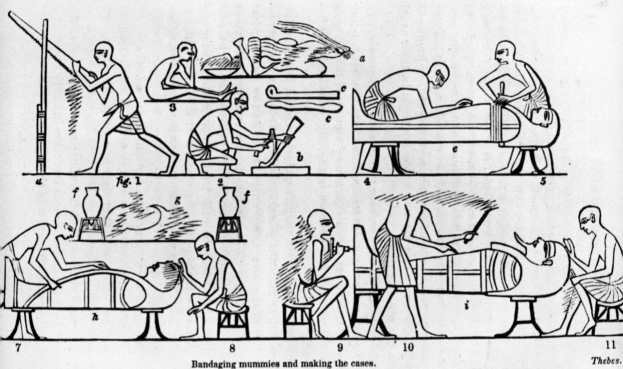

Bandaging mummies and making the cases.

Thebes.

Fig. 1, sawing wood.   2, cutting the leg of a chair, indicating the trade of the carpenter.   3, a man fallen asleep.
ready for cutting.   *d*, onions and other provisions; which occur again at *g*, with vases *ff*.   4, 5, and 7, binding mummies.
   6, brings the bandages.   9, using the drill.   8, 10, and 11, painting and polishing the case.

Hay, a Scottish traveler and antiquarian, first visited Egypt in 1824, after meeting the famous artist
Frederick Catherwood, who was soon to gain im-
mortality for his paintings of lost Mayan temples
in Mesoamerica. Hay was a man of independent
means who developed a great love for the Nile.
For more than ten years, from 1828 to 1839, he
recorded the ruins of the Nile in a systematic
fashion assisted by a series of highly competent
and enthusiastic artists, among them Catherwood;
Joseph Bonomi, who became expert at reproduc-
ing hieroglyphs; and Owen Browne Carter, an
architect employed to plan the major sites. The
work started at Memphis and Gizeh and went on

Mummies—an illustration from
Wilkinson's *Manners and Customs of the Ancient Egyptians*
(1837)

265

Richard Lepsius (1810–1884) in later life

at a leisurely pace, resulting in a huge corpus of invaluable information, most of which remains unpublished among the Hay papers in the British Museum. The descriptions and drawings of the survey team remain a critical source of information on monuments which have been largely destroyed since Hay's time.

Official interest in serious survey work and the recording of hieroglyphs received considerable impetus from the publication of Champollion's and Rosellini's volumes on Egypt, which were enthusiastically received. The king of Prussia became interested in Egypt in 1842, partly as a result of the eloquence of Alexander von Humboldt, the world-famous traveler and naturalist. Karl Richard Lepsius, a thirty-one-year-old lecturer at the University of Berlin, was chosen to lead a three-year expedition to the Nile. The artist Bonomi and James Wild, an English architect, joined Lepsius and his Prussian staff in an exhaustive survey of the major archaeological sites.

The expedition was a great success, largely because Lepsius himself spent a long time in thorough preparation. He visited all the major collections of Egyptian antiquities in Europe, taught himself Champollion's grammar and proved its validity to his satisfaction, and learned lithography and copper engraving before leaving for Egypt. Although the main intention was to survey monuments and collect antiquities, Lepsius did dig at the site of the Labyrinth in the Fayyum and even made accurate drawings of the archaeological layers at the site, a startling innovation for the time.

Lepsius and his colleagues left Egypt with 15,000 casts and Egyptian antiquities which formed the nucleus of an Egyptian museum in Berlin. Lavish publications ensued, including a twelve-volume set of 894 folio plates, *Denkmäler aus Ägypten und Äthiopien,* probably the largest work on Egyptology ever published. Five further volumes of descriptive text were edited after Lepsius's death in 1884. Together, the subsidized publications of the Lepsius expedition represent a magnificent and valuable source on the monuments of Ancient Egypt, still of great use even today.

By the late 1840s, most of the major monuments of Upper Egypt had been surveyed, at least cursorily. Lower Egypt and the delta were still archaeologically unknown, for no one had attempted excavations in the deep sands of the Nile floodplain. But the scientific excavation of Egyptian sites as a whole had hardly begun, except for some accurate planning of the pyramids by Colonel William Howard Vyse, a military gentleman with a strong belief in the Bible and a penchant for using gunpowder to find the hidden entrance to the pyramid of Mycerinus. Egyptologists were, for the most part, concerned with chronology and inscriptions, for major academic controversies surrounded both the dating of Ancient Egypt and the decipherment of hieroglyphs.

Excavation was still largely the domain of the dealer and tomb robber, and the resultant destruction was catastrophic and on an immense scale. The volume of protest against wholesale destruction was still muted and hardly loud enough to be heard, for most major European museums and consular officers were busily engaged in searching for new finds. A few solitary voices were raised, among them that of an American, George Robins Gliddon, at one time American vice-consul in Alexandria and later a well-known author and lecturer on Ancient Egypt whose travels took him as far west as St. Louis. In 1849 he wrote one of the first appeals to the archaeological conscience, an obscure and little-remembered memoir, *An Appeal to the Antiquaries of Europe on the Destruction of the Monuments of Egypt,* which seems to have been largely ignored.

Gliddon's appeal is a long and turgid documentation of the destruction to the monuments of the Nile since the Napoleonic wars, damage wrought by both vandals and antiquarians, but more espe-

The Nilometer by David Roberts, 1846

cially by Mohammed 'Ali and his government.
Philae had remained intact only because of the
turbulent waters of the First Cataract. The Nilometer had lost its steps, taken to build a palace.
Thebes had been decimated ever since Wilkinson's investigations in 1836. Gunpowder had been
used on the Karnak temples, and a small bribe
could obtain sculptured blocks from the portico.
The wooden door on Sethy's tomb, so carefully
erected by Belzoni, was removed by Albanian soldiers after Henry Salt's death. A quarter of the
temple of Dendereh had been quarried away for a
saltpeter factory in 1835. Only the protests of the
French consul stopped the devastation. "Strange,"
wrote Gliddon somberly, "that the Columns
erected by a Hadrian to the service of religion,
should now uphold a distillery for rum!"

Much of Gliddon's wrath was directed at the
pasha, whom he accused of deliberate neglect, exploitation of the temples for building stone, and

Colonel Howard Vyse's excavations at the pyramids, 1835

269

political use of firmans as favors to influential visitors. The irony was that much of the quarried stone was used to construct factories that never went into production.

By the time Gliddon's pamphlet appeared, public opinion had begun to favor some conservation measures. Champollion had complained in 1829; the French Consul Jean François Mimaut, in a new diplomatic departure, in 1839. Lord Algernon Percy, an aristocratic collector, had been moved to comment on the scale of destruction two years earlier, while in 1839–1840 a long list of damage and devastation was cataloged by the British government in a formal report to the pasha. But a public exposé of the situation was delayed in the hope that something would be done by the Egyptian government. This report arose from a major study of consular and commercial activities by diplomats in Egypt compiled by Lord Bowring, which was highly critical of the antiquities trade. When the report was released in 1842, Lord Palmerston excised those parts which dealt with some of the archaeological activities of consuls, although by the mid-1830s diplomats were too busy to spend time on archaeology and the pasha's Antiquities Law of 1835 was at least in existence—on paper.

Gliddon's pompous effusion had little apparent effect on the sins of the tourist or treasure hunter, despite his railings against the hammer-wielding chipper of monuments or the "Anglo-Indian gentleman" who cut bas-reliefs off the walls of Amun-hotpe III's tomb so he could draw them more effectively on board his Nile boat. When the artist had finished, the originals were thrown into the river. Even as Lepsius and his draftsmen were in Upper Egypt, an eccentric French artist and traveler named Achille Constant Théodore Emile Prisse d'Avennes stole to the temple of Karnak and removed the magnificent Table of Kings, a series of carved stone blocks recording the portraits and cartouches of many Egyptian kings. Prisse had no firman and was in open defiance of the antiquities ordinance.

By dint of working at night and in great secrecy, Prisse succeeded in packing the stones into eighteen crates before he was denounced to the governor of Esneh. Prisse's tent was placed under guard until, a month later, he bribed the governor and quietly moved the stones on board a boat after nightfall. On the way downstream he met Lepsius on his way to Karnak and entertained the eminent scholar with coffee as he sat on one of the priceless packing cases. Even the French consul declined to have anything to do with Prisse, whose finds were eventually deposited in the Louvre.

In a sense, one could not blame the museum officials and archaeologists of the day for their cavalier attitudes toward treasure hunting. All around them, they saw the pulverizing of temples and pyramids for building stone, the tourist accosted by the dealer with a handful of antiquities. Surely it was better, they argued, to let scholars and dealers take their precious finds to Europe, where they would be safe from plunder and destruction. As long as there was no museum in Cairo, this position was to some extent a thoroughly defensible one, even more so after the rapid dissolution of the first Cairo Museum in the Ezbekiya Gardens. The pressure to copy and record as well as to preserve by export was strong among respectable scientists of the day.

Thousands of inscriptions and papyri were thrown away, burned, or destroyed in the frantic digging for large antiquities. Every museum in Europe wanted large antiquities, beautiful papyri, or major manuscripts. But no one could be bothered to develop systematic techniques for recovery of material from archaeological sites.

Manuscripts were what brought another young Frenchman to the Nile, with momentous consequences for Egyptian archaeology. Auguste Mariette was born in Boulogne, France, on February

Emile Prisse d'Avennes at the time of his Karnak exploits

271

11, 1821. After an uneventful but happy child-hood, he went to England at the age of eighteen to teach French at a private school in Stratford-upon-Avon. This job lasted a year, an experimental venture at ribbon designing an even shorter time. So Mariette returned to Boulogne and became a teacher at the local college where he had received his own education. He soon discovered he had a talent for writing and spent his spare time preparing articles on all manner of subjects for newspapers and magazines. Until he was twenty-two, Mariette had no exposure to Egypt or to Egyptology. Then in 1842, the father of a recently deceased artist and explorer, Nestor L'Hôte, who had been a member of Champollion's expedition and died on a later desert journey, was transferred to Boulogne. His son had left an enormous mass of papers and copies which urgently needed organization and publication. L'Hôte's father, a customs officer, was related to the Mariettes, and he asked Auguste to examine the papers. Mariette was soon fascinated by the new world that opened up in front of him; he became engrossed by the intricacies of hieroglyphs and decipherment.

Soon he was spending every moment of his spare time with his new hobby and writing an article on the few Egyptian objects in the Boulogne Museum. On the strength of this piece, he got the city to back his application for official support for an expedition to Egypt. This was promptly turned down, so Mariette impulsively resigned his teaching and editing jobs and moved to Paris. There he pored over the Karnak Table of Kings in the Louvre and wrote a closely reasoned seventy-page paper on the inscriptions which impressed the Egyptologist Charles Lenormant at the College de France so much that he obtained a minor job at the Louvre for the energetic young man. Soon Mariette was spending his days cataloging papyri and his evenings reading everything about Egyptology and mastering hieroglyphs to a professional standard.

The temple of Esneh. "The Portico was excavated by Mohammed 'Ali in 1842; not in any spirit of antiquarian zeal, but in order to provide a safe underground magazine for gunpowder."—Amelia Edwards.

Then in 1850 his big chance came. Lenormant continued to approve, and his protégé was soon instructed to collect rare Coptic manuscripts in Egypt. Excitedly, Mariette took ship to Alexandria and contacted the Coptic patriarch in Cairo, only to find him deeply hostile to foreign collectors. Some years before two Englishmen had got some monks drunk and made off with an entire library of manuscripts. He was not about to let any other books out of ecclesiastical hands.

Mariette was momentarily at a loss, for it was clearly profitless to look for manuscripts. So he turned his thoughts toward excavation, for a supplementary clause in his instructions authorized him to excavate archaeological sites to enrich the museum collections. By the end of October 1850 Mariette had gathered some equipment and was camped in the midst of the Necropolis at Sakkareh. He had no firman from the pasha, little money, and only the most limited authority from the Louvre. But he was inspired by the head of a sphinx projecting from the sand, similar to other examples from Sakkareh that he had seen in Cairo and Alexandria. It was then that Mariette's wide reading paid off, for he suddenly remembered that the Greek geographer Strabo had referred to a Serapeum at Memphis, in a sandy place where an avenue of sphinxes leading to the tomb of the holy Apis bulls was constantly being buried under drifting sand. Inspired, he gambled everything and gathered thirty workmen at the sphinx to dig for the Serapeum.

The excavations were immediately successful. Sphinx after sphinx was uncovered as the workers followed the avenue. Tombs, seated statues, a phallic god, and two temples of Apis, one Greek and the other Egyptian, eventually came to light, the latter containing a magnificent statue of Apis. Soon French government funds were running out, but the French consul, Arnaud Lemoyne, was so captivated by the energy of the young man that he advanced him money to con-

The famous Sitting Scribe figure from the Serapeum, found by Mariette. This illustration comes from his *Choix de Monuments* (1856).

tinue while Mariette applied to his superiors for more funds. His gamble paid off, for an increased subvention was soon on its way.

Within a few weeks of the financial crisis Mariette was digging up a huge cache of bronze statues of Osiris, Apis, and other Egyptian gods under the temple floor, a discovery that aroused the envy and fascination of Egyptian and foreigner alike. All Cairo was excited, and the dealers jealous. Soon Abbas Pasha, the son of Mohammed 'Ali, stepped in and tried to confiscate the antiquities, but the French consul smoothed things over and there was a token handover of antiquities. A firman was granted on condition that France renounce all claims to future discoveries, which, since the French government had just voted 30,000 francs to pay for further excavations, caused considerable alarm in Paris.

Mariette was undeterred and went on digging. In November 1851, he finally reached the tomb of Apis, sealed by a magnificent sandstone door. The young archaeologist was soon inside, gasping at the huge granite coffins of the bulls, whose lids had been removed and scattered by tomb robbers. But an enormous amount of material still remained, all of which, under the conditions of the firman, was to go to the pasha's museum, where it would probably be given away, Mariette knew, to distinguished foreign visitors in exchange for political favors. So he resolved on stratagem and set up his packing cases at the bottom of a deep pit whence a secret trapdoor led to the tombs below. For several months Mariette packed the items from his early excavations ceded to France by day and the contents of the theoretically still-unopened tomb below him by night. The finest relics from the Serapeum duly arrived at the Louvre, while Mariette blandly showed disappointed officials the empty tombs he had just discovered.

Over a period of many months Mariette explored the innermost recesses of the Serapeum. He was lucky enough to find an unplundered burial of Apis, deposited in the time of Ramesses II. Even the footprints of the funeral workmen were preserved in the dust of the tomb, while the sarcophagus contained both the undisturbed mummy and rich jewelry and gold. The Serapeum finds caused a sensation in Paris when they were exhibited at the Louvre and brought Mariette fame and recognition all over the world. He was promoted to assistant keeper and soon published a series of plates of the Serapeum, entitled *Choix de Monuments*, that gave a foretaste of what full publication of his excavations might lay before the public.

A perennially restless man like Mariette could never be happy in one place for long. His contacts among Egyptologists were now wide. A warm and gregarious man, he had become a close friend of the German Egyptologist Emil Brugsch, an expert on demotic script. Brugsch came on a chance visit to the Serapeum, and a lifetime of friendship was forged. Both Brugsch and Mariette were convivial souls, full of bonhomie and fond of good living. Although Mariette was never especially revealing about his personal life in Egypt, Brugsch fills in some gaps. He recalled Mariette's mud house at the Serapeum, which teemed with women, children, monkeys, and his laborers. The furniture was Spartan at best. "Bats flew into my cell," complained Brugsch. "I tucked my mosquito net under the mattress and commended myself to the grace of God and all the saints whilst the jackals, hyenas and wolves howled around the house."

One man who was interested in Mariette was that remarkable diplomat and visionary Ferdinand de Lesseps, the genius behind the construction of the Suez Canal. De Lesseps was attracted by Mariette's ambitious and burning energy, and listened to his proposals for saving the monuments of the Nile. He spoke with Said Pasha, the new ruler of Egypt after the assassination of Mariette's old adversary, Abbas Pasha, in 1854. Three years later, the pasha invited the French government to send Mariette to Egypt on the occasion of the visit of the Prince Napoleon to the Nile. It was only when he arrived that Mariette discovered that he was to dig for fine antiquities to be presented to the royal visitor. Mariette did not hesitate for a moment. Money and an official steamer were at his disposal. He started digging at Sakkareh and was soon at Thebes and Abydos, where Brugsch soon joined him in a happy field reunion. The excavations were richly rewarded, but the royal visit was canceled. Fortunately de Lesseps stepped in and persuaded the pasha to appoint Auguste Mariette director of ancient monuments in Egypt and curator of a new museum of antiquities to be built in Cairo. Such an appointment was long overdue and was bitterly opposed by dealers and diplomats up to their necks in the antiquities trade.

Nevertheless, Mariette's position was extremely precarious. He had to depend on the pasha's good will for money. The museum premises consisted of "a deserted mosque . . . small filthy sheds, and a dwelling-house alive with vermin" in which the Mariettes lived. But Mariette was blissfully happy and gathered his family and faithful supervisors around him in an orgy of excavation. Labor was cheap and abundant, for he was able to requisition the entire male population of a village if he wished. His ruthless methods were unpopular, but they certainly produced results. At one point, men were digging under his direction at thirty-seven different locations simultaneously from the delta to the First Cataract.

Mariette's discoveries were extraordinary, but excavated with complete abandon. He was mainly concerned with spectacular finds, which he needed to fill his museum and to satisfy the pasha. Dynamite was among his techniques; careful recording and observation mattered nothing, only objects. More than three hundred tombs were emptied at Gizeh and Sakkareh alone. At Edfu he moved the Arab village off the roof of the buried temple onto the plain and exposed this magnificent shrine to full view for the first time in centuries. At Thebes, Mariette's laborers cleared the buried temple of Queen Hat-shepsut at Deir el Bahri, nearly getting in a fight with the Marquis of Dufferin and Ava, who was quietly removing a large number of carved stone fragments from the temple of Montu-hotpe nearby. The great temple of Hat-Hor, the temple of Amun at Karnak, and more than 15,000 small antiquities were exposed in Mariette's excavations.

Conservation was a new idea, and one that at this point merely implied cessation of quarrying and channeling as many looted and excavated antiquities into official hands as possible. Mariette tried to achieve this by forbidding any excava-

278

tions in Egypt except his own and making exportation of antiquities a virtual impossibility. He made every effort to get funds for a new museum, but his difficulties were formidable. The pasha had no real interest in archaeology. He had ap-

The mortuary temple of Queen Hat-shepsut, Deir el Bahri

Mariette's excavations at the same site

pointed Mariette to appease the powerful de Lesseps and Napoleon III, who, he felt, would be kept quiet by some gesture toward antiquity. He was likely to cut off funds without warning or give away a choice item in the national collections to a favored visitor. The only way Mariette could keep interest alive was by producing a steady stream of gorgeous finds to titillate the pasha's fancy. This, of course, led to a frantic rush for new discoveries, which corrupted the whole course of archaeology on every official excavation, as other Egyptologists later found out to their cost.

Then, early in 1859, Mariette received word in Cairo that the gold-decorated sarcophagus of Queen A-hetep, mother of the pharaoh Ah-mose, had been found intact at Thebes. He also learned that the local governor had seized the coffin, ripped out the jewelry, and sent it to Cairo as a

280

special, and highly political, gift to the pasha. Mariette was incensed and immediately took a steamer upstream with an official order enabling him to stop all vessels on the Nile suspected of carrying antiquities. Passions flowed strongly when the two steamers met. For half an hour the argument raged furiously over the gold, until Mariette in a fury took the law into his hands and laid about him with his fists. One man was nearly thrown in the river, another cajoled at gunpoint, until the jewelry was handed over. Mariette rushed to the pasha, presented him with a scarab and a necklace for one of his wives, and averted a tense political situation. The pasha was so delighted with the finds—and, one suspects, the discomfiture of his governor—that he ordered a new museum built to house the queen's possessions. A new museum building was soon a reality and filled with Mariette's treasures.

Mariette's long career involved him in diplomacy as well as archaeology. For a while the French government used him on a diplomatic mission to persuade Said Pasha to visit France in connection with a financial loan. Mariette disliked his diplomatic role, but eventually accompanied Said to France, where they visited his home town of Boulogne and received a tumultuous welcome. Said was so pleased that he gave Mariette the title of bey and a pension. But this friendship was abruptly cut short by the death of Said Pasha six months later. Bulak Museum was now a showpiece. Mariette was much in demand to escort foreign dignitaries and maintained academic ties with serious Egyptologists all over Europe. He had even closer ties with government officers, dealers, and humble villagers throughout the Nile Valley, contacts that he used to keep an eye on his precious monuments. He worked with an inspired frenzy and was at his desk or out in the field every day at dawn. At lunch or dinner, however, he would relax, for his wife Eleanore maintained an open house, which was always crowded with

The Khedive Ishmail (1830–1895) with his son Tewfik

friends and visitors. Work became the only antidote when his devoted wife died of the plague in 1865. Perhaps it was fortunate that the khedive ordered him to Paris for a year to set up the Egyptian exhibit in the International Exhibition of 1867.

Paris was entranced with the splendor of Mariette's exhibits, which purported to reconstruct life in Ancient Egypt. The collections at Bulak were ransacked for their finest pieces. Queen A-hetep's jewelry formed the centerpiece and sensation of the Paris Exhibition. The jewelry excited the cupidity of no less a regal personage than the Empress Eugénie herself. She promptly intimated to the khedive that she would be graciously pleased to receive the jewels as a gift. It was a great moment for Egyptian archaeology when the khedive temporized, for, he said, "there is one more powerful than I at Bulak. You should apply to him." Neither bribes nor threats could sway Mariette, not even the displeasure of a powerful empress or an indignant khedive. The jewelry returned safely to Egypt.

Preservation was much on Mariette's mind in his later years. "It behooves us to preserve Egypt's monuments with care," he once wrote. "Five hundred years hence Egypt should still be able to show to the scholars who shall visit her the same monuments that we are now describing." Tourists were a thorn in Mariette's flesh. One American tourist in particular aroused his justifiable ire by touring Upper Egypt in 1870 "with a pot of tar in one hand and a brush in the other, leaving on all the temples the indelible and truly disgraceful record of his passage."

Vandalism was a serious problem, too. Ti's tomb at Sakkareh, for example, "suffered more damage by the hand of tourists during the last ten years, than it had during the whole of the previous six thousand years of its existence." Small wonder that Mariette dug up as much as he could to save Egypt's antiquities for posterity. In all, we are

told, Mariette employed more than 2,780 laborers during his career, a number far larger than any one man could supervise at all closely. Workshops for handling the new flood of antiquities were set up at Edfu, Thebes, Abydos, and Memphis, an innovation far ahead of facilities available in other Near Eastern countries.

Mariette's prodigious energies were not devoted entirely to antiquities. He was deeply involved in the glittering ceremonies that accompanied the opening of the Suez Canal on November 17, 1869. His old adversary, the Empress Eugénie, opened

"The Turkish mosque and Palace of the Pasha of Egypt in the Park." A scene at the Paris International Exhibition, 1867.

283

the waterway in the French royal yacht *Aigle*.
Mariette must have gained some quiet satisfaction
in escorting Her Royal Highness up the Nile. The
khedive enlisted Mariette's literary talents for a
quite different task, the writing of the libretto for
Verdi's *Aïda*, a grand opera with an Ancient Egyptian theme composed to commemorate the opening of the canal. Mariette shared this memorable
task with C. du Lode, a fellow Frenchman.

The last decade of Mariette's long career was a
series of archaeological and personal tragedies. Financial troubles dogged his excavations as the
khedive plunged Egypt so deeply into debt that
the British and French deposed him in 1879. The
year before, the Bulak Museum was flooded and
much lost, including many of Mariette's books and
priceless notes on the Serapeum. Although his international reputation grew and he was honored

**"The Cairo Opera House with
the statue of Ishmail Pasha"**

**The opening of the Suez
Canal**

by the Académie des Inscriptions, Mariette's children died one by one, leaving him with a depleted family and little to live for.

A haunting picture of the elderly and quieter man was left by a French nobleman in 1872: "A man of great stature, broadly built, aged rather than old, an Athlete roughed out of the mass like the colossi over which he watches. His deep-toned face has a dreamy and morose look, yet how many times, sitting on the bank of the Nile, did he speak with feeling of this strange Egypt, its river, its nocturnal skies."

After the British and French takeover, life became more settled and at least Mariette's salary was paid regularly. But his health was failing, for diabetes was weakening his formidable constitution. He struggled back to Cairo from Europe in late 1880 and died peacefully in the house by his beloved museum on January 18, 1881. The Serapeum was still unpublished, but the tide had turned. A permanent museum, filled with the glories of Ancient Egypt, had ensured that the course of Egyptology was changed forever and that the rape of the Nile would slow, if never completely cease. A grieving Egypt gave him a state funeral and buried the man it owed so much at the door of his museum.

Auguste Mariette in 1861

A scene from the opera *Aïda* in about 1878

287

18 "In the British Museum He Is Placed beyond the Reach of All Such Evils"

Auguste Mariette's death coincided with a major change in the political scene, sparked both by the khedive's incompetence and by a popular insurrection in Cairo. The British and French governments took an ardent interest in the affairs of Egypt, more so because of the major investments represented by the Suez Canal and other industrial development. At any sign of unrest, Allied warships would appear off Alexandria, as if to remind the Turks that others were the masters of the Nile.

A military revolt in September 1881 resulted in the formation of an abortive popular government which lasted but a year. The British demanded the resignation of the new ministry, nominally headed by the Khedive Tewfik, but in fact led by

288

Ahmed Arabi, a young army officer. Public order deteriorated, and Europeans were assaulted in the streets of Alexandria. So the British sent the Mediterranean fleet and an expeditionary force to the Nile. General Sir Garnet Wolseley and his army made short work of the Egyptians. By September 1882, the British had restored order in Egypt, reinforced with all the authority and panoply of Victoria's mighty armies. A nominal khedive was controlled by the British agent and consul general, Sir Evelyn Baring, later to become Lord Cromer. This powerful and righteous man, a model of calm Victorian authority, effectively ruled Egypt for twenty-four years. Although he had no formal authority over the khedive, his word was law and his policies emanated from London. Lord Cromer was an economist who spent his entire career in Egypt placing that debt-ridden country on a firm financial basis through a series of harsh austerity measures that hit all government departments, including the Antiquities Service, hard. British civil servants took over the running of defense, police matters, foreign affairs, finance, and public works. But the French remained influential in education, the arts, and archaeology.

Sir Evelyn Baring (Lord Cromer) (1841–1917)

The French government had been much concerned at Mariette's failing health and had taken prompt steps to ensure a continuity of French influence over the Antiquities Service. Gaston Maspero, a young Egyptologist and an expert in hieroglyphs, who had become friends with Mariette when a young student in Paris in 1867, came to Egypt two weeks before Mariette died to assume his post at the Bulak Museum. Maspero was born in Paris in 1846, the son of an Italian refugee from Milan. He acquired an interest in Egyptology at an early age and was soon specializing in hieroglyphs, although he did not visit Egypt until he was thirty-four years old.

Maspero was a giant among pioneers of Egyptology, a man whose incredible energy and industry

289

exceeded even that of Mariette. His prodigious talents were turned to all aspects of Egyptology from excavation to hieroglyphs, while his popular works on Egyptology and other subjects were widely read in Europe and had much to do with the emergence of more responsible attitudes toward Ancient Egypt.

Under Maspero's directorship the huge collections of the museum were organized and rearranged. Lord Cromer and Maspero together built up the Antiquities Service from an embryonic organization into a more viable institution with five regional inspectors and exercised regulation of all excavations in Egypt. Some foreign excavators were now allowed to work under the eye of the inspectorate, although the illegal traffic in antiquities and forgeries continued on the side, encouraged by museum and private collectors who were often highly unscrupulous in their methods.

The dealers of Luxor always had a ready market for whatever antiquities were for sale. From the 1860s onwards the tourist traffic through Thebes increased steadily, and the tomb robbers of Kurneh made a comfortable living from the many boats that called at Luxor and Karnak. The supply of mummies and other antiquities seemed almost inexhaustible, especially those supplied by one Ahmed Abd el Rasul and his brother Mohammed which were smuggled into Thebes in bundles of clothing or in baskets of vegetables. What had happened was that Ahmed had accidentally discovered an exceptionally rich cache of mummies and grave furniture at the base of an abandoned shaft into the rocky hillside while looking for a lost goat. For nearly ten years Ahmed and his brother mined the cache for small quantities of fine antiquities which they floated onto the open market a few at a time, to avoid deflating the prices in a rising market. The small items of jewelry bearing the royal insignia that appeared on the Luxor market were soon snapped up by greedy American and English tourists. News of the exceptional

"The Temple of Luxor, restored," Gaston Maspero's reconstruction. "Let us add here," wrote Mariette in a guide to the monuments, "that Luxor is the center of a more or less legitimate traffic in antiquities. . . . Luxor possesses certain manufactories where statuettes, stelae, and scarabaei are imitated with a dexterity which often deceives even the most experienced antiquarian."

purchases reached Gaston Maspero, who sensed that a spectacular find had been made near the Valley of Kings. Many of the pieces which were exchanging hands were unique and of such royal associations that some pharaohs' mummies were obviously involved.

Maspero acted with caution, for Luxor officialdom was far from incorruptible in 1881. First he telegraphed the Luxor police, asking them to keep an eye on local antiquities dealers. Then he dispatched one of his staff to Luxor in the disguise of a rich tourist with money to spend. Maspero's agent quietly bought a few choice pieces to gain the trust of the dealers and soon became one of the obvious people to offer the best antiquities to. One day a dealer brought him a funerary statuette from a XXI Dynasty tomb which was so fine that it could only have come from a royal burial. After extended haggling the agent bought the piece, but not before he had been introduced to Ahmed Abd el Rasul. Both the inquiries of the police and the agent's experience were by now pointing the finger of suspicion both at the Rasul family and at Mustapha Aga Ayat, a Turk who had succeeded in having himself appointed consular agent for Belgium, Great Britain, and Russia, a post that gave him diplomatic immunity and a convenient cover for dealing in antiquities. It was to this man that the Rasul family had sold most of their finds.

While Aga Ayat was immune from prosecution, the Rasuls were not, and the brothers were arrested in April 1881 and sent in chains to the mayor of Keneh for examination. The two men pleaded their innocence with eloquence, pointing out that no antiquities had been found in their houses—they were not that stupid—and producing a swarm of witnesses who swore to the high-minded conduct of the Rasul family. Daud Pasha, the mayor, soon released the brothers, as torture and persuasion had produced no firm evidence, and, one suspects, Daud knew the family only too well. Everyone returned home to Kurneh appar-

292

Gaston Maspero, Emil Brugsch Bey, and Mohammed Abd-el-Rasul at the mouth of the Deir el Bahri cleft. A picture from the *Century* magazine, May 1887. "As we ascended from the tomb, I grouped my companions at its mouth, and once again caused the camera to secure a link of history. Professor Maspero reclined on the rocks at the right; Emil Brugsch Bey stood at the palm-log; and Mohammed was posed in front holding the very rope in his hand which had served in hoisting royalty from its long-hidden resting-place."

ently satisfied. But a massive family quarrel soon erupted over the sharing of the proceeds of the cache, with Ahmed claiming a larger share of the loot to compensate for his suffering under torture. Soon the quarrel became common knowledge around Thebes, and the Antiquities Service started fresh inquiries. Mohammed soon realized that his only route to safety was to confess to everything. Three months after the trial he was back in Keneh, where he confessed all to Daud Pasha, obtained immunity from punishment, and dictated every detail of the family conspiracy into official court records. A few days later Mohammed led a

293

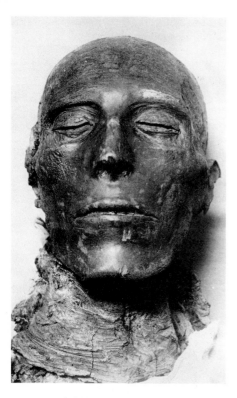

The head of Sethy I. XIX Dynasty.

small party to the site of the cache. Maspero himself was out of Egypt, so Emil Brugsch went along as the official representative of the government. Brugsch was understandably nervous as he climbed the steep hillside to the deep shaft where the cache lay, for he feared reprisals from the villagers. Armed to the teeth, he was lowered down the shaft on a long rope with a supply of candles to light the chamber. Within a few minutes he was confronted by an extraordinary sight, dramatically described by Maspero from Brugsch's report. He had been led to believe that Ahmed's find was a tomb of wealthy officials, but

the Arabs had disinterred a whole vault of Pharaohs. And what Pharaohs! Perhaps the most illustrious in the history of Egypt, Thutmose III and Seti I, Ahmose the Liberator and Ramses II the Conqueror. Monsieur Emil Brugsch, coming so suddenly into such an assemblage, thought that he must be the victim of a dream, and like him, I still wonder if I am not dreaming when I see and touch what were the bodies of so many personages of whom we never expected to know more than the names.

The chamber was scattered with libation vessels of bronze and canopic jars. Coffins of eminent queens were bundled together in heaps.

When he had recovered from his astonishment, Brugsch acted with dispatch. Three hundred workmen were immediately hired to work on the clearing and transportation of the precious finds from their hiding place under the careful supervision of the official party. The government steamer *el-Menshieh* was pressed into service to carry the precious cargo to Cairo. Within forty-eight short hours the first batch of the forty pharaohs and a host of precious antiquities had been loaded on board and were on their way downstream. As the steamer left Thebes, so Maspero tells us, the women followed the boat wailing and the men fired off their rifles in honor of the ancient monarchs. Other, more cynical observers wondered if

294

the locals were bewailing the loss of a highly satisfactory source of income. Later, some of the mummies were unwrapped and archaeologists were able to gaze on the features of the most famous monarchs of Ancient Egypt. Sethy I was the best preserved, with "fine kingly head." "A calm and gentle smile still played over his mouth, and the half-open eye lids allowed a glimpse to be seen from under the lashes of an apparently moist and glistening line, the reflection from the white porcelain eyes let into the orbit at the time of burial." Belzoni would have been both fascinated and pleased that the owner of his most spectacular discovery had survived for posterity.

The incident of the pharaohs' mummies caused Maspero to redouble his vigilance. He employed extra guards and instituted new controls to restrict the activities of dealers and the agents of major European museums who were their principal clients. But this did not deter the European or American museum curator in search of new and spectacular pieces for his public galleries. Many of them resorted to underhand dealing to satisfy their backers.

One of the most flamboyant museum collectors of the late nineteenth century was Wallis Budge, who started his long career as assistant keeper of Egyptian and Assyrian antiquities in the British Museum. Budge was a constant visitor to Egypt, the Sudan, and Mesopotamia, where he bought antiquities for the museum. He was also a prolific excavator and writer. His collection methods can quite simply be described as outrageous. They certainly infuriated Lord Cromer, Maspero, and British as well as French officialdom, an impressive enemy list in the changing intellectual climate of the late nineteenth century, but one that Budge shrugged off under the guise of loyalty to the British Museum and its great aims. This inveterate traveler first visited Egypt on a collecting trip in 1886. He had acquired a working knowledge of Egyptian antiquities and their market value from

Samuel Birch

295

Wallis Budge

the famous Samuel Birch, keeper of Oriental antiquities at the British Museum, who had become a famous Egyptologist without ever visiting Egypt. Armed with this knowledge and 250 pounds, Budge arrived to a dusty reception from Sir Evelyn Baring, who had been greatly irritated by the recent activities of British archaeologists and dealers. Budge was undeterred and determined to work by devious means, through the dealers, if necessary.

Soon he had made useful official and unofficial contacts in Cairo and Thebes. Tombs were cleared, most of them admittedly already half empty. Some of the fine things from them had "somehow disappeared," but Budge was able to lay his hands on quite a few nice pieces. Senior military officers joined his excursions around Aswan; companies of Royal Engineers were mobilized to help in excavations and provide tackle for moving large statues. In one instance, eight hundred Ancient Egyptian skulls were collected piecemeal for a physical anthropologist at Cambridge and stacked at one end of Budge's hut awaiting packing. The hyenas were so eager to get at the heads that they broke into the hut and stole several dozen of them. The only way Budge could export the skulls was by declaring them to customs as "bone manure." "When dealing with customs' officials," Budge remarked, "I discovered that, after all, there is a good deal in a name."

Budge's reputation as a collector was unwittingly enhanced by the field representative of the Bulak Museum, who cautioned all the locals that Budge was a wealthy and unscrupulous collector. So they promptly offered him all manner of antiquities in the privacy of his hut at night. Such was the reputation of the British Museum that the dealers would even give Budge a valuable piece and tell him to send the money from England later. Many of his best acquisitions came through the British consul at Thebes, who introduced Budge to the Rasul family. He was regaled with

296

graphic accounts of the tortures used to extract the secret of the Deir el Bahri cache from them. By the end of the trip he had acquired twenty-four large cases of antiquities which were covertly exported, despite furious objections from Sir Evelyn Baring and the Antiquities Service, simply by placing them under military control. And the military were all for excavation and archaeology, considering, like Budge, the native dealers as reasonable men trying to make a living, and the Antiquities Service a corrupt body whose members sold antiquities for themselves. The trustees of the British Museum passed a special minute in April 1887 commending Budge for his "energy."

Most of Budge's collecting took place in Mesopo-

The Step Pyramid of Zoser at Sakkareh

297

Book of the Dead. Papyrus of
Ani. Ani's heart is weighed
against *ma'et*.

tamia, but his Egyptian exploits were daring
enough. On his next visit to Cairo, the Antiquities
Service had him watched by the police, who were
instructed to report the names of any dealers that
visited him. Nothing deterred, Budge set off on his
buying tour with the police in tow. At Akhmim,
he bought some fine Coptic manuscripts from a
Frenchman who arranged a large supper for the
police while the two collectors transacted their
business.

There were further complications at Luxor.
Budge was taken in the depths of night to a tomb
on the western bank, where an important find of
papyri had been made, including one large roll 78
feet long, a complete Book of the Dead, written
and painted for "Ani, the real royal scribe, the
registrary of the offerings of all the gods, overseer
of the granaries of the lords of Abydos, and scribe
of the offerings of the Lords of Thebes." Budge
recorded the seal on the rolled papyrus and carefully unrolled a portion of the roll. "I was amazed
at the beauty and freshness of the colors of the
human figures and animals, which in the dim light
of the candles and the heated air of the tomb,
seemed to be alive." Several other important
papyri came from the same location. Budge secured the lot, sealed them in tin containers, and
hid them in a safe place.

A few hours later, while drinking coffee with
the dealer who had taken him to the papyri,
Budge found himself under arrest. The Antiquities
Service had placed guards on every dealer's house
in Luxor at the order of Eugène Grébaut, Maspero's successor as director. Grébaut's runner,
who brought the news of the arrest, revealed that
the director's boat was stuck on a sandbank in the
Nile 12 miles away. It so happened that the captain's daughter was being married that day. Naturally the boat could not be refloated successfully.
Grébaut then tried to ride to Luxor, but no donkeys were available, for the villagers drove them
all into the fields so that they could not be hired.

298

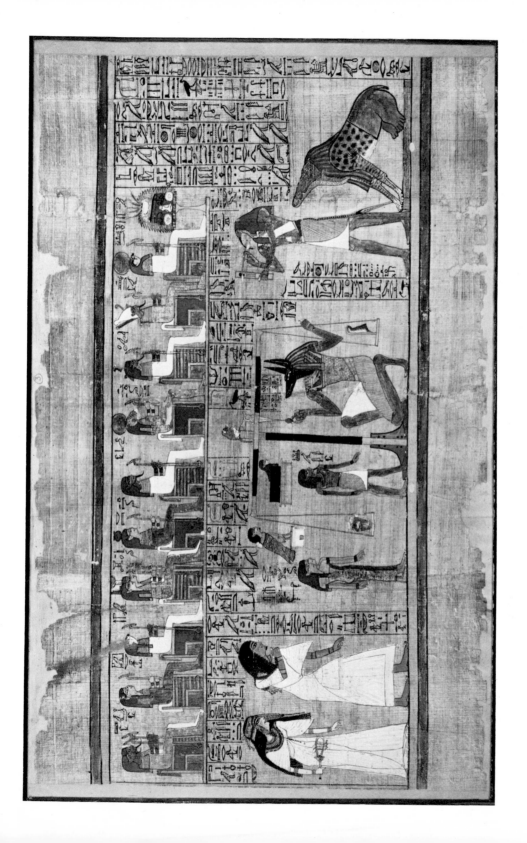

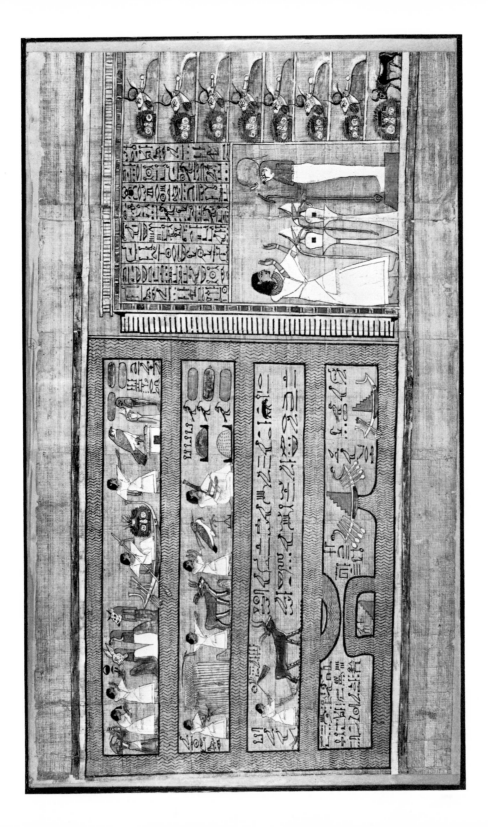

Soon news arrived that the steamer had been re-floated and that Grébaut was on his way. The chief of police now sealed off all the dealers' houses, including a small house abutting onto the wall of the Luxor Hotel, in the basement of which Budge's antiquities had been hidden. At first the dealers tried to get the guards drunk with brandy, but they steadfastly refused to leave their posts. So the dealers commended the guards on their fidelity and promptly resorted to another stratagem. A crew of hefty gardeners entered the hotel garden at sunset, dug a tunnel under the two-foot-thick wall of the hotel that adjoined the house, and entered the basement full of antiquities through a carefully shored-up tunnel. "As I watched the work with the manager it seemed to me that the gardeners were particularly skilled house-breakers, and that they must have had much practice," remarked Budge proudly.

The whole operation was completed in silence, without alerting the guards on the roof of the house, and meanwhile a hearty meal was prepared for their consumption while the antiquities were spirited out through the tunnel. "In this way," boasted Budge, "we saved the papyrus of Ani, and all the rest of my acquisitions from the officials of the Service of Antiquities, and all Luxor rejoiced." One cannot entirely blame Budge for his cynicism. Grébaut's own staff members were selling the antiquities he had collected on the way upstream to local dealers and spiriting them off the steamer while the director ate dinner. Budge was soon in Cairo, where, with a final touch of irony, he managed to arrange for the police, who were watching him, to carry his precious boxes of papyri and tablets into Cairo. The very same day the papyri were on their way to England in official military baggage.

Budge's activities were perhaps only typical of many European museum officials of the time. He developed a healthy contempt for the Antiquities Service and its servants. Although he got on well

Other scenes from this famous papyrus

301

A barber's shop in Cairo

with Maspero, and sometimes worked in collaboration with the museum, his relationships with dealers over the years proved far more rewarding. Even the *Egyptian Gazette* disapproved of Budge, describing him as being "well known as a somewhat unscrupulous collector of antiquities for his museum." His tactic was to pay fair prices and to spend plenty of money. Dealers were encouraged as they ransacked pre-Dynastic cemeteries after scientific digs had been completed. Coptic manuscripts, acquired after "much talking and coffee drinking," made the British Museum one of the finest repositories of Coptic materials in Europe.

Despite stricter enforcement of antiquities regulations by an infant service that was now growing into manhood, Budge's expeditions were models of illegal purchase, excavation, and what can only be described as dubious archaeological tactics. His rationale for wholesale removal and purchase of

302

antiquities was simple: he was attempting to prevent the destruction of Ancient Egypt. "The principal robbers of tombs and wreckers of mummies have been the Egyptians themselves," he wrote. "The outcry against the archaeologist is foolish, and the accusations made against him are absurd. . . . If one archaeologist won't buy, another will, and if no archaeologist will buy, then the owners of the mummies will break them up and burn them piecemeal."

Then, in a splendidly pompous piece of logic, he went on: "Whatever blame may be attached to individual archaeologists for removing mummies from Egypt, every unprejudiced person who knows anything of the subject must admit that when once a mummy has passed into the care of the Trustees, and is lodged in the British Museum, it has a far better chance of being preserved there than it could possibly have in any tomb, royal or otherwise, in Egypt."

After a lengthy description of the dreadful fate which could await a mummy, he continued: "The Egyptian prayed fervently and unceasingly against all these possible, nay probable, evils, as any one can see who takes the trouble to read the charms . . . buried with him. In the British Museum he is placed beyond the reach of all such evils." Furthermore, Budge added, the identity and deeds of the mummy would acquire far more exposure through public but safe display, photographs, guides, and picture postcards. In enlisting the support of the Ancient Egyptians themselves, Budge flattered himself that he had moral right on his side and that looting Egyptian sites was entirely legitimate, provided something was left in the Egyptian collections for the local people to gaze upon and study.

19   "A Boating Trip Interspersed with Ruins"

By the second half of the nineteenth century, Egypt had become a fashionable place for a winter vacation among both the wealthy and the less affluent. Regular steamship service between Italy and Alexandria, with a schedule that was as regular as clockwork, now made it possible to travel in three and a half days a distance that had taken the fastest Roman galley six days. By 1872 the tourist could travel from Alexandria to Cairo by train before taking a small steamer up the Nile to Aswan and Philae. Most of the major Nile monuments could be glimpsed in three weeks by tourists with limited time to spare and no inclination for the more leisured journey by dahabeah, which took three months and was ideal for the artist wishing to camp among the ruins. A trip up the Nile,

Lady Lucie Duff-Gordon (1821–1869)

thanks to Thomas Cook and other pioneer travel agencies, became a safe if slightly exotic experience, rather like some of the widely touted package tours to remoter parts of our own shrunken world.

But for many visitors Egypt was still the "donkey-ride and a boating-trip interspersed with ruins" epigrammatically described by the French archaeologist Jean Ampère. Such tourists came to be entertained and informed, traveling in a single chartered dahabeah, or sometimes, like Belzoni's friend Lord Belmore half a century before, in a convoy of hired vessels. Those with time to spare often went as far south as Abu Simbel. The dry climate of Egypt also attracted some permanent residents, too, émigrés from dank European Novembers determined to nurse weak chests and extract some grim enjoyment from the desert scene.

One such involuntary émigrée was the formidable Lady Lucie Duff-Gordon, who settled at Luxor in a ramshackle residence known as the French House. Her ruined and Spartan dwelling was perched on the roof of a temple near the Nile. From 1863 to 1869 Lucie Duff-Gordon surveyed the local scene, entertained both the great and the lowly, and assimilated herself into local peasant society to an extent that shocked many of her contemporaries. She wrote a steady stream of lively letters to her family, which were published in two widely read volumes that achieved great popularity. They are remarkable reading, unusual for their humility and careful perception of local society. The outrageous deeds of the pasha's government and the hideous oppression of the common man were exposed with tart comment and pitiless detail that heightened public reaction toward excesses. At the same time the trivial domestic round of harvest and famine, of dust storm and interesting visitor, came to light in a charming way that captivated her audience.

The Duff-Gordon letters, a revelation to people unfamiliar with the teeming life of the Nile's

306

banks, caused quite a stir. Antiquities were to her as much part of the landscape as the people. She met an old foreman who had worked for Belzoni and visited Sethy I's tomb in the Valley of Kings. In one letter to her husband, who had thanked her for the gift of a lion, she admitted she "stole him for you from a temple, where he served as footstool for people to mount their donkeys. A man has stolen a very nice silver antique ring for me out of the last excavations—don't tell Mariette. . . . My fellah friend said, 'Better thou have it than Mariette sell it to the French and pocket the money; if I didn't steal it, he would'—so I received the stolen property calmly."

By 1870, three hundred American tourists were

"Lady Duff-Gordon's house on the roof of the Temple at Luxor before the excavations"

307

registering at the consulate in Cairo in a year. Mark Twain had recently published his *Innocents Abroad,* a widely read and at times entertaining account of his travels. Time was short, and he only managed the pyramids and the Sphinx before turning for home. Yet he admired the lushness of Egypt, "the boundless sweep of level plain, green with luxuriant grain, that gladdens the eye as far as it can pierce through the soft, rich atmosphere." One member of his party tried to hammer a memento off the face of the Sphinx, but Mark Twain was content with accusing the Egyptians of feeding mummies to their railway engines. Seventeen years before, the French novelist Gustave Flaubert had enjoyed a bawdy and somewhat riotous voyage up the Nile and had been less polite. He accused the inhabitants of Edfu of using the temple as a public latrine and suffered from the fleas.

The Suez Canal had transformed British knowledge of Egypt, for Cairo became a stopping-off point for the passenger on his way to years of service in India. Shepheard's Hotel in Cairo, described caustically by Mark Twain as "the worst on earth except the one I stopped at once in a small town in the United States," became the popular Mecca of the leisured traveler in Egypt. Its services included excursions to the pyramids and every luxury for the jaded tourist, despite Mark Twain's strictures. Almost half those who stayed there were Anglo-Indian civil servants or military personnel on their way to and from India. The remainder were winter residents, or tourists on a short visit. One such short-term visitor in November 1873 was Amelia B. Edwards, popular novelist, lecturer, and passionate traveler, a tourist whose perception of Ancient Egypt influenced that of thousands of Victorians.

Amelia Edwards was one of that now extinct breed of prolific romantic novelists whose literary output more than compensated for the lack of radio and television a century ago. During her sixty-one years, an immense number of articles,

Exploitation of the peasants. The digging of the Suez Canal by forced labor. Lady Duff-Gordon did much to make the public aware of the pasha's excesses.

Shepheard's Hotel in Cairo

lectures, books, reviews, and pamphlets streamed
from her facile pen. The daughter of an army
officer who served under the Duke of Wellington
in the Peninsular War, she showed a remarkable
talent for writing and drawing in childhood and
possessed a fine voice of potentially professional
standard. Her first poem was published when she
was seven.

Ultimately Amelia Edwards became a journalist,
contributing articles on all manner of subjects to
popular periodicals such as *Chambers's Journal*
and *Saturday Review.* Eight novels flowed from
her pen between 1855 and 1880, and she edited

310

popular books on history and art, most of which sold well and allowed her to live the life of leisured travel and writing which was the right of a successful author a century ago.

An interest in history and early civilization led Edwards to an extended tour through Syria and Egypt in 1873–1874. The trip changed her life and led to her best-known book, *A Thousand Miles up the Nile,* published three years later. *A Thousand Miles* was a deservedly popular travel book which went through several editions and displays Edwards's lush writing style at its best. She describes a typical, fairly luxurious trip to the Second Cataract in two dahabeahs. The party consisted of five English gentlefolk, traveling in company with two English ladies in another craft. They seem to have been typical "Nile-goers,

A dahabeah. "Some are luxuriously fitted up, room even being found for a piano."

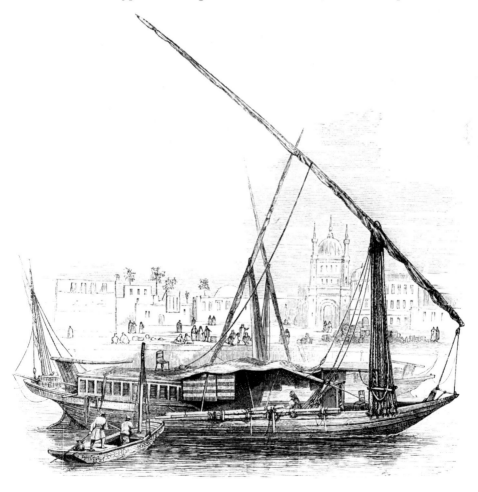

Amelia Edwards (1831–1892)

young and old, well-dressed and ill-dressed, learned and unlearned," eager for any new experience, and, like so many Victorians, secure in their own society and conscious of the superiority of its values, religion, and morals over those of "foreigners" and certainly the Egyptians.

Amelia Edwards made full use of her river journey and wrote a book which in places is delightfully evocative both of the unchanging Nile scene and of the tourist life of a century ago. *A Thousand Miles* is informative, yet bears its knowledge lightly. The facts are accurate, carefully checked by Samuel Birch of the British Museum and by Wallis Budge (who regarded the lady with some distrust). But her own impressions come through strongest. Her feelings in the Great Hall at Karnak flow out in vivid prose, as she compares the columns to a grove of huge trees:

But the great trees, though they have taken three thousand years to grow, lack the pathos and mystery that comes of human labor. They do not strike their roots through six thousand years of history. They have not been watered with the blood and tears of millions. Their leaves know no sounds less musical than the singing of birds, or the moaning of the night wind as it sweeps over the highlands of Calaveros. But every breath that wanders down the painted aisles of Karnak seems to echo back the sighs of those who perished in the quarry, at the oar, and under the chariot-wheels of the conqueror.

Edwards was entranced by the fine view of the island as their boat approached the temples of Philae.

The tourist at large: a burial chamber by torchlight in the Serapeum of Memphis

The approach by water is quite the most beautiful. Seen from the level of a small boat, the island, with its palms, its colonnades, its pylons, seems to rise out of the river like a mirage. Piled rocks frame it on either side, and purple mountains close up the distance. As the boat glides nearer between glistening boulders, those sculptured towers rise higher and even higher against the sky. They show no sign of ruin or of age.

312

All looks solid, stately, perfect. One forgets for the moment that anything has changed. If a sound of antique chanting were to be borne along the quiet air—if a procession of white-robed priests bearing aloft the veiled ark of the God, were to come sweeping round between the palms and the pylons—we should not think it strange.

The party made their way by the now well-known river journey to Abu Simbel and the Second Cataract. An eighteen-day stay at Abu Simbel was broken by a four-day excursion to the Second Cataract, where they followed in Belzoni's footsteps and climbed the rock of Abu Sir. The summit of the rock was carved with the names of dozens of visitors, including Giovanni Belzoni. Unlike the Italian, Edwards and her companions enjoyed "draughts of ice-cold lemonade" from a goatskin at the summit.

But it was Abu Simbel that made the greatest impression. Every morning Edwards rose to greet the sunrise and the miracle of daylight at Abu Simbel. "Every morning I saw those awful brethren pass from death to life, from life to sculptured stone. I brought myself almost to believe at last that there must sooner or later come some one sunrise when the ancient charm would snap asunder, and the giants must arise and speak."

The travelers cleared a small painted shrine with the aid of fifty locals and experienced for themselves the excitement of original discovery, gazing on paintings which had been covered up for centuries. Like Belzoni, more than fifty years before, they had some hectic bargaining with the kachif, who had to be content with "six pounds for his men, and for himself two pots of jam, two boxes of sardines, a bottle of eau-de-Cologne, a box of pills, and half a sovereign."

By the time of Edwards's visit Abu Simbel was positively crowded. At one point there were no fewer than three sketching tents pitched at the great temple and a fleet of dahabeahs ranged

314

along the shore. Everywhere along the river there was bustle at the temples and major monuments. At Thebes there were many boats, "gay with English and American colours." American and English tourists were most commonly met with, but Germans, Belgians, and French were also encountered. The dealers of Luxor flocked to each boat as it moored.

They waylaid and followed us wherever we went; while some of the better sort—grave men in long black robes and ample turbans—installed themselves on our lower deck, and lived there for a fortnight. . . . There we always found them, patient, imperturbable, ready to rise up, and salaam, and produce from some hidden pocket a purseful of scarabs or a bundle of funerary statuettes. Some of these gentlemen were Arabs, some Copts—all polite, plausible, and mendacious.

The Rock of Abu Sir. "We found Belzoni's name," wrote Amelia Edwards, "but looked in vain for the signatures of Burckhardt, Champollion, Lepsius, and Ampere."

315

The landing at Aswan

Earlier Edwards had been shocked by the change in tourist attitudes toward "antikas," including her own. The violated graveyards at Sakkareh came as quite a shock, but, she wrote,

we soon became quite hardened to such sights, and learnt to rummage among dusty sepulchers with no more compunction than would have befitted a gang of professional body-snatchers. These are the experiences upon which one looks back afterwards with wonder, and something like remorse; but so infectious is the universal callousness, and so overmastering is the passion for relic-hunting, that I do not doubt we should again do the same things under the same circumstances.

316

The dealers at Thebes now did a roaring trade, not only in genuine antiquities, the best of which were reserved for really wealthy collectors and the agents of foreign museums, but also in forgeries. Everything was grist for the forgers' mill— inscribed tablets, alabaster statuettes, and, of course, scarabs, antiqued by feeding them to turkeys as a bolus, a process from which they "acquire by the simple process of digestion a degree of venerableness that is really charming." A frenetic pace of excavation and forgery caused Luxor to hum. The illegal excavators lived in fear of the governor, but carried on their illicit trade as they had done for centuries. They dwelt among the

Towing the dahabeah

The tourist at large—"in an Egyptian street"

tombs, as they had lived in Belzoni's time, driving donkeys or lifting water during the day and excavating in the tombs at night. Everybody had "antikas" to sell, from the turbaned official on a commercial visit to the "gentlemanly native" encountered at dinner with a scarab in his pocket.

The forgers were in big business, but they lived in constant fear of discovery by the tourist. Quite by chance Edwards and a companion wandered

318

into a forger's workshop while looking for a consulate. They were admitted to a large, unfurnished room where three tables were strewn with scarabs, amulets, and funerary statuettes in every stage of completion. The tools of the trade lay around the unfinished objects, together with a large mummy case used for the wood. No one was in the room, but a few minutes later a well-dressed Arab arrived breathlessly and ushered his unwelcome guests out of the house, explaining that the consulate had been moved. "I met that well-dressed Arab a day or two after," wrote Edwards, "and he immediately vanished round the nearest corner."

By this time the Antiquities Service was maintaining a small gang of official excavators in the burial grounds, under the superintendence of the governor. The mummies they found were forwarded to Bulak unopened. One day Edwards was able to witness the discovery of some burials. Early in the morning the visitors rode out to the Ramesseum, crossing the Nile by boat and then eating their breakfast on donkeyback as they rode across the plain. It was a gorgeous morning. The young barley shimmered and rippled for miles in the morning sun, and the Colossi of Memnon glistened in the freshness of the new day. Wild flowers were ablaze in the barley. It was a memorable excursion, heightened by the discovery of a carved sarcophagus the moment they arrived at the excavations. The mummy was in almost perfect condition, deposited in a brick-lined vault. The governor himself was supervising the excavations, and invited Edwards to lunch with him in a nearby tomb, now converted into a stable where the mummies were temporarily stored. The lunch consisted of sour milk and "a tray of the most uninviting little cakes," and it was eaten to the accompaniment of reeking manure.

Edwards seems to have declined refreshment, for the party lunched in the Ramesseum, one of many jolly lunches in the leisured Egypt of a cen-

tury ago. Rugs were spread among the columns. Waiters flitted to and fro. At a decent distance milled a crowd of hopeful vendors, the "brown and tattered Arabs," each with a string of forged scarabs, pieces of mummy case, or fake statues to sell. Here, as throughout the voyage, the respectful (and not so respectful) natives paid court to the representatives of civilization vigorously maintaining their standards in the wilderness.

The tourist life of a century ago reverberates solidly through the lush pages of Amelia Edwards's tour de force. We are suitably entranced, educated, enlightened, and shocked through its pages. Once returned to England, she plunged into a whirlwind of activity, lecturing to clubs and societies and writing article after article about her experiences on the Nile. She professed horror at the vandalism and destruction of the temples and tombs of Ancient Egypt, deplored the lack of sound excavation techniques, and was grief-stricken over the destruction of temples by quarrymen.

Although Amelia Edwards's pen was a powerful weapon in molding public opinion about Ancient Egypt, there was already a devoted interest in things Egyptian among the educated public. Country gentlemen purchased the most learned monographs on Thebes; historical novels featuring the pharaohs sold tens of thousands of copies; books linking the archaeology of Ancient Egypt with the biblical story were popular birthday and Christmas gifts. Interest in all the early Classical and prehistoric civilizations was at fever pitch, thanks to the work of Heinrich Schliemann at Troy and of Austen Henry Layard and others in Mesopotamia. A Classical education was still considered to be an essential attribute of an educated person, as was a thorough knowledge of the scriptures. Egypt figured prominently in both, and everyone was excited by pyramids, mummies, and the hieroglyphic controversies. Long before Amelia Edwards's time, Egyptology, thanks to Wilkinson,

"Digging for mummies." Amelia Edwards recalled that "it gave one a kind of shock to see it first of all lying just as it had been left by the mourners; then hauled out by rude hands, to be searched, unrolled, perhaps broken up as unworthy to occupy a corner in the Boulak collections."

Lepsius, and other scholars, as well as thousands of religious tract writers, was having an increasing impact on the popular culture of Europe, on architecture, fashion, and, to a lesser extent, on serious literature. Unfortunately, many of these literary efforts were grossly misleading, for it was almost impossible for a middle-class Victorian writer with narrow and well-defined cultural values to understand contemporary Egyptian culture, let alone that of the Ancient Egyptians.

Amelia Edwards took up the cudgels on behalf of scientific archaeology in an incredible burst of literary productivity that lasted from her return from Egypt until her death in 1892. Three years after her return from the Nile *A Thousand Miles* was published to popular acclaim. A stream of articles and progress reports on Egyptology appeared in dozens of journals and newspapers under the Edwards name, arguing that the only solution to the orgy of destruction that called itself archaeology was systematic recording of monuments and properly scientific excavations. Amelia Edwards was so concerned that she stopped writing fiction altogether and concentrated on Egyptology to the exclusion of other topics. Her efforts, after public disinterest, were granted a polite interest.

Professional Egyptologists in England were, however, deeply concerned about the state of affairs on the Nile. An abortive attempt to found a Society for the Protection of Ancient Buildings in 1880 had come to nothing. But in March 1882, Amelia Edwards conceived the idea of an Egypt Exploration Fund designed to carry out scientific excavations in Egypt. She managed to assemble a group of powerful backers, among them Reginald Stuart Poole, a distinguished Orientalist, and Sir Erasmus Wilson, a well-known surgeon who had financed the transportation of the obelisk known as Cleopatra's Needle from Alexandria to London. This enterprise had cost 10,000 pounds, a colossal sum in those days. A prestigious meeting at the

British Museum resulted in the foundation of the
Egypt Exploration Fund under the presidency of
its major benefactor, Wilson. Edwards and Poole
became the secretaries. Advertisements were
placed in prominent newspapers announcing the
formation of the group, appealing for funds, and
giving details of sites to be explored. The objectives of the Egypt Exploration Fund were: "to organize expeditions in Egypt, with a view to the
elucidation of the History and Arts of Ancient
Egypt, and the illustration of the Old Testament
narrative, so far as it has to do with Egypt and
the Egyptians." The Egypt Exploration Fund was
among the first organizations to apply for excavation permits, with serious research and potential
publication as the primary objective, not looting
and spectacular finds.

The crew of a dahabeah making music. "For the crew no
sleeping accommodation whatsoever is provided. They roll
themselves up in their *bur-
nouses* and lie down on the
foredeck like bundles of old
clothes, for which I have not
infrequently mistaken them."

The erection of Cleopatra's Needle in London, September 1878

1. The obelisk on September 11
2. Windlass to lower the base of the obelisk
3. Obelisk descending to a vertical position on September 12
4. The obelisk erect on its pedestal

In the 1880s archaeological excavation was still a highly unscientific pastime, a form of licensed—or unlicensed—destruction that concentrated on large and impressive finds rather than the careful examination of a site and its contents. The objective was to find as much as possible in as short a time as practicable. Mariette's field techniques had been horrifying and quite unscientific. So were those of Maspero and many other respected early Egyptologists. Flinders Petrie, a British pioneer of modern excavation methods on the Nile, used to lecture with ghoulish horror about Mariette's digs and techniques. It is fair to say that Mariette was typical of his age, and Petrie was no paragon by modern standards. But change was in the air. The spectacular discoveries of Austen Henry Layard and others in Mesopotamia, the decipherment of cuneiform hieroglyphs, Richard Lepsius's meticulous researches, and, above all, Heinrich Schliemann's wonderful finds at Troy and Mycenae had painted a vivid picture of Mediterranean civilization. Now German scholars were following in Lepsius's footsteps and adopting much more rigorous excavation and recording procedures. A mass

Launching Cleopatra's Needle at Alexandria, 1877

of new and highly significant information had emerged from the more careful excavations of recent years, as field archaeology gradually matured from a treasure hunt into an exact science.

There had been some more careful pioneers in Egypt, too. A quiet Scotsman named Alexander Henry Rhind had planned to pursue a sedate career at the Scottish bar. But ill health forced him to winter in Egypt in 1855. Rhind spent two seasons at Thebes searching carefully for a complete and undisturbed tomb which he could excavate and record in detail, for he deplored the fact that "attention was given almost exclusively to obtaining possession of the relics without sufficiently careful reference to the circumstances under which they were discovered." The devastation and havoc wrought by Drovetti and Salt at Thebes was such that there seemed to be little chance of locating more than a few undisturbed tombs. Finally he located a solitary sepulcher "in which the response of the last occupants had remained entirely unbroken."

Rhind excavated the site with considerable care. He left a step-by-step description of his dig, the contents of the tomb, and the position of the objects in the grave. He recorded the robbing of the tomb and its reuse and the identity of the last people to be buried there. The papyri found on the bodies gave him the names of the deceased, and the whole excavation was carefully described in his book *Thebes: Its Tombs and Their Tenants* (1862).

Unfortunately Rhind died at the early age of thirty on his way home after a third journey to Egypt. Although he was not the first man to describe an undisturbed Egyptian tomb, there is no doubt that Rhind would have become one of the great archaeologists of Egypt had he lived.

The members of the Egypt Exploration Fund chose a Swiss archaeologist, Henri Edouard Naville, as their first excavator in British Egypt. Naville had learned his Egyptology from Lepsius.

326

By the time he was invited to work for the Fund, Naville had already acquired a European reputation. His first excavations were at Tell el Maskhuta in the delta, near the new Cairo-Suez canal. The trustees of the Fund had made a deliberate decision not to work in Upper Egypt, but to concentrate on the unknown delta areas where spectacular results might be expected.

Naville's excavations at el Maskhuta aroused considerable public interest. For years the site had been regarded as one of the two cities built by the Israelites for Ramesses II, settlements known as Ramesses and Pithom. A link with the scriptures was definitely an objective of the first season, and one that Naville purported to obtain. He uncovered the remains of a temple, part of a city, fortifications, and a military camp, dating the settlement to between the fifteenth century B.C. and the fourth century A.D. It seemed that Ramesses II had built the city, but there was no sign of the Israelites. Naville studied the artifacts from the city and decided that the Egyptians had dedicated it to the god Atum, from which it was an easy step to "Pi Atum" or Pithom. The trustees were delighted; they touted Naville's sensational discoveries in a loud voice, hoping for increased public support and more abundant funds. Although many Egyptologists refused to accept Naville's conclusions, the public was convinced that modern archaeology had strengthened the authenticity of the scriptures.

Naville was possessed, like so many early Egyptologists, with an extraordinary energy and capacity for hard work. He preferred to excavate large monuments and temples, for his training had been in the rather crude traditions of Mariette and Maspero. But he was a man of formidable intelligence and strong views, whose work placed the Egypt Exploration Fund at the forefront of serious research organizations. His excavations at Wady Tumilat in 1885–1886 and Bubastis in 1886–1889 were the subject of considerable interest.

An Egyptian princess. The frontispiece of Georg Ebers' most famous novel.

This famous archaeologist continued to work for the Fund until 1913, carrying on a running feud with German Egyptologists. A broadly built, jolly man, Naville, although trained by the German Lepsius, detested the Teutonic ways of scholarship, with their detailed classifications and card indexes.

Despite memorable academic feuds, the German school made magnificent contributions to Egyptology in the late nineteenth century. Many German Egyptologists owed their early training not only to Richard Lepsius but also to Georg Moritz Ebers, professor of Egyptology at Leipzig. Ebers, a prolific writer on Egyptian subjects, was also an able teacher. But his great contribution was a series of popular historical novels with Ancient Egyptian themes, the most famous of which, *An Egyptian Princess* (1864), was translated into sixteen languages, and sold more than 400,000 copies by 1922. Ebers's Egyptian princess was quite a character, courted by Cambyses, startlingly beautiful and sensitive, regal and yet human, the perfect heroine for the suppressed maidens of his time. They could not fail to admire a princess whose "royal purple added to her beauty, the high flashing tiara made her slender, perfect figure seem taller than it really was." Ebers made careful use of the narrative to introduce accurate descriptions of Egyptian artifacts and customs as background color. His florid romances were read by all lovesick young ladies at the turn of the century.

Adolf Erman, director of Egyptian Antiquities in the Berlin Museum, was a man whose influence on Egyptology has been described in *Who Was Who in Egyptology* as "cyclonic and the greatest since Champollion." Erman, predominantly a philologist, altered the grammar and teaching of Egyptian linguistics to the extent that existing ideas on Ancient Egyptian were completely revolutionized. He showed the relationship between Ancient Egyptian and archaic Semitic languages, divided Ancient Egyptian into Old, Middle, and Late versions, and was a pioneer in providing accurate interpretations and translations. In a sense, Erman was a polymath of Egyptology, for he was interested in archaeology and history as well as languages. One of his most important works was his *Daily Life in Ancient Egypt,* a brilliant account of the Ancient Egyptians which drew almost entirely on Egyptian sources and is still widely read today.

Many events were conspiring to bring archaeology in Egypt to the threshold of a dramatic change for the better. The tremendous authority of the French and German Egyptologists and their dramatic linguistic achievements, much-improved communications, and a flood of new information about the Ancient Egyptians were all pointing up the need for accurate and well-recorded archaeological information. Ebers's novels were widely read, and Amelia Edwards's articles and books were avidly devoured by a public better informed on Egypt than ever before. The mighty flag of the British Empire flew over the Nile, ensuring a stable political environment for excavation and scholarship.

Amelia Edwards toured the United States in 1889–1890, speaking about the work of the Fund and enlisting American support for the excavations. Her tour was a great success, her lectures well received. "Since 1883," she wrote, "the French in Upper Egypt, the English in Lower Egypt, have labored simultaneously to bring to light the buried wealth of the most ancient of nations." She went on to state confidently that there were "more ancient Egyptians under the soil of Egypt than there are living men and women above it." Six years before, the Egypt Exploration Fund had engaged a young Englishman to excavate for them in the delta, an association that lasted but three years. The young man, Flinders Petrie, was destined to become one of the seminal figures in archaeological excavation in the Nile Valley.

Adolf Erman (1854–1937)

20 "Inscriptions, Objects, Positions, and Probabilities"

The site of one of Mariette's excavations. "Everywhere one hears the tootling of pipes and the sound of voices."

Flinders Petrie was born in 1853, into a family with a long tradition of travel, casual scientific inquiry, and surveying. His formal education was largely neglected, but the young Petrie picked up an excellent practical knowledge of surveying and geometry from his father. He was soon walking around the English countryside, armed with his father's sextant and a looking glass, plotting prehistoric earthworks. "I used to spend five shillings and sixpence a week on food, and beds cost about double that," he wrote. "I learned the land and the people all over the south of England, usually sleeping in a cottage." All this was invaluable experience for Petrie's later life in the desert, as were his hours of browsing among coins and books in the British Museum.

Both Petrie and his father had long nurtured a strong interest in the pyramids of Egypt, partly from reading the astronomer Piazzi Smyth's *Our Inheritance in the Great Pyramid,* a notorious speculative work on pyramidology which the young Petrie bought by chance at the age of thirteen. Father and son planned an expedition to make a more detailed survey of the Great Pyramid than had ever been attempted before. They cut their teeth with Stonehenge in 1872, producing a plan that was the definitive effort for many years. Then Flinders Petrie left for Egypt in November 1880, embarking on a new life at the age of twenty-seven. To his great regret, his father never joined him on the Nile, preferring a quiet life of research and reflection at home. After a stormy passage, Petrie and his instruments arrived at Alexandria a month later. Within a week, he was comfortably ensconced in a rock tomb at the pyramid of Gizeh. Permits were no problem, since he had no plans to excavate, and he was thus independent of Mariette and the Egyptian Antiquities Service.

Petrie's pyramid survey was a novel undertaking by Egyptian standards. He spent many weeks setting up accurate survey points and studying the construction of the pyramids. There was ample leisure to observe the excavation methods of the redoubtable Mariette and his colleagues.

Mariette most rascally blasted to pieces all the fallen parts of the granite temple by a large gang of soldiers, to clear it out instead of lifting the stones and replacing them by means of tackle. . . . Nothing seems to be done with any uniform and regular plan, work is begun and left unfinished; no regard is paid to future requirements of exploration, and no civilized or labor-saving devices are used. It is sickening to see the rate at which everything is being destroyed, and the little regard paid to preservation.

The Englishman's survey work soon attracted attention among more serious archaeologists.

332

Many visitors found their way to his sepulcher home, among them the great General Lane Fox Pitt-Rivers, a pioneer in meticulous excavations, who strongly encouraged Petrie's efforts. Petrie was particularly amused by the pyramid cranks and their measurements; one of them even tried to file down the granite to conform to his specifications.

In the intervals between surveying, he collected potsherds and small objects. Maspero told Petrie to take out small objects in his pockets, as they would not be searched. Perhaps it was just as well that Maspero was so casual, for Petrie was now convinced that the smaller objects, such as glazed pots, held some of the keys to Ancient Egypt. It was this conviction and the sickening destruction around him that convinced Petrie that he should turn his attention from survey to excavation. His survey work had received the approval of the Royal Society, and he now applied to the Egypt Exploration Fund for financial support. Everyone was against the unknown maverick at first, including the formidable Amelia Edwards. But his pyramid work carried the day, and the Fund reluctantly agreed to some sponsored but unfunded research. Soon Petrie was writing to Edwards: "The prospect of excavating in Egypt is a most fascinating one to me, and I hope the results may justify my undertaking such a work. I believe the true line lies as much in the careful noting and comparison of small details, as in more wholesale and off-hand clearances."

Egyptian archaeology was in a parlous state. Petrie, who had become aware of the gaps in archaeological knowledge through contacts in the British Museum, was shocked. Samuel Birch, the Orientalist, begged him to bring back at least a box of pottery from each of the "great sites," to use as a means of developing an Egyptian chronology. "A year's work in Egypt made me feel it was like a house on fire, so rapid was the destruction going on. My duty was that of a salvage man,

333

to get all I could, quickly gathered in, and then when I was sixty I would sit down and write it up." Nothing had any meaning to the archaeologists of the day except an inscription or a sculpture. Precision was unknown, looting still commonplace.

Petrie was soon back in Egypt, excavating at Tanis and other sites, including Naukratis, "where the whole ground is thick with early Greek pottery, and it seemed almost a sacrilege to walk over the heaps with the fine lustrous black ware crunching under one's boots." Unlike most of his predecessors, Petrie employed his laborers directly and housed them, to prevent blackmail by the sheiks, who wanted to act as intermediaries and force the men to pay them to let them work. The result was that many of his labor problems were drastically reduced. He soon found that Mariette had used different methods, for the Frenchman had simply requisitioned laborers from local villages, leaving his foremen to collect the levies. So the foremen promptly drafted the richest villagers, who had to bribe them to be exempted. Eventually the poorest laborers were hired compulsorily and marched off to work. Most local excavations were haphazard affairs. "An Arab's notion of digging is to sink a circular pit, and lay about him with his pick hither and thither, and I have some trouble to make them run straight narrow trenches," wrote Petrie. His own methods, while better, would horrify many modern archaeologists. There were three categories of worker: trenchers, shaft sinkers, and stone cleaners. Each group was supported by a small gang of earth carriers. Petrie's notion was to maintain better supervision of the labor force, although it is difficult to see how he achieved this. He even employed girls as pick workers. "One of them is rather a boistrous damsel, and how she paid out the old man she had to work with! She slanged him unlimitedly, and kept time to her tongue by banging him with her basket."

334

Work started at 5:30 in the morning and continued until 6:30 P.M., except for a rest period during the heat of the day. Petrie would retire to his tent for breakfast and watch the excavations with a telescope. Otherwise, he was always on the site keeping an eagle eye on the workmen. In contrast, Mariette had visited his dig once every few weeks, ordering the clearing of large areas before his next visit. The foremen were given total charge and made huge profits by bribery and levying labor. They were terrified that excavations would be abandoned if they were unproductive. When their digging did not produce enough results they promptly went to the Cairo dealers and bought sufficient numbers of small antiquities to keep Mariette's interest alive. Important finds were kept back until a psychologically opportune moment, and then produced out of context with a strict profit motive in mind. It was small wonder that the Cairo Museum's boast that they obtained everything found from foreign excavations was, at best, regarded by everyone as a hollow bluff.

Petrie's excavations yielded useful results. He cleared part of a temple and great enclosure built by the pharaoh Psouseunes I, XXI Dynasty, and discovered a large quantity of pottery and baskets full of papyri, some of which were later mounted between glass and translated. Many of his finds were exported to England and placed on exhibit in the Royal Archaeological Institute. Even more significant, Petrie spent the passage home writing up the results of his work for prompt publication. Amelia Edwards was constantly asking for copies of his working journals, from which she wrote attractive articles on Petrie's fieldwork for the London *Times*. It was an auspicious and successful beginning to a lifetime of excavation in Egypt and Palestine.

Although Flinders Petrie's excavations were much more strictly supervised than those of his predecessors, his techniques were still rough and ready by modern standards. Huge labor forces

The forecourt of the temple of Sethy I at Abydos

moved mountains of archaeological deposits. At the Naukratis excavation in 1885, Petrie employed 107 men with only two European supervisors to watch over them. So many small objects were recovered that small change ran out and complicated accounts were needed to keep track of the baksheesh paid to the workmen for their finds. Basically Petrie was buying the contents of the site in competition with the dealers, as all serious excavators had done before him. He tried to regulate the traffic by paying fixed prices for different categories of object. If the finder refused Petrie's price, then the object was refused, a policy that was reasonably successful.

It was at Naukratis that Petrie discovered the critical importance of accurate dating of objects and the strata they came from. After a time he developed such a good rapport with the workmen that accurate dating of many accidental finds was possible. He began to date temples and other structures by correlation with the layers of foundation deposits under the buildings. Many of the objects found in the soil packed into deep foundation trenches were coins or inscribed ornaments which could be precisely dated, once their context was accurately established. This was a real innovation, never tried in Egypt before.

In 1887 Petrie headed an important archaeological expedition to the Fayyum. By now he had severed his connection with the Egypt Exploration Fund and was operating as an independent agent. His main objective was the pyramid of Hauwareh, which Belzoni had admired nearly seventy years before. Working conditions were uncomfortable. Petrie camped in a small tent. "Imagine," he wrote, "being limited to a space six and a half feet long, and about as wide as the length. . . . Besides bed I have nine boxes in it, stores of all kinds, basin, cooking stove and crockery, tripod stand . . . and some antiques; and in this I have to live, to sleep, to wash, and to receive visitors." Important mummies were stored under his bed for safety.

The large number of workmen engaged seemed to like the work: "There is a constant tootling of pipes, singing, clapping, shouting, and general jollity going on." A tunnel into the center of the pyramid was combined with a detailed survey of the monument. Nothing came from the tunnel, for the diggers reached a massive chamber roof which was impenetrable with the time available for excavation. But by this time Petrie was more interested in the Roman mummies coming from a nearby cemetery, which he dated to A.D. 100–250. The mummies bore remarkable portraits painted in colored wax on their wood panels, portraits that had been hung on the wall of a house during life and then bound to the mummy after death. The deceased were kept in family vaults near the

home for at least a generation and then moved in batches into pits in a large cemetery near the pyramid.

The splendid collection of portraits was shipped, together with sixty crates of other finds, to Bulak Museum, where everything was dumped outside to rot in the spring rains. Much to Petrie's disgust, the museum kept all the best portraits and most of the fine textiles. But he was able to mount a fascinating exhibition of the exported portraits and mummies in a large room of the Egyptian Hall in Piccadilly, the very same hall used by Giovanni Belzoni for his celebrated exhibition. Indeed, one of the more aged visitors to the exhibitions was able to recall the original show and the giant Italian. Petrie's exhibition was a great success and thronged with large crowds. Egyptology had truly become a respectable and widely appreciated science.

The following season saw Petrie back inside the pyramid. He also found a German treasure hunter hard at work in the Fayyum with official sanction. Petrie learned that the German had had little success so was turning his eyes toward the sites that Petrie had planned to investigate in a few weeks; he was forced to put two men digging at the Illahun pyramid tombs and two more at Ghurab in order to stake out a claim. The supervision of these additional sites involved him in a 17-mile walk twice a week, exercise that Petrie described as "very unsatisfactory." It took a month to break through the roof of the Hauwareh burial chamber, which turned out to be fashioned from a solid block of quartzite, 20 feet long, 8 feet wide, and 6 feet deep. Two empty sarcophagi lay in the chamber, which was waist high in water, but a cartouche bearing the name of Amun-em-het III (c. 1800 B.C.) soon established the ownership of the tomb.

The Hauwareh excavations continued with the clearance of the original entrance of the burial chamber. All the passages were clogged with mud,

A bas-relief from Flinders Petrie's 1894 expedition. "Weighing the precious metals. Frankincense trees in pots."

339

**Mummy of Artemidorus, a
Greek settler**

and Petrie had to strip off his clothes and slide through, making measurements on the way. Eventually gangs of men were organized to clear the defiles, and the original doorway of the pyramid was located. A magnificent collection of *ushabtis* and a large sarcophagus came to light in a burial chamber 40 feet deep in the pyramid. All the finds were waist deep in water so salty that even a drop caused the eyes to smart. Petrie removed the *ushabtis* from their storage place by lying in the water and using his feet to dig. The sarcophagus proved even harder to move. Bolt holes were drilled in the lid, and the men hauled on rope tackles as Petrie, submerged up to his nose in the salt water, cleared the sand around the sarcophagus with his feet. "I was hauled up looking 'like a buffalo' as the men said," he recalled. The coffin was eventually moved into the light, where Petrie did not have to wade waist deep "amid rotten wood and skulls."

The hectic season of 1888 continued with work at el Lahun and the workmen's town of el Kahun, built in the XII Dynasty to house the families of those building the pyramid. Petrie cleared many houses, finding copper tools, lamp stands, pieces of wooden furniture, and flint sickles as well as other domestic trivia, which enabled him to build up a picture of the average workman's life during the XII Dynasty. Previous excavators on the Nile had indulged a preoccupation with large monuments and tombs, at the expense of the archaeology of towns and villages. The finds from the Kahun dig provided much of the basis for Adolph Erman's famous book *Daily Life in Ancient Egypt*, published in 1895.

The finds at Ghurab were less spectacular, but the town site yielded invaluable dating evidence. The town was partially cleared, especially a large walled enclosure close to the temple which seemed to have been occupied by foreigners. Petrie noticed some foreign pottery on the surface and was soon finding other shards of a similar

type in houses. It turned out to be Mycenaean ware, of the type found by Schliemann at Mycenae in Greece and by others on the Aegean islands, conclusive evidence of contacts between the Nile and the Aegean as early as 1500 B.C. Three years later, Petrie was able to visit Mycenae for himself, where he recognized actual Egyptian imports which belonged to approximately the

The Egyptian Hall in Victorian times. A little more dilapidated, but still in use by the Egyptologists.

341

The plaster bust of Queen Nefertity, XVIII Dynasty (1355 B.C.). The famous bust found at Amarneh.

same period—the XVIII Dynasty—as the Ghurab finds. He declared that the Egyptian imports gave a date for the beginnings of Mycenaean civilization of about 2500 B.C., with the later stages of the civilization dating to around 1500–1000 B.C. This was one of the first examples of the refined use of the technique of cross-dating, whereby imported objects of historically known age were used to date archaeological sites in countries a long

342

way from the actual point of origin of the imports. This technique is still widely used by European prehistorians.

Mycenaean archaeologists were enthusiastic. Petrie's own pupil Ernest Gardner declared that Petrie had "done more in a week than the Germans had done in ten years to clear up the matter from an Egyptian basis." The chronology stood unchallenged for many decades and formed an important basis for Sir Arthur Evans's chronological work at the palace of Minos in Crete. For the first time an archaeologist had realized that Ancient Egyptian civilization had not flourished in isolation, but had enjoyed commercial relations with many other societies, relations that would be reflected in the archaeological record.

An alabaster sphinx of XVIII to XIX Dynasty age excavated by Petrie

Unlike earlier collectors, Flinders Petrie had a broad comparative knowledge of Near Eastern and European archaeology. He moved in a comfortable circle of cultivated and well-versed scholars who were generalists rather than specialists, deeply interested in a wider world than merely that of their own site, or the Nile alone. The Schliemanns, Evanses, and Petries of the late nineteenth century enriched one another's academic researches by a constant interchange of visits and informal discussions, as well as by trading artifacts and corresponding with a Victorian alacrity that leaves the busiest twentieth-century scholars in awe of their work schedules.

Petrie was well aware of the fame that was now coming his way, but he seemed more concerned with loftier goals. "So far as my own credit is concerned," he wrote to a friend at the end of the season, "I look mostly to the production of a series of volumes, each of which shall be incapable of being altogether superceded, and which will remain for decades to come—perhaps centuries—as the sources of facts and references on their subject." This was a contrast to his predecessors who rarely bothered to publish anything or to record the provenience of their finds.

Petrie was acutely aware of the need for records, descriptions, and more records. He felt that he brought five specific skills to his work, which he set down publicly: first, "The fine art of collecting, of securing all the requisite information, of realising the importance of everything found and avoiding oversights, of proving and testing hypotheses constantly, as work goes on, of securing everything of interest not only to myself but to others." Second, "The weaving a history out of scattered evidence using all materials of inscriptions, objects, positions, and probabilities. . . ." He listed material culture, archaeological surveying, and "weights" as his other specialties. Prompt publication, accurate plans, excavations, and records, and precise chronology were the primary

344

goals of all Petrie's work, a striking contrast to Mariette, who took forty years to publish anything about the Serapeum.

Meanwhile, Petrie was getting drawn into the political arena in Cairo over the thorny issue of excavation permits and the export of antiquities. Since Mariette's time, French interests had dominated antiquities administration. According to Petrie, the administrative structure was both corrupt and incompetent. Permits were given to dealers and unqualified excavators. The museum was in a shocking state. The staff was disinterested and left valuable mummies and sculptures in crowded passages and in the open air to rot and decay. Several staff members were covertly in league with Cairo dealers. On one occasion Petrie actually witnessed a transaction between a leading dealer and a keeper at the museum whom a friend had observed "with his arms full of paper parcels." "The Museum had curious ways of doing business without cheques," remarked Petrie.

By this time, however, there was a rising outcry in England against the destruction of monuments in Egypt, largely as a result of Petrie's exhibitions and Amelia Edwards's eloquent lectures and writings. A Society for the Preservation of Monuments was soon formed, with powerful backers. They proposed the appointment of an independent inspector from England, a proposal that was quashed by the French.

The trouble could be laid to an Antiquities Committee, dominated by the French and particularly by Wallis Budge's old adversary Grébaut, who was in league with the dealers— or at least Petrie so alleged. The Committee promptly responded to Petrie's scheme by introducing new regulations for the export of antiquities which made it quite impossible for any foreign expedition to work in Egypt. Even Petrie was prevented from digging, at which point "the fat was in the fire, and letters, howlings and questions in Parliament were all coming thick," wrote Petrie

345

with glee. "Intense political pressure ensued, the result of which was stricter but more realistic regulations, which defined more closely the specifications regarding exportation, insisted on publication, and made it harder for dealers to make sizable profits."

Petrie's next excavation was at Tell el Amarneh, where he discovered the magnificent painted pavements and frescoes of the heretic pharaoh Akhen-Aten's palace, and the remarkable "Amarneh correspondence," which he described in his *Ten Years' Diggings*, published in 1892. The painted pavements were so important that Petrie arranged for a building to be erected over the palace pavement, which measured about 250 feet square. A walkway was erected over the paintings so that visitors could pass through without damaging the art. Tourists flocked to see the paintings, which were some of the first domestic Egyptian palace art to be exhibited. However, the Department of Public Works never built a path to the exhibition shed, and the visitors trampled down valuable crops. So one day an angry peasant hammered the paintings to fragments and all was lost. Fortunately Petrie had followed another of his basic precepts and recorded the scenes in color and black-and-white drawings on one-tenth scale. It was at this site that Petrie first met, and supervised the work of, a young man of seventeen named Howard Carter, who was later to make history in the Valley of Kings with his discovery of the undisturbed tomb of Tut-ankh-Amun.

Britain's greatest Egyptologist had begun his work with no financial support at all. But in 1892 Amelia Edwards died, leaving her money to endow a professorship of Egyptology at the University of London. Flinders Petrie was the first holder of the chair, an appointment he celebrated with the discovery of pre-Dynastic Egypt.

For years, Egyptologists had been puzzled at the apparent lack of ancestors for Dynastic civilization on the Nile. It was thought that the first

Funerary offerings to the Queen Hat-shepsut. Found by the Petrie expedition in 1894.

347

rulers of a unified Egypt had arrived in the Nile Valley from Mesopotamia, bringing their distinctive civilization with them. Then in 1894 Petrie got wind of a vast cemetery near the town of Nekadeh where numerous skeletons accompanied by pottery and other grave furniture were coming to light. The pots found with these skeletons were quite unlike those associated with Old Kingdom graves, but were skillfully made and the work of a well-established Egyptian culture. At first the newly appointed professor thought that the burials were those of Libyan invaders, but he soon realized that the cemetery had been filled in prehistoric times, and he set out with his usual gusto to excavate it. Nearly two thousand graves were uncovered in the 1894 season alone. A few years later a royal grave found at Nekadeh itself provided a link between the prehistoric burials and the culture of the earliest Dynastic peoples. So the roots of Ancient Egyptian civilization were now traced back to prehistoric cultures in the Nile Valley, and the migration theories of earlier times fell into disrepute. As always, Petrie developed his own methods to clear the cemetery.

Boys were sent to hunt for soft places in the ground; so soon as they had cleared round the edge of a tomb pit they were moved on. Then ordinary men were put on to clear the pit until they should touch pottery in position. Next first class men were put in to clear round the pottery and skeleton, but not to move anything. Lastly the skill of Aly Suefy came in to remove every scrap of earth and leave the pits, bones and beads, all bare and exposed.

The pottery from the graves was carefully studied by shape and decoration. Petrie found that there were gradual changes in the shapes of vessels and particularly in the handles on a certain type of jar. These changed from functional designs, obviously for daily use, to more decorative forms and finally degenerated into a series of painted lines. Similar jars came to light at Diospolis Parva and other pre-Dynastic sites, again associated with characteristic grave furniture.

Aerial view of Amarneh

The archives at Amarneh during excavation

349

The palette of Narmer, which shows the legend of the unification of Egypt

Columns at the temple of Sethy I at Abydos

Eventually so many graves were found that Petrie was able to build up a series of "stages" of characteristic grave furniture groups, to which he assigned "sequence dates," based on the stylistic changes in the pots. His earliest stage was "ST 30," for he rightly assumed that he had not yet found the earliest pre-Dynastic societies. Fifty

350

Sir Flinders Petrie arranging an exhibit of Palestinian pottery in London

stages later he came to "ST 80," which coincided with the beginning of Dynastic time. These sequence dates provided the first attempt at a chronology for prehistoric Egypt and were applied by Petrie and others to finds throughout the length of the Nile Valley.

Petrie regarded sequence dating as one of his major contributions to archaeology. "This system enables us to deal with material which is entirely undated otherwise; and the larger the quantity of it the more accurate are the results. There is no reason now why prehistoric ages, from which there are groups of remains, should not be dealt with as surely and clearly as the historic ages with recorded dates." This optimistic statement appeared in Petrie's *Methods and Aims in Archaeology*, published in 1904, a book in which he enumerated his fundamental rules of excavation, honed

352

by many seasons of self-instruction in the Nile Valley. In fact, later research has shown that sequence dating is nothing more than a refined form of ordering undated finds. But, for its time, it was a bold and revolutionary attempt to place Egyptian archaeology on a better chronological footing.

Petrie's zestful researches took him the length and breadth of the Nile Valley. He kept up a running battle with the Antiquities Service and the museum, whose relationships with dealers he strongly distrusted. His autobiography, *Seventy Years in Archaeology*, is replete with stories about the sins of his French colleagues. One Gallic archaeologist worked the royal tomb at Abydos, kept no plans, and boasted that he "burnt up the remains of the woodwork of the Ist Dynasty in his kitchen." His finds were scattered among his financial partners in Paris and sold by auction. A succession of incompetent directors of Antiquities had followed Gaston Maspero, and things came to a head when Victor Loret, the latest of an incompetent line of officials, casually remarked, when told of an example of pillage, "That's impossible! There's a law!"

Eventually Maspero was appointed to a second term as director at the princely salary of 1,500 pounds a year and expenses. He allowed Petrie to go to Abydos to clear up the mess. He promptly found the tombs of four of the eight kings of the I Dynasty and a queen, identified them, and cleared more than three hundred graves of their servants as well. Even more remarkable was the publication record. The work at Abydos began in November 1899 and was completed in March 1900. By June 22 of the same year Petrie had completed the proofs of the index. The published report was available almost as soon as the finds were ready for display, surely a record for archaeological publication. The I Dynasty finds were duly exhibited in London, and Petrie at last noticed a difference in public attitude. "A new public feeling appeared; instead of only caring for things of beauty or remarkable appearance, people hang over the tables, fascinated by the fragments of the Ist Dynasty. Some workmen would spend their whole dinner hour in the room."

The tussles with dealers and tomb robbers continued throughout the earlier part of Petrie's long career. Abydos was a bad spot for pillagers. While Petrie was engaged in tracing twelve successive rebuildings of the great temple by examining minute differences in trench wall colors, the locals had other things on their minds. One man succeeded in removing a statue weighing more than 100 pounds from the courtyard of Petrie's house. He was tracked down by the distinctive impressions of his feet in the ground and arrested, but got off by bribing the police. On another occasion a man loitered outside the Petries' mess hut at night and fired a pistol at Mrs. Petrie from point-blank range. Fortunately the bullet missed.

Extraordinary precautions were taken during the excavation of a plundered tomb at el Lahun in 1914. The sarcophagus in the tomb was empty,

Sir Flinders Petrie on safari in Palestine at the age of 83. Petrie and his wife (in helmet at left) had just completed a 1,200-mile journey in the old green bus in the background.

and Petrie did not expect to find anything dramatic. But a few rings of fine gold tubing came to light at the side of the sarcophagus. Immediately Petrie dismissed the men and left only a single trusted workman in the trench, joined by Guy Brunton, one of Petrie's students. Together they carefully removed the soil from the gold and began to uncover a spectacular treasure. Brunton lived in the tomb day and night, gently extracting all the objects from the soil without damaging them. Each item was carefully washed and photographed before being packed away. Petrie was so anxious to avoid pillage that he warned all his party not to talk or write about the gold hoard. The collection turned out to be a royal treasure of the XII Dynasty. It was finally bought by the Metropolitan Museum of New York after prolonged but fruitless negotiations with British museums.

The pace and breathtaking scope of Petrie's archaeological life amazes the modern student. Each winter he excavated in Egypt, spending the spring and summer in Europe writing up the previous season's work and exhibiting the finds. At least a book a year flowed from his prolific pen. Dozens of lectures as well as his regular University of London series were delivered every year. In forty-two years Petrie excavated more sites than Mariette and made more major discoveries than any other archaeologist before or after him. The cities of Naukratis and el Kahun, the el Amarneh material, the tombs of Abydos, and the jewels were only a few of his finds. Pre-Dynastic Egypt was resurrected from Nekadeh and Diospolis Parva. He found the famous stela of King Mery-en-Ptah, which provided the first known Egyptian references to Israel, a find that prompted one of his colleagues to murmur, "Won't the reverends be pleased." Petrie was an innovator, an Egyptologist who was ahead of his time and yet forced to support his excavations by selling his finds to European museums. Unfortunately he had a somewhat

355

tactless and quarrelsome personality. Distinguished public figures did not impress him, and
he was not afraid to describe the aged and authoritative writer James Baikie, well-known author
of *A Century of Excavation in the Land of the
Pharaohs* and other widely read books on Ancient
Egypt, as "a genial man . . . who argued on Greek
accent all day with all comers, and sang Scotch
songs with but small provocation." His lack of
formal education led him in later life to ignore
the valuable work of his contemporaries and to
insist that he was always right, never an endear-
ing quality in an archaeologist.

Petrie did far more than found an English
school of Egyptology and introduce reputable excavation methods into the Nile Valley. He trained
a whole generation of new Egyptologists, schooled
in hieroglyphs and his excavation methods. Many
of them improved on his techniques. Howard
Carter worked with Petrie. Ernest Arthur Gardner
learned his excavation at Naukratis and went on
to direct the British School of Archaeology in
Athens, where he helped Petrie with his work on
cross-dating Mycenaean imports from Egypt. Sir
Alan Gardiner, one of the greatest British Egyptologists in this century, was befriended by Petrie
and spent a lifetime studying hieratic texts. His
Egyptian Grammar (1927) is one of the fundamental source books for all students of Ancient
Egyptian languages. Guy Brunton, the young assistant who dug up the treasure of el Lahun, went on
to become one of Petrie's most distinguished fol-
lowers, renowned for his careful excavations on
pre-Dynastic tombs and villages. Gertrude Caton
Thompson, a remarkable archaeologist who excavated the sites of the earliest known Egyptian
farmers in the Fayyum depression in the 1920s
and then went on to study the Stone Age hunters
of the Khargeh oasis, learned excavation from
Petrie. The list of his former pupils reads like a
who's who of archaeology.

The annual Petrie excavations continued for

**Tombstone from the door of
the Coptic shrine in Edfu**

357

most years until 1926, when he abruptly transferred his attentions to Palestine. New and stringent regulations to control excavations by anyone except those employed directly by the National Museum or the Antiquities Service effectively prevented Petrie from further digging in the Nile Valley. In part these regulations came into effect as a result of the discovery of the tomb of Tut-ankh-Amun, which focused attention on the liberal conditions under which foreign expeditions were allowed to work in Egypt and to remove most of their finds with them at the expense of the national collections. After prolonged arguments, the contents of Tut-ankh-Amun's sepulcher were retained in Cairo and foreign excavation was restricted. But Petrie's work in a sense was done, for forty years of excavation, training, and publication had improved standards of field archaeology and brought forward a whole new generation of Egyptologists, including some native Egyptian scholars to man the Antiquities Service. Petrie himself had put more of Ancient Egypt on record than any man before him and continued to work every year in the Near East until the outbreak of the Second World War. He lived on to the age of eighty-nine as a respected if fiery phenomenon of twentieth-century archaeology.

Like so many other Egyptian excavators, even those hungry for plunder and buried treasure, he seems to have been at his best in the field. He returned to the quiet and serenity of the desert to escape the batterings of a scholarly world where minor quarrels and petty intrigues were all too common.

The real tranquility and room for quiet thought in this sort of life is refreshing. I here *live*, and do not scramble to fit myself to the requirements of others. In a narrow tomb, with the figure of Nefermaat standing on each side of me—as he has stood through all that we know as human history—I have just room for my bed, and a row of good reading in which I can take my pleasure when I retire to the blankets after dinner. Be-

hind me is that Great Peace, the Desert. It is an entity—
a power—just as much as the sea is. No wonder men
fled to it from the turmoil of the ancient world.

The history of Egyptology is full of men of
energy—Denon, Belzoni, Mariette, Petrie, and
others—who excavated the length and breadth of
the Nile Valley. Each seems to have had a fascination with the desert environment with its quiet serenity and unchanging sunshine. This tranquil
backdrop was the scene of an unparalleled scramble for antiquity which had no rivals in the feroc-
ity and ruthlessness of its aims.

**The finds from the tomb of
Tut-ankh-Amun are carefully
removed from the Valley of
Kings under guard. Such precautions are always needed,
even today.**

21 Epilogue

Over a hundred and fifty years have passed since Giovanni Belzoni shook the dust of Alexandria off his feet for the last time. But many familiar scenes would greet his eyes if he were to return to the Nile today. The pyramids still tower above the floodplain, while the Sphinx crouches at their feet surrounded by curious tourists. The sun still rises in a gray dawn, lights up the vast spaces of the desert, and highlights the fertile green and cultivated land by the banks of the Nile. The shimmering heat of midday embraces the heavy air of temple and royal tomb in the same way that it has for centuries. White-sailed river vessels retrace the course taken by Belzoni's ramshackle boats and pass the scenes of his greatest exploits. There is a sense of timelessness about

360

the Nile that transcends the passage of years or the stirring events of history. The visitor to the Nile can smell the same smells as the Ancient Egyptians, of hot dust and damp reeds, of the river itself as it flows smoothly toward the north. Every year, like clockwork, the Nile comes down in flood, ensuring the fertility of crops and perpetuating agricultural practices that are often little modified from pharaonic times. One can almost sense that elusive feeling of equilibrium and *ma'et,* that sense of rightness so highly prized by the Ancient Egyptians as they identified with their unchanging environment.

Belzoni had come to the Nile at a time when the full extent of the glories of Ancient Egypt had just been revealed to the world for the first time. The collections of Napoleon's savants had electrified the scholars of Europe and a craze for things Egyptian had swept the cultivated drawing rooms of European capitals. The Rosetta Stone had reached the British Museum; the Louvre in Paris had just unpacked its spoils from the Nile. A surge of nationalistic lust for the precious and exotic was filling these museums and those in other countries with all manner of curiosities and the finest artistic achievements of Western civilization. And Egyptian antiquities were at the top of the curators' shopping lists. Thus the scramble for Ancient Egypt began, a campaign of looting conducted in the name of diplomacy and leisured cultural inquiry, which soon degenerated into an orgy of destruction, greed, and outright profiteering. As in other parts of the world, archaeology began as treasure hunting and then slowly evolved into a scientific discipline armed with all the specialist methods and techniques of the twentieth-century fieldworker. But by the time the scientific archaeologist arrived, much of Ancient Egypt was gone forever, devoured by the voracious maw of the treasure hunter, unscrupulous collector, or curious tourist.

Napoleon's men were only human in their de-

Royal throne from the tomb of Tut-ankh-Amun

sire to collect Egyptian antiquities, for the urge to collect and possess is one of the more passionate of human desires. Time and time again the early archaeologist was overcome with a passion to excavate, loot, or just remove the past to another place, where he could caress it and contemplate its glories without the disturbing qualities of its original context. Soon European nationalism and the petty ambitions of diplomats and statesmen became involved in the collecting business, as many nations sought to acquire a fine repository of the most beautiful, exotic, and valuable manifestations of Ancient Egyptian civilization. It became fashionable to be knowledgeable about Ancient Egypt in all its nostalgic and fascinating glory. Egypt was the epitome of ancient civilization, that of a strong and powerful society that had oppressed the Israelites, suffered from the Mosaic plagues, and taken a conspicuous place in the established order of world history. Unfortunately, knowledge coincided with ownership and profit in many people's minds.

In a sense one cannot blame the museum curator or collector of a century and a half ago for the attitudes that they possessed. Everywhere they looked they saw statuary and temples being broken up and tombs being looted for jewelry. In Egypt nothing was safe. But a papyrus carefully unrolled in the secluded comfort of the British Museum was safe from destruction, cushioned with the awesome security of the greatest museum in the world. After all, as Wallis Budge pointedly remarked, a mummy displayed in the British Museum was very privileged compared with his cousins in the looted tombs of Thebes. No one could desecrate a British Museum mummy or tear it apart. The outrageous tactics of private purchase and surreptitious excavation in defiance of authority were condoned in the comfortable certainty that they were the only practicable way to save Ancient Egypt from extinction. What need, asked many people, did the Egyptians have for their

362

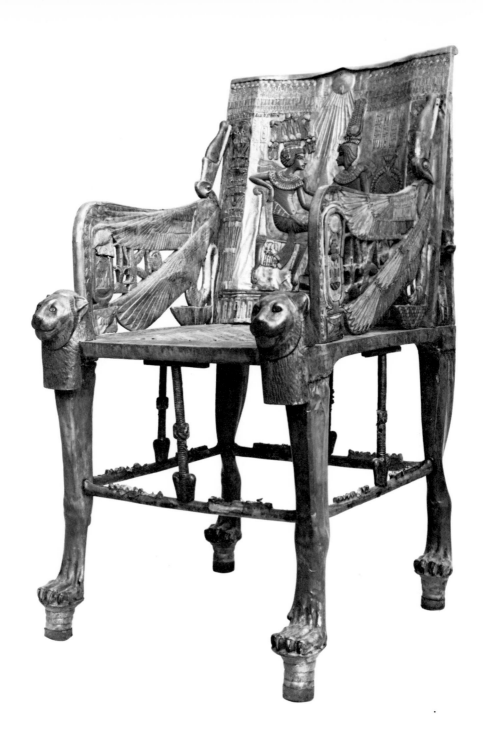

past? After all, the pasha's government was destroying and giving it away all the time. And the fellahin seemed to have no respect for tomb or temple or any identity with the Ancient Egyptians themselves, only in the value of their corpses. There was none of the local nationalistic sentiment that had stirred vigorous public outcry in Greece when Lord Elgin removed the marble friezes that bear his name in the British Museum from the portico of the Parthenon. The well-heeled museum collector and tourist of a century and a half ago was fully aware that the Ancient Egyptians themselves had helped themselves to the contents of royal tombs. They had violated their most sacred places and the royal sepulchers for gold and a guaranteed source of wealth that would enable them to meet life's day-to-day needs. The ancients had treated the past with a casual cynicism that had been inherited by their successors, a cynicism that was matched with equal contempt by the nineteenth-century collector. It is a miracle that anything at all has survived for us to enjoy.

Without question, however, much of Ancient Egypt's magnificent splendor was saved from oblivion by the aggressive policies of Wallis Budge and others—witness, to mention only a few instances, not only Belzoni's collections, but also the Papyrus of Ani, the best and most complete version of the Book of the Dead, and the thousands of Coptic manuscripts in the Louvre and the British Museum. By displaying their acquisitions, the officials of major European museums, however unscrupulous their methods, made possible a heightened awareness of the need to learn about Ancient Egypt and to save it for posterity before it all vanished forever.

Fortunately, when one looks back over the history of Egyptology one views a landscape peopled by giants. Jean François Champollion and John Gardner Wilkinson unlocked the secrets of hieroglyphs. Auguste Mariette excavated for the

364

Louvre and then became the first jealous guardian of Ancient Egypt for serious scholar and tourist alike. Flinders Petrie introduced modern excavation methods to the Nile. The genius of Champollion and the passionate vigor of Mariette resulted in the gradual creation of an organization designed to thwart destruction and inevitable oblivion. Egypt became the first Near Eastern country to possess a national museum, even if it began life as a ramshackle shed in a back garden in Cairo, and even if its contents were occasionally donated to influential visiting dignitaries. Gradually the diplomats turned from antiquities to political activities, while more and more people came to look rather than loot. Egypt itself became an interesting place to visit, with the great pyramids and temples as part of a backdrop for a thoroughly entertaining vacation.

In a sense it was the tourist and the educated dilettante who saved Ancient Egypt. Egypt's first Antiquities Ordinance was promulgated in 1835 and was largely ignored by those it sought to control, for there were no mechanisms or facilities to enforce it. Ironically, it was the looted antiquities in European museums that caused a rising tide of public opinion to react against the orgy of destruction. People had admired the fine statuary in the Louvre, felt that such fine achievements belonged to the world at large and that everyone had the right to enjoy them. There was a slow realization that fanatics like Mariette were correct, and that the flamboyant director of the Bulak Museum was right to offend the covetous Empress Eugénie with her imperious demands. Besides, tourism was good business for everyone: for the prosperity of foreign trade, for European political interests in the Near East, for the Egyptians, and for the tourists themselves. How could there be any tourism if there were no temples, tombs, or museum collections for the visitor to admire?

The studied logic and efficient bureaucracy of British rule in Egypt finally created, albeit slowly,

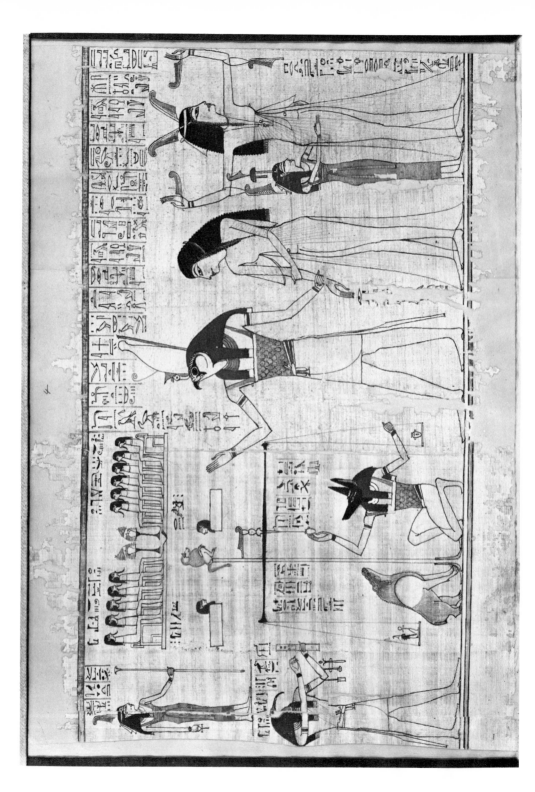

a change in public attitudes within Egypt itself. Amelia Edwards journeyed through Egypt at the beginning of a long period of relative political stability, when the Antiquities Service began to develop a network of guards and active intelligence agents employed to prevent illegal collecting and the further rape of Ancient Egypt. Of course, there were incidents of scandalous corruption and brazen tomb robbing, some of them associated with respectable museums, but the tide of public attitude and archaeological morality had turned imperceptibly in favor of preservation and scientific excavation. Even those who chose to paint their names on the great temples were publicly excoriated for their conspicuous sins. It became harder to remove antiquities from Egypt and more fashionable to consider the Cairo Museum as one of the foremost repositories for Ancient Egypt in the world, a museum soon to be staffed by Egyptians themselves.

The stolid façade of the British Empire fostered a rising sense of nationalism in Egypt, as elsewhere, a latent resentment of foreign rule and British imperialism, a greater identity with the long and fascinating kaleidoscope of history that the Egyptians could look back upon. This nationalism manifested itself in political events, which are familiar to us all, but also in an abhorrence of a "cultural imperialism" that chose to remove the choicest achievements of antiquity to foreign climates. The magnificent discovery of the undisturbed tomb of Tut-ankh-Amun in 1922 merely fueled the sentiment against foreign excavation and exploitation of Ancient Egypt, although Lord Carnarvon gave the royal tomb's contents to the Cairo Museum. By the 1920s foreign expeditions were rarely found in Egypt, for there were few rewards for well-financed museum expeditions that depended on rich finds to attract generous benefactors. A long drawn-out stand-off between the acquisitors of major foreign museums and the Egyptian Antiquities Service reflected a hardened

Weighing the soul of the Princess Ankh-ai against *ma'et.* **A papyrus in the British Museum.**

attitude, one where sharing of a unique cultural heritage with other nations was morally unacceptable. Few scholars were able to dig in Egypt on the scale that archaeologists like Petrie had regarded as commonplace. It is only in recent years that Egypt has opened its doors to foreign archaeologists again, this time on a carefully controlled scale.

But now the international climate for archaeology has changed, in a world that is ardently nationalistic and increasingly jealous of its diverse cultural heritages. People are far more aware of archaeology, conscious, like the Egyptians, of the enormous contribution that the discipline can make to the proper study of humankind. Today, the wealth of Ancient Egypt is spread through the museums of several continents. Mummy after mummy, sarcophagus after sarcophagus, statue after statue, museum storerooms and galleries, are filled with the dusty remains of Egyptian antiquity. Most were acquired by private collectors and then donated to the museums, or acquired in massive field seasons, supported by private donations, where often quantity was more important than quality. The large expeditions and casual collecting forays of half a century ago have been replaced by an illegal antiquities traffic that feeds on the law of supply and demand and the avaricious acquisition policies of large museums and wealthy collectors. Journalist Karl Meyer has documented this nefarious trade with its long ancestry in the activities of Belzoni and his kind in *The Plundered Past,* a devastating indictment of the mechanics of the twentieth-century antiquities trade. Meyer describes public consciousness of the seriousness of the problem as being at about "stage zero," for the importance of archaeology and its significance to humankind is something that is theoretically easy to understand, has been rarely discussed at length in print, and is far harder to comprehend in practice. It is certainly almost impossible to persuade taxpayers to pay for archaeology when the thorny

368

issue of limited resources and ordered priorities comes up.

The Egyptian government has been restrictive in its permit granting and nationalistic in its recent attitudes toward Ancient Egypt. Some limited sales of duplicates have been officially sanctioned and massive efforts made to conserve what remains of Ancient Egypt. This has not prevented the reported looting of dozens of tombs as recently as 1973 and further damage to the temple of Dendereh. Papyri are still a primary target for tomb robbers, and it has been alleged by a French journalist that Soviet technicians have smuggled plenty of antiquities out of Egypt in their diplomatic baggage in recent years. There seems to be no ready solution to the endless destruction of Ancient Egypt.

The Egyptians have appealed to the world as well, arguing that the finest achievements of the Ancient Egyptians are an international legacy. World support was invited to save the temple of Abu Simbel and other Nubian antiquities from the rising waters of Lake Nasser. The Aswan High Dam project spawned an enormous archaeological activity that combed the thousands of square miles to be flooded by the new lake. International consciences were stirred and a world appeal raised the funds to move the brooding statues of Ramesses II's temple to a new site on higher ground above the lake. The delicate move was carried out by an international consortium of contractors and archaeologists. The sun still rises every morning and shines through the original temple entrance so laboriously excavated by Belzoni and his friends, even if the site of the temple is altered and all traces of the unruly kachif's village are gone forever. For once antiquity triumphed over accelerating development in a world where the rapacious needs of industrial growth and the greed of collectors still dominate public attitudes toward archaeology. As a reward for their work the expeditions that surveyed Lake Nasser

Seated figure of a cat

369

were allowed to take many of their finds away with them. But at least many of the sites were recorded properly before being lost forever.

The United States was given the temple of Dendur as a reward for its efforts in Nubia. Such is institutional greed that it soon became the target of intense competition between the Metropolitan Museum of Art, the Smithsonian Institution, and the Kennedy family who wished to erect it by the chilly and damp banks of the Potomac beside the Kennedy Center. At the same time as the Met acquired the temple of Dendur, it had just finished selling off thousands of its smaller Egyptian antiquities—mummies, scarabs, beads, and pottery acquired through large-scale digs in earlier years. This authorized disposal of a priceless archive of basic research material seems to be atypical of most major museums, but fully justifies the cynicism of many Egyptians about foreign exploitation of their ancient past. Was Wallis Budge really right when he said that mummies were safe in the British Museum? At the moment he still is, but no one knows what will happen in a world where there may soon be little of Ancient Egypt left for us to study or enjoy.

The passion for collecting dies hard, especially in times of recession or mushrooming art prices. Nor does it perish in the face of attitudes like those of New York art dealer André Emmerich who was bold enough to say in public a few years ago that he thought the United States "more than any other [country] has a special claim to the arts of all mankind." We live in what are sometimes called enlightened times, but they can hardly be described as enlightened in terms of antiquity, as long as these sorts of attitudes pervade public thinking. Many archaeologists are wondering if there is a future for the past and some fear that Ancient Egypt is faced with total extinction. But let us take heart from the immortal and inspired words of the great Jean François Champollion:

370

Egypt is always herself, at all stages in her history, always great and powerful in art and enlightenment. Going back through the centuries, we see her always shining with the same brilliance, and the only thing we lack to satisfy our curiosity is a knowledge of the origin and growth of civilization itself.

As these pages have shown, at least something has been done to satisfy Champollion's, and our, curiosity.

ACKNOWLEDGMENTS
SOURCES
ILLUSTRATION ACKNOWLEDGMENTS
INDEX

ACKNOWLEDGMENTS

This book owes its genesis to Patricia Cristol
of Charles Scribner's Sons, who suggested the idea
in the first place. I am deeply grateful to her both
for the idea and for her constant advice, encouragement, and assistance. I also owe a considerable
debt to the many colleagues and friends who have
read all or parts of the manuscript while it was in
draft. Many photographic agencies and museums
have assisted with photographs, and individual acknowledgments are made elsewhere. Their willing
cooperation is greatly appreciated. Pat Griffith undertook much of the laborious typing work, and
her insights into the rough draft were invaluable.
Jé Goolsby of Santa Barbara kindly drew the map.
Only someone who has studied Egyptian archaeology in depth knows how much anyone writing

on the history of Egyptology owes to his prede-
cessors. I want to acknowledge the debt that I
owe to the many authors who have written about
Belzoni and others. Their number includes C. W.
Ceram, Leslie Greener, Stanley Mayes, John
Wortham, and the hundreds of other Egyptologists,
amateur and professional, who have worked in the
Nile Valley.

This book would never have been completed
without the services of the UCLA and University
of California, Santa Barbara, libraries.

SOURCES

I have consulted hundreds of books, articles, and reviews in writing this book. The major sources for the research may, however, be of interest to a reader interested in delving more deeply into Egyptian archaeology.

Chapter One: Of the many books on Ancient Egyptian civilization, I have found Cyril Aldred's *The Egyptians* (New York, 1961) a concise, fluent, and well-illustrated account of political events and social life on the Nile. John A. Wilson, *The Culture of Ancient Egypt* (Chicago, 1951), is a readily accessible essay for American readers. Both these books are well referenced, especially for basic sources on art, architecture, and religion. The tomb robbers of the XX Dynasty have been the subject of exhaustive study by T. E. Peek, *The Great Tomb-Robberies of the Twentieth Egyptian Dynasty* (Oxford, 1930), while James Breasted's *Ancient Records of Egypt* (Chicago, 1906) also contains translations of tomb-robbing records. Howard Carter's classic popular description, written with A. C. Mace, *The Tomb of Tut-Ank-Amen* (London, 1923–33) is essential reading for anyone interested in royal tombs. I. E. S. Edwards, *The Pyramids of Egypt* (London, 1947), is the classic survey of the pyramids.

Chapter Two: The early history of tourism in the Nile Valley begins with Herodotus' *History*. George Rawlinson's translation (New York, 1910) is probably most popular. F. Gladstone Bratton, *A History of Egyptian Archaeology* (London, 1967), is informative on the early Greek authors, while Roman tourism in Egypt has been described by Ibrahim Amin Ghali, "Touristes romains en Egypte et Egyptiens à Rome sous le Haut-Empire," *Cahiers d'histoire Egyptienne*, XI (1969), 43–62.

Chapters Three and Four: There is a proliferating literature on this period of Egyptian archaeology. John David Wortham, *The Genesis of British Egyptology* (Norman, Okla., 1971), is a basic source on the period, Leslie Greener's *The Discovery of Egypt* (New York, 1966) is an entertaining account of this and other phases of Egyptology. I have relied heavily on its wide range of sources. Karl H. Dannenfeldt, "Egypt and Egyptian Antiquities in the Renaissance," *Studies in the Renaissance*, VI (1959), 7–27, is a beautifully written study of early Egyptologists. The early history of hieroglyphs is surveyed by Erik Iversen, *The Myth of Egypt and Its Hieroglyphics in European Tradition* (Copenhagen, 1961). See also the French Institute's series of early travel accounts: *Voyageurs Occidentaux en Egypte* (9 volumes to date).

Chapter Five: J. Christopher Herold has written the definitive account in English of Napoleon's expedition, *Bonaparte in Egypt* (New York, 1962). C. de la Jonquière's *L'Expédition d'Egypte, 1798–1801* (Paris, 1828) is the standard French history. Vivant Denon's travels are best read in French, but the English translation, *Travels in Upper and Lower Egypt* (London, 1803), is readily available. It is worth going a long way to pore over Esmé Jomard's *Description de l'Egypte*. Only those who have admired the plates at first hand can appreciate its true significance. Prosper Jollois, *Journal d'un Ingénieur attaché a l'Expédition d'Egypte, 1798–1802* (Paris, 1904) is informative on Desaix's campaign. Henry Dodwell's *The Founder of Modern Egypt* (Cambridge, 1931) remains the scholarly and definitive account of Mohammed 'Ali's career. Henry Salt has been ignored by biographers except for J. J. Halls's typically nineteenth-century eulogy, *The Life and Correspondence of Henry Salt, Esq., F.R.S.* (London, 1834).

Chapters Six to Fifteen: The literature about Giovanni Belzoni is diffuse, and the number of travelers who refer to his work in their travelogues is enormous. In writing this account I have relied very heavily on his own *Narrative of the Operations and Recent Discoveries Within the Pyramids, Temples, Tombs, and Excavations, in Egypt and Nubia* (London, 1820). Belzoni's book is long, at times boring, and stylistically clumsy. But it glows with vivid action and restlessness. There is a gusto about it that led me to regard it as a primary source. Everyone who writes about Belzoni will rely heavily on Stanley Mayes's definitive biography, *The Great Belzoni* (New York, 1961). This is a comprehensive study which involved extensive research into primary sources about Belzoni (a rarity). I found it an invaluable source of background reading, references, and a reliable guide to a complex man. It contains a useful appendix on Belzoni's finds in the British Museum, which helped me through a spellbound afternoon in the Egyptian Galleries. Maurice Willson Disher's *Pharaoh's Fool* (London, 1957) concentrates on Belzoni's theatrical exploits, while Colin Clair's *Strong Man Egyptologist* (London, 1957) is a small-scale biography.

John Lewis Burckhardt's *Travels in Nubia* (London, 1819) gives one an insight into this gifted traveler, while a bibliography of travelers who mention Belzoni's work can be found in Mayes's biography. Drovetti's life remains undescribed except for some articles in Italian, but Charles Irby and James Mangles's *Travels in Egypt and Nubia* (London, 1823) adds much to Belzoni's own account of Abu Simbel. The history of that monument can be learned from William MacQuilty, *Abu Simbel* (London, 1965). Berenice was visited by Lieutenant R. Wellstead, Royal Navy, about fifteen years after Belzoni's expedition: "Notes on the Ruins of Berenice," *Journal of the Royal Geographical Society*, VI (1836). The best account of Belzoni's last years is that by

Mayes, who based his research on contemporary documents. But Samuel Smiles's *A Publisher and His Friends* (London, 1891) contains a brief comment on Belzoni. References to Belzoni are commonplace in most surveys of Egyptology; his wider historical significance is discussed by Glyn Daniel, *A Hundred Years of Archaeology* (London, 1950).

Chapter Sixteen: A major source for this, and indeed most of the chapters, was Warren R. Dawson and Eric P. Uphill, *Who Was Who in Egyptology* (London, 2nd ed., 1972). This is a basic compendium of all known deceased Egyptologists, including Lelorrain and other such characters. It is invaluable to any student of the subject. The story of decipherment has been told many times, notably by C. W. Ceram in *Gods, Graves and Scholars* (New York, 1953) and by Leslie Greener in his *Discovery.* My primary source was H. Hartleben, *Champollion, sein Leben und sein Werk* (Berlin, 1906), apart, of course, from Champollion's own writings and those of his companions.

Chapter Seventeen: John Gardner Wilkinson's best monument is his own *Manners and Customs of the Ancient Egyptians* (London, 1837), for a definitive biography has yet to appear. Hay's work is also largely unpublished, but Richard Lepsius is readily accessible through his own works, the monumental *Denkmäler* and other volumes. Gliddon's monograph is very rare, and an authoritative biography of Auguste Mariette is badly needed. I relied on Edouard Mariette's *Mariette Pacha* (Paris, 1904) and on Gaston Maspero's *Auguste Mariette, notice biographique et oeuvres diverses* (Paris, 1904). Mariette's own writings, especially his *Voyage dans la Haute Egypte* (Paris, 1893), are also informative. The salient features of his life have been ably summarized by Greener, Bratton, and many other authors, including James Baikie, *A Century of Excavation in the Land of the Pharaohs* (London, 1923).

Chapter Eighteen: Wallis Budge was a prolific author, and his *By Nile and Tigris* (London, 1920) is a more than adequate chronicle of his doings. Gaston Maspero was an able and vigorous writer, and his guides and popular books are a useful and entertaining collection, notably *L'Archéologie égyptienne* (Paris, 1887). The po-

litical background to these years has been recalled by
Lord Cromer, *Modern Egypt* (London, 1908).

Chapter Nineteen: No one should miss Amelia
Edwards, *A Thousand Miles up the Nile* (London, 1877),
a delicious piece of evocative Victoriana, or her lec-
tures, *Pharaohs, Fellahs, and Explorers* (New York,
1901). The tart comments of Lady Lucie Duff-Gordon,
Letters from Egypt (London, 1865), are a useful perspec-
tive. American visitors to the Nile are chronicled by
John A. Wilson, *Signs and Wonders upon Pharaoh*
(Chicago, 1964). George Ebers's romantic novels I found
heavy going. A list of some of them appears in John
Wortham's *Genesis of British Egyptology* (Norman,
Okla., 1971), of great use for this and the next chapter.

Chapter Twenty: Flinders Petrie described himself in
a steady stream of books. I have used *Seventy Years in
Archaeology* (London, 1931) and *Ten Years Digging in
Egypt, 1881–1891* (London, 1892), and I dipped into
some of his monographs. An outline bibliography appears in *Who Was Who.* An assessment of Petrie's
work can be found in Glyn Daniel, *A Hundred Years of
Archaeology* (London, 1950). The later development of
Egyptology can best be seen through the pages of specialized periodicals such as the *Journal of Egyptian
Archaeology.*

Illustration Acknowledgments

Page 2: Hirmer Fotoarchiv, Munich
Pages 4–5: Hirmer Fotoarchiv, Munich
Page 7: Griffith Institute, Ashmolean Museum, Oxford
Page 10: Turin Museum
Page 12: Radio Times Hulton Picture Library, London
Page 16: Samuel Manning, *The Land of the Pharaohs* (1876)
Page 17: Hirmer Fotoarchiv, Munich
Page 19: Hirmer Fotoarchiv, Munich
Page 22: Hirmer Fotoarchiv, Munich
Page 25: Samuel Manning, *The Land of the Pharaohs* (1876)
Page 26: Hirmer Fotoarchiv, Munich
Page 29: Trustees of the British Museum
Page 30: Hirmer Fotoarchiv, Munich
Page 31: Courtesy of the Brooklyn Museum, Charles Edwin Wilbour Fund
Page 37: S. Marmounier, Chambéry
Page 38: Metropolitan Museum of Art, New York, Rogers Fund and contribution of Edward S. Harkness, 1921
Page 40: Samuel Manning, *The Land of the Pharaohs* (1876)
Page 41: Hirmer Fotoarchiv, Munich
Page 42: David Roberts, *Egypt and Nubia* (1846)
Page 43: Metropolitan Museum of Art, New York, Museum Excavations, 1919–1920, Rogers Fund, supplemented by contribution of Edward S. Harkness

INDEX

(Page numbers in boldface indicate illustrations)